Lecture Notes in Artificial Intelligence   13812

Subseries of Lecture Notes in Computer Science

More information about this subseries at https://link.springer.com/bookseries/1244

Thomas Guyet · Georgiana Ifrim ·
Simon Malinowski · Anthony Bagnall ·
Patrick Shafer · Vincent Lemaire (Eds.)

Advanced Analytics and Learning on Temporal Data

7th ECML PKDD Workshop, AALTD 2022
Grenoble, France, September 19–23, 2022
Revised Selected Papers

 Springer

Editors
Thomas Guyet (iD)
Inria Grenoble - Rhône-Alpes Research
Centre
Villeurbanne, France

Georgiana Ifrim (iD)
University College Dublin
Dublin, Ireland

Simon Malinowski (iD)
University of Rennes
Rennes, France

Anthony Bagnall (iD)
University of East Anglia
Norwich, UK

Patrick Shafer (iD)
University of Rennes
Rennes, France

Vincent Lemaire (iD)
Orange Labs
Lannion, France

ISSN 0302-9743   ISSN 1611-3349   (electronic)
Lecture Notes in Artificial Intelligence
ISBN 978-3-031-24377-6   ISBN 978-3-031-24378-3   (eBook)
https://doi.org/10.1007/978-3-031-24378-3

LNCS Sublibrary: SL7 – Artificial Intelligence

This Springer imprint is published by the registered company Springer Nature Switzerland AG
The registered company address is: Gewerbestrasse 11, 6330 Cham, Switzerland

Preface

Workshop Description

The European Conference on Machine Learning and Principles and Practice of Knowledge Discovery in Databases (ECML-PKDD) is the premier European machine learning and data mining conference and builds upon over 20 years of successful events and conferences held across Europe. ECML-PKDD 2022 took place in Grenoble, France, during September 19–23, 2022. The main conference was complemented by a workshop program, where each workshop was dedicated to specialized topics, cross-cutting issues, and upcoming research trends. This standalone LNAI volume includes the selected papers of the 7th International Workshop on Advanced Analytics and Learning on Temporal Data (AALTD) held at ECML-PKDD 2022.

Motivation – Temporal data are frequently encountered in a wide range of domains such as bio-informatics, medicine, finance, environment and engineering, among many others. They are naturally present in emerging applications such as motion analysis, energy efficient buildings, smart cities, social media, or sensor networks. Contrary to static data, temporal data are of complex nature, they are generally noisy, of high dimensionality, they may be non-stationary (i.e., first order statistics vary with time) and irregular (i.e., involving several time granularities) and they may have several invariant domain-dependent factors such as time delay, translation, scale, or tendency effects. These temporal peculiarities limit the majority of standard statistical models and machine learning approaches, that mainly assume i.i.d data, homoscedasticity, normality of residuals, etc. To tackle such challenging temporal data we require new advanced approaches at the intersection of statistics, time series analysis, signal processing, and machine learning. Defining new approaches that transcend boundaries between several domains to extract valuable information from temporal data is undeniably an important topic and it has been the subject of active research in the last decade.

Workshop Topics – The aim of the workshop series on AALTD[1] was to bring together researchers and experts in machine learning, data mining, pattern analysis, and statistics to share their challenging issues and advances in temporal data analysis. Analysis and learning from temporal data covers a wide scope of tasks including metric learning, representation learning, unsupervised feature extraction, clustering, and classification.

For this seventh edition, the proposed workshop received papers that cover one or several of the following topics:

---

[1] https://project.inria.fr/aaltd22/.

- Advanced Forecasting and Prediction Models
- Classification of Univariate and Multivariate Time Series
- Data Augmentation for Time Series Classification
- Application Methods
- Temporal Alignment
- Anomaly Detection
- Temporal Data Clustering

Outcomes – AALTD 2022 was structured as a full-day workshop. We encouraged submissions of regular papers that were up to 16 pages of previously unpublished work. All submitted papers were peer-reviewed (double-blind) by two or three reviewers from the Program Committee, and selected on the basis of these reviews. AALTD 2022 received 22 submissions, among which 12 papers were accepted for inclusion in the proceedings. The papers with the highest review rating were selected for oral presentation (6 papers), and the others were given the opportunity to present a poster through a spotlight session and a discussion session (6 papers). The workshop had an invited talk on "Causal Discovery in Observational Time Series"[2] given by CNRS researcher Emilie Devijver of the CNRS/LIG-APTIKAL department, France[3].

We thank all organizers, reviewers, and authors for the time and effort invested to make this workshop a success. We would also like to express our gratitude to the members of the Program Committee, the Organizing Committee of ECML-PKDD 2022 and the technical staff who helped us to make the AALTD 2022 a successful workshop. Sincere thanks are due to Springer for their help in publishing the proceedings. Lastly, we thank all participants and speakers at AALTD 2022 for their contributions. Their collective support made the workshop a really interesting and successful event.

November 2022

Thomas Guyet
Georgiana Ifrim
Simon Malinowski
Anthony Bagnall
Patrick Schäfer
Vincent Lemaire

---

[2] https://project.inria.fr/aaltd22/invited-speakers/.

[3] https://lig-aptikal.imag.fr/∼devijvee/.

Organization

Program Committee Chairs

Anthony Bagnall	University of East Anglia, UK
Thomas Guyet	Inria, France
Georgiana Ifrim	University College Dublin, Ireland
Vincent Lemaire	Orange Innovation, France
Simon Malinowski	Université de Rennes, Inria, CNRS, IRISA, France
Patrick Schäfer	Humboldt University of Berlin, Germany

Program Committee

Timilehin Aderinola	Multimedia University, Malaysia
Mustafa Baydoğan	Boğaziçi University, Turkey
Antonio Bevilacqua	University College Dublin, Ireland
Alexis Bondu	Orange Innovation, France
Padraig Cunningham	University College Dublin, Ireland
Bhaskar Dhariyal	University College Dublin, Ireland
Johann Gamper	Free University of Bozen-Bolzano, Italy
Dominique Gay	Université de La Réunion, France
David Guijo-Rubio	Universidad de Córdoba, Spain
Paul Honeine	Université de Rouen, France
Thach Le Nguyen	University College Dublin, Ireland
Brian Mac Namee	University College Dublin, Ireland
Matthew Middlehurst	University of East Anglia, UK
Thu Trang Nguyen	University College Dublin, Ireland
Charlotte Pelletier	Université de Bretagne-Sud, IRISA, France
Pavel Senin	Los Alamos National Laboratory, USA
Diego Silva	Universidade Federal de Sao Carlos, Brazil
Ashish Singh	University College Dublin, Ireland
Chang Wei	Monash University, Australia

Causal Discovery in Observational Time Series
(Invited Talk)

Charles K. Assaad[1], Emilie Devijver[2], and Eric Gaussier[2]

[1] EasyVista, 38000, Grenoble, France
cassaad@easyvista.com
[2] Univ. Grenoble Alpes, CNRS, Grenoble INP, LIG, 38000 Grenoble, France
{emilie.devijver, eric.gaussier}@univ-grenoble-alpes.fr

Abstract. Time series arise as soon as observations, from sensors or experiments for example, are collected over time. They are present in various forms in many different domains, as healthcare (through, e.g., monitoring systems), Industry 4.0 (through, e.g., predictive maintenance and industrial monitoring systems), surveillance systems (from images, acoustic signals, seismic waves, etc.) or energy management (through, e.g. energy consumption data).

In this paper, we propose an overview of existing methods for inferring a causal graph for time series. Their behaviors are illustrated on different benchmark datasets.

keywords: Causal discovery · Time series.

1 Motivation

Machine learning methods lack the ability to capture how the world works, to react to events different from the training set, or to go beyond correlation relationships. Causality is thus crucial for explanatory purpose, since an effect can be explained by its causes, regardless of the correlations it may have with other variables [1]. In this paper, we focus on the causal discovery for multivariate observational time series [2].

We consider a d-variate time series X of continuous values. For a fixed t, each X_t is a vector $(X_t^1, \ldots, X_t^d)$, in which X_t^p is the measurement of the pth time series at time t. In Fig. 1 (top), we draw a running example with four time series with a diamond structure.

A classical assumption for time series, needed when we want to do estimation from a finite sample size, is the consistency throughout time: a causal graph for a multivariate time series X is said to be *consistent throughout time* if all the causal relationships remain constant in direction throughout time. Under this assumption, the window causal graph is equivalent to the full time causal graph, the summary causal graph can summarize the information while being easier to infer and to interpret, and the extended summary causal graph is an intermediate representation, where instantaneous relations are discriminated from lagged relations. Those notions are illustrated in fig. 1 for the running example of diamond structure.

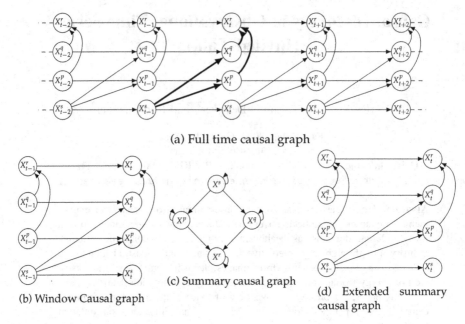

(a) Full time causal graph

(b) Window Causal graph

(c) Summary causal graph

(d) Extended summary causal graph

Fig. 1. A diamond structure with self causes. The full time causal graph is represented (top), and the diamond structure is highlighted in bold for a specific timepoint. Three representations of the diamond structure are then given under the consistency throughout time assumption: the window causal graph with a window of size 2 (bottom left), the summary causal graph (bottom middle) and the extended summary causal graph (bottom right).

We assume in this study that every relevant variable is observed (causal sufficiency), but note that many methods have been proposed in the literature to solve this problem as well.

2 Methods

Several methods have been proposed in the literature, relying on different assumptions. We describe here several families on which we will focus on:

- **Granger methods** are inferring the Granger causality, which is not exactly the causality, but used in many applications. The goal is to detect variables that are the most relevant for prediction (no matter of spurious correlations).
- **Constraint-based approaches** exploit conditional independencies to build a skeleton between variables, which is then oriented according to a set of rules that defines constraints on admissible orientations. Remark that the solution is a Markov equivalence class, being not able to detect which graph is the true one among equivalent orientations. Those methods are based on the causal Markov condition and the faithfulness assumption.

– **Noise-based methods** describe the causal system by a set of causal equations, where each equation explains one variable of the system in terms of its direct causes and some additional noise. They are based on causal Markov condition and minimality assumption.

Several methods for each class have been discussed in [2].We want to highlight two new methods, not presented in the survey.

First, NBCB [3] is a method that takes benefit of the constraint-based approaches to focus on conditional independencies and to the noise-based methods to relax the unfaithfulness assumption. It achieves competitive performances on generated and real datasets.

Second, PCGCE [4] is a constraint-based method that infer an extended summary causal graph (the first method to introduce this kind of graph, to our knowledge) based on conditional independencies. The main advantage is on the validation and interpretation of the inferred graphs by experts: it is usually difficult for experts to have a deep look on the lag of the causal effect, which is here only differentiate for instantaneous relations. It has also a reduced time complexity, compared with the window causal graph.

3   Experimental Results

We compare different methods in Table 1 on three real datasets: the temperature dataset[1] , about indoor and outdoor temperatures; the diary dataset[2] about prices of milk, butter and cheddar cheese ; and FMRI[3], that measures the neural activity of 50 regions of interest in the brain based on the change of blood flow.

We study MVGCL [5], a standard implementation of multivariate Granger causality, from the Granger methods; PCMCI [6] to illustrate the performance of constraint-based methods ; VarLiNGAM [7] and TiMINo [8] to illustrate noise-based

Table 1. Results for three real datasets. We report the mean and the standard deviation of the F1 score.

	Temperature	Diary	FMRI
NBCB [3]	1	0.8	0.40 ± 0.21
PCGCE [4]	0	0	0.31 ± 0.20
MVGCL [5]	0.66	0.33	0.35 ± 0.08
PCMCI [6]	1	0.5	0.22 ± 0.18
VarLiNGAM [7]	0	0.0	0.49 ± 0.28
TiMINo [8]	0	0.0	0.32 ± 0.11

---

[1] Data is available at https://webdav.tuebingen.mpg.de/cause-effect/.

[2] Data available at https://future.aae.wisc.edu.

[3] Data available at https://www.fmrib.ox.ac.uk/datasets/netsim/index.html, a preprocessed version at https://github.com/M-Nauta/TCDF/tree/master/data/fMRI.

methods, based on non-gaussian distribution assumption for Var-LiNGAM, and the two new methods NBCB [3] and PCGCE [4].

The considered real datasets do not necessarily satisfy every classical assumption, then it is difficult to conclude to a best method without giving precision on the context. We argue that NBCB is challenging, because it relaxes classical assumptions by mixing two worlds. PGCGE is also performing well on FMRI, but it needs large sample size to achieve good performance, which is not the case in Temperature and Diary datasets.

4 Conclusion

We review in this paper some methods to infer causal graph for time series.If a general conclusion cannot be drawn from the 3 real datasets studied here, we illustrate that all the families of methods may be interested, depending on the assumptions underlying the datasets. Causal sufficiency, which is often not satisfied in real datasets, has also been studied [9]. Recent papers discuss the use of causality in machine learning [10] to improve the generalization of inferred models, and this is an interesting open question for time series.

Acknowledgements. This research was partly supported by MIAI@Grenoble Alpes (ANR-19-P3IA-0003).

References

1. Spirtes, P., Glymour, C., Scheines. R.: *Causation, Prediction, and Search*.MIT press (2000)
2. Assaad, C. K., Emilie Devijver, E., Gaussier, E.: *Survey and evaluation of causal discovery methods for time series*. JAIR, 73 (2022)
3. Assaad, C. K., Emilie Devijver, E., Gaussier, E.: *A Mixed Noise and Constraint Based Approach to Causal Inference in Time Series*, ECMLPKDD (2021)
4. Assaad, C. K., Emilie Devijver, E., Gaussier, E.:*Causal Discovery of Extended Summary Graphs in Time Series*, UAI (2022)
5. Arnold, A., Liu, Y., Abe, N.: *Temporal causal modeling with graphical granger methods*. In: Proceedings of the 13th ACM SIGKDD International Conferenceon Knowledge Discovery and Data Mining, KDD 2007, pp. 66–75, New York, USA (2007)
6. Runge, J.: *Conditional independence testing based on a nearest-neighbor estimator of conditional mutual information*. In: AISTATS, pp. 938–947 (2018)
7. Hyvarinen, A., Zhang, K., Shimizu, S., Hoyer. P. O.: *Estimation of a structural vector autoregression model using non-gaussianity*. J. Mach. Learn. Res., **11**, 1709–1731. ISSN 1532-4435 (2010)
8. Peters, J., Janzing, D., Scholkopf, B.: *Causal inference on time series using restricted structural equation models*. In: Advances in Neural Information Processing Systems, Vol. 26, pp. 154–162 (2013)

9. Malinsky, D., Spirtes, P.: *Causal structure learning from multivariate time series in settings with unmeasured confounding*, In: Proceedings of 2018 ACM SIGKDD Workshop on Causal Disocvery, Vol. 92 of PMLR, pp. 23–47, London, UK. PMLR

10. Kaddour, J., Lynch, A., Liu, Q., Kusner M. J., Silva, R.: *Causal Machine Learning: A Survey and Open Problems*, arXiv (2022)

Contents

xvi   Contents

Oral Presentation

Adjustable Context-Aware Transformer

Sepideh Koohfar$^{(\boxtimes)}$ and Laura Dietz

University of New Hampshire, Durham, NH, USA
{Sepideh.Koohfar,Laura.Dietz}@unh.edu

Abstract. We propose a multi-horizon forecasting approach that accurately models the underlying patterns on different time scales.

Our approach is based on the transformer architecture, which across a wide range of domains, has demonstrated significant improvements over other architectures. Several approaches focus on integrating a temporal context into the query-key similarity of the attention mechanism of transformers to further improve their forecasting quality. In this paper, we provide several extensions to this line of work. We propose an adjustable context-aware attention that dynamically learns the ideal temporal context length for each forecasting time point. This allows the model to seamlessly switch between different time scales as needed, hence providing users with a better forecasting model. Furthermore, we exploit redundancies arising from incorporating the temporal context into the attention mechanism to improve runtime and space complexity. The code for reproducing the results is open sourced and available online (https://github.com/SepKfr/Adjustable-context-aware-transfomer).

Keywords: Time series forecasting · Temporal systems · Neural networks

1   Introduction

Time series forecasting is an important problem across many domains, such as economics [4,34], retail [7,29], healthcare [19], and sensor network monitoring [23]. In such domains, users are interested in future forecasts based on the historical data to glean insights. Multi-horizon forecasting is a critical demand for many applications, such as early severe weather events forecasting and travel planning based on traffic congestion.

Recurrent Neural Networks (RNNs) have been applied to model repeating patterns in time series [24,25], however RNNs and their variants are not able to leverage information from the longer past as needed to model long-term dependencies. Previous studies have demonstrated that RNNs including Long Short Term Memory networks (LSTMs) [12] might also fail to capture long-term patterns of dependency when information from the past is gradually overwritten by information from recent observations [15].

Transformers [30] can incorporate any observations of the series (potentially skipping over non-relevant data points) which renders them more suitable for

T. Guyet et al. (Eds.): AALTD 2022, LNAI 13812, pp. 3–17, 2023.
https://doi.org/10.1007/978-3-031-24378-3_1

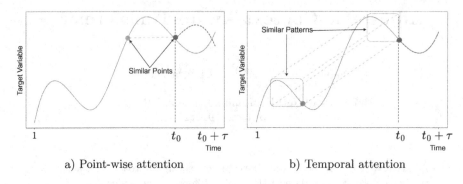

a) Point-wise attention   b) Temporal attention

Fig. 1. A synthetic example of predicting the future after the dashed red line given the preceding data. The attention mechanism would choose the points that are most similar to the query point at t_0 (depicted in blue) and predict a similar trajectory. In the case of (a) point-wise attention, this would be the green point, which would result in an erroneous forecast following the blue dashed line, where the correct forecast is depicted in black. In the case of (b) temporal attention the similarity is depending on the context, depicted as rectangle, and the pink rectangle is determined to exhibit most similar behavior. This results in an accurate forecast, depicted as blue dashed line. (Color figure online)

capturing similarities in the longer past. We hypothesize that these similarities are critical for achieving accurate forecasts. However, the basic attention mechanism in transformers estimates the similarity based on a point-wise vector of the query and key, each representing individual time steps, thereby ignoring the temporal context surrounding the query and key. As depicted in Fig. 1 estimating similarities based on point-wise vectors without incorporating the temporal context might lead to misleading predictions, when observations have high point-wise similarities but exhibit different temporal behaviours (Fig. 1 left).

Many approaches are based on the hypothesis that in a multi-layer model, the temporal context can be absorbed into the representation of the query and key from a previous layer. However, there are two shortcomings. 1) Previous layers suffer from the same lack of temporal understanding. 2) Such a mechanism operates indirectly which provides little insights for more explainability. We strive for a direct approach that is even effective as a single-layer model, as it obtains better performance while using fewer resources.

Li et al. [18] address this shortcoming with a Convolutional Neural Network (CNN) transformer. CNNs are used as a preliminary layer to inform points with context information to feed into the transformer stack. However, our experimental results demonstrate that integrating a fixed length temporal context limits the degree of flexibility to detect similarities on different time scales in order to improve the forecasting quality.

We dive into these issues and investigate the importance of incorporating a flexible temporal context into the attention mechanism. Our contributions are summarized as follows:

- We propose the *adjustable context-aware* attention, an attention mechanism that dynamically learns the optimal temporal context length for each query and key pair to obtain the best forecasting results. We propose the adjustable Context-aware Transformer (ACAT) which replaces the basic attention mechanism with our adjustable context-aware attention.
- We increase the efficiency of our approach by exploiting redundancies in temporal contexts. While it seems counter intuitive to first introduce then remove redundancies, the result is a more efficient model overall.
- We successfully apply our proposed architecture to real world time series datasets to validate its potential in generating more accurate predictions.

2   Problem Definition

Given the input data prior to time step t_0, the task is to predict the variables of interest for multiple steps into the future from t_0 to $t_0 + \tau$.

Given the previous time series observations of variables of interest $\boldsymbol{y}1 : t_0 = [\boldsymbol{y}1, \boldsymbol{y}2, \dots, \boldsymbol{y}t_0]$, and time series covariates that are known over both the historical and forecasting period $\boldsymbol{x}1 : t_0 + \tau = [\boldsymbol{x}1, \boldsymbol{x}2, \dots, \boldsymbol{x}t_0 + \tau]$, we predict the variables of interest for the next τ time steps $\boldsymbol{y}t_0 + 1 : t_0 + \tau = [\boldsymbol{y}t_0 + 1, \boldsymbol{y}t_0 + 2, \dots, \boldsymbol{y}t_0 + \tau]$. Where $\boldsymbol{y}i \in \mathcal{R}^{d_y}$ and $\boldsymbol{x}i \in \mathcal{R}^{d_x}$.

For a univariate problem each $\boldsymbol{x}i$ contains the information of static time-based covariates such as hour of the day and day of the week. However, we also include other exogenous covariates to $\boldsymbol{x}i$, when dealing with a multivariate problem. In this paper we focus on generating univariate predictions where the total number of target variables at each step is one ($d_y = 1$), although the problem can be generalized to predict multiple target variables at a time step ($d_y > 1$).

3   Related Work

Time series forecasting methods can be categorized into classical and neural network methods. Prominent examples of classical methods include ARIMA [3] and state space models (SSMs) [8]. ARIMA and SSMs require the expertise of practitioners to manually select the autocorrelation structure, seasonality, trend, and other explanatory variables. Additionally, the core assumption of classical methods, such as stationarity and homoscedasticity of the time series data, make them unsuitable for sporadic and nonuniform large data.

Neural network methods have been widely applied to time series forecasting to model the non-linearity in large-scale data across related time series. Deep neural networks have been proposed to model the interacting patterns among time series and they have demonstrated strong performance improvements over traditional time series models [1,22,24]. Many deep learning architectures depend on RNNs to model non-trivial time series data [10,24,25,32]. Deep AR [25] generates parameters of a one-step-ahead Gaussian distribution using stacked layers of LSTM [13]. The Deep State Space Model (DSSM) [24] uses LSTMs to generate parameters of a linear state space model at each time step. Multi-horizon Quantile Recurrent Forecaster (MQRNN) [32] uses an RNN architecture as an encoder to generate a context vector for multi-layer perceptrons to generate multi-step forecasts.

Transformers have shown superior performance in modeling long-term dependencies compared to RNNs [9,18]. The Attention mechanism has been applied to a variety of tasks such as translation [30], image classifications [31], music generation [14], and tabular learning [2]. Recently, the attention mechanism has gained popularity in the time series community as well [6,18,20,21,27]. To include temporal information in the query-key similarity of the attention mechanism, several works benefit from CNNs [17,18,26]. CNN-trans [18] uses a convolutional processing layer to integrate the temporal context into the attention mechanism to build an autoregressive transformer-based model. Temporal Convolution Attention-based Network (TCAN) [28] follows a similar approach by applying dilated convolution to the output of a temporal attention layer to model the short- and long-term temporal behavior. However the aforementioned approaches use a convolutional filter with a fixed size controlled by a hyperparameter. In natural language processing domain, Chen et al. [5] demonstrate the usefulness of a max pooling layer on top of different CNN filters by proposing a Dynamic Multi-pooling Convolutional Neural Network (DMCNN). Albeit in a different domain, this idea is related in spirit to our approach.

Recently, new approaches have developed efficient transformer models to predict for long-time series forecasting problems. Informer [33] uses KL-divergence and ProbAttention to select the most prominent queries and reduces the complexity to $O(L \log L)$. Autoformer [11] includes the series decomposition as an inner block of transformers and replaces the attention mechanism with the auto-correlation among sub-series to achieve $O(L \log L)$ complexity. Our contribution is complementary to these extensions since our attention mechanism can serve as a substitute for auto-correlation and attention block in ProbAttention.

4   Methodology

In this section, we detail shortcomings to point-wise attention and elaborate on principles of context-based temporal attention. We develop a self-adjusting model that will select the most appropriate filter size for each forecasting decision. We remove redundancies of this model via a subsampling approach.

4.1   Background: Issues Arising from Point-Wise Attention

Given time series data, a basic single-layer transformer model with masked scaled dot-product QKV attention would predict the layer output y_i at time step i as $y_i = \mathtt{softmax}(\sum_{j \le i} a_{ij} v_j)$ with attention $a_{ij} = \mathtt{softmax}\left(q_i^\mathsf{T} \cdot k_j / \sqrt{d}\right)$ where query, key, and value vectors are derived via $q_i = \mathtt{proj}(x_i)$, $k_j = \mathtt{proj}(x_j)$, and $v_j = \mathtt{proj}(x_j)$ using three different multi-layer perceptron-style projections of inputs to vectors with dimension d.

We call this form of attention point-wise, because it does not incorporate the temporal context, as we are solely considering the information at time points i and j. Figure 1 illustrates a forecasting issue that might arise because of the point-wise attention mechanism in transformers. The canonical approach to incorporate the temporal context into the attention mechanism is to use a multi-layer model. The hope is that in a multi-layer architecture, the previous layers provide an appropriate representation of the temporal context. However, previous layers are also suffering from the problem induced by point-wise attention. Therefore, while multi-layer transformers can theoretically learn a good temporal representation, the architecture is an impediment to good performance. In the following we address this issue with a simple-to-implement approach to directly incorporate the temporal context and demonstrate in the experimental evaluation that even a single layer of our approach can outperform a multi-layer transformer model.

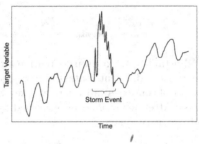

Fig. 2. An example of the temporal behaviour of the target variable taken from the watershed dataset. The center of the plot depicts a stormy period with higher dynamical behavior. Shorter context sizes are more appropriate for modeling temporal behavior in these periods.

4.2 Temporal Attention

The first step towards a better model is to include the temporal context into the attention. This idea has been discussed under the name convolutional attention [18] or temporal attention [28].

This is achieved by deriving query and key vectors from the context of length L preceding the time step i. Denoting this temporal context $i_{<L} = [(i - (L - 1)), \dots, i]$, the only modification to the temporal attention is how query and key vectors are obtained: $q_i = \text{proj}(x_{i_{<L}})$ and $k_j = \text{proj}(x_{j_{<L}})$. The attention follows as: $a_{ij} = \text{softmax}\left(q_i^{\mathsf{T}} \cdot k_j / \sqrt{d}\right)$.

Note that $x_{j_{<L}} \in \mathbb{R}^{d_x \times L}$ is a matrix, which can be interpreted as being re-shaped into a vector.

While this kind of attention is considering the temporal context, the issue is that this context is of a fixed length L, which needs to be either pre-determined or tuned as a hyperparameter. The common belief is that even if the ideal context length L^* would be unknown, choosing a sufficiently large context length $L \geq L^*$ is sufficient. It is based on the hope that end-to-end training will set the parameters of the MLP-projection to ignore parts that are not needed.

However, we hypothesize that the noise introduced by excessively large context sizes will inhibit good performance and potentially mislead the model. In the following we propose an alternative and demonstrate in the experimental section that this leads to significantly better forecasting performance.

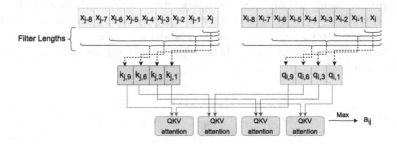

Fig. 3. An example of the adjustable context-aware attention architecture with context lengths $\mathcal{L} = \{1, 3, 6, 9\}$. We consider different context sizes to project the input data at time step i and j to create a set of context-aware query and key vectors (the projections is indicated in dashed arrows). Attention score a_{ij} is governed by the highest similarity to query at time step i and key at time step j.

4.3   Adjustable Context-Aware Attention

Our goal is to provide the model with the flexibility to choose the optimal context length L for the temporal attention. In the following we refer to optimality with respect to the overarching model's hold-out performance of forecasting target variables, via the query-key similarity.

Rather than learning a single one-size-fits-all context length parameter L, we hypothesize that a successful model would need to switch between different lengths dynamically, depending on the situation. For example, as depicted in Fig. 2 for the watershed domain, behavior of the target variable is much more dynamic during storm events than during dry periods. Hence the ideal context length would be much shorter during a storm event than during dry periods. Hence, we will consider multiple context sizes $\mathcal{L} = \{l_1, \ldots l_n\}$ when computing the attention score. We will make the selection of the ideal context length part of the prediction problem using the following model.

for all context length $l \in \mathcal{L}$ obtain:

- query vector $\boldsymbol{q}_{i,l} = \texttt{proj}\left(\boldsymbol{x}_{i_{<l}}\right)$
- key vector $\boldsymbol{k}_{j,l} = \texttt{proj}\left(\boldsymbol{x}_{j_{<l}}\right)$.

Then use the context length that maximizes the attention score:
$$a_{ij} = \max_{l \in \mathcal{L}} \texttt{softmax}\left(q_{i,l}^{\mathsf{T}} \cdot k_{j,l}/\sqrt{d}\right).$$

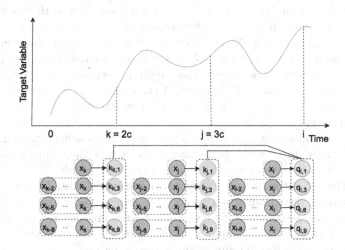

Fig. 4. An overview of our subsampling scheme with $c = 9$. Context sizes are from $\mathcal{L} = \{1, 3, 6, 9\}$. Each key with context length $l \in \mathcal{L}$ subsumes the information of its l preceding inputs. Hence, even though keys from time step $j-1$ to $j-8$ are skipped, the information of x_{j-1} to x_{j-8} is represented in key $k_{j,9}$ via the context-aware attention.

The intuition is that all wrong filter lengths will miss to detect the similarity, therefore if a filter length triggers a similarity, during training, the back propagation encourages a low similarity across all filter lengths for intervals with different temporal behavior. This adjustable context-aware attention score is used inside the transformer model. Note that, with this approach, the query q_i and the key k_j are represented by multiple context-aware query and key vectors for different context lengths in $\mathcal{L}$. Figure 3 depicts an overview of our proposed attention mechanism.

We claim that this provides the attention mechanism with the flexibility to dynamically determine the optimal query-key similarity and hence leads to better forecasting results. We will provide empirical evidence for this claim in the experimental evaluation.

The downside of this approach is its demand in resources. To calculate the attention weights, our model needs to explore all possible context-aware query and key pairs. For an attention model with Q queries and K keys, computing the attention weights requires $O(|\mathcal{L}| \cdot Q \cdot K)$ space and time—not accounting for the cost of projections. This is in contrast to $O(Q \cdot K)$ for the original point-wise attention. We address this next.

4.4 Efficient Adjustable Context-Aware Attention

In order to increase the efficiency our adjustable context-aware attention, we first propose a subsampling scheme for the keys used for attention then explain how our model still incorporates the information from skipped time points.

Let c be the subsampling rate, our transformer would only consider keys with index $j \in \mathcal{J}_c = [0, c, 2c, 3c, \dots]$. For example $c = 2$ would skip every other key, where with $c = 5$, only every 5'th key is considered. However, multiple filter lengths are available at each of these indices, therefore, as an example the information between 0 and c is represented via k_c.

Hence the predicted output y_i at time i is obtained as:

$y_i = \mathtt{softmax}(\sum_{j \in \mathcal{J}_c} a_{ij} v_j)$.

In neural networks with point-wise attentions, such a subsampling approach would potentially degrade the performance, as each of the skipped time steps might be potentially crucial for an accurate forecasting result.

Due to the use of the temporal attention in our model, data between skipped keys, for example data from $2c + 1$ to $3c - 1$ is represented via k_{3c}. This is also depicted in Fig. 4. In contrast, if we would not subsample keys, this would lead to lots of redundancies as any input x_j is incorporated into multiple key vectors $k_j, k_{j+1}, k_{j+2} \dots$ due to the temporal attention paradigm.

Context lengths $\mathcal{L}$ and subsampling rate c have opposing effects on the overall complexity, which renders the total memory usage and runtime to $O(\frac{|\mathcal{L}|}{c} \cdot Q \cdot K)$. While $\mathcal{L}$ and c can be independently chosen, in our experimental setup, we use $c = \max \mathcal{L}$. The effect on the overall network is that for the query at time step i and the key at time step j, the network selects the context length l that is sufficient to identify whether the temporal behavior of time step j is helpful to forecast at time step i.

In other words, during periods where a short context is sufficient to identify that the behavior is different, a small context window will be chosen and c keys will be skipped as it is identified as not helpful. Also whenever the similarity is only apparent when inspecting longer contexts, the longer context will be chosen by the network and c keys can be skipped to avoid redundancies. We want to remark that this approach is designed to work with target variables that are smooth over time, with signals that can exhibit rapid or slow changes.

4.5 Overarching Architecture

Our model adapts an encoder-decoder architecture used by Vaswani et al. [30].

Encoder. While a stack of ACAT layers could be used, we use an encoder of only a single layer. The encoder is comprised of a multi-head adjustable context-aware self-attention and a feed forward network sub-layer. The encoder is used to encode the information of previous observation (including the target variables) into hidden representations.

Decoder. The decoder is a single layer comprised of a masked multi-head adjustable context-aware self-attention, a multi-head adjustable context-aware cross-attention, and a feed forward network sub-layer. Masked multi-head attention is applied by setting masked dot-products to $-\infty$. This prevents the current time step from attending to future time steps. The decoder generates predictions based on the encoder's hidden representation of previous observations and current known inputs. Alternatively a stack of ACAT decoder layers could be used, here we demonstrate the efficacy of even a single layer.

5   Experiments

5.1   Datasets

We empirically perform experiments on three datasets, including two univariate publicly available datasets and one multivariate dataset that we provide in our github repository.

- **Electricity:**[1] The univariate UCI Electricity Load Diagrams dataset, containing the electricity consumption of 370 customers aggregated on an hourly level.
- **Traffic:**[2] The univariate UCI PEM-SF Traffic Dataset, containing occupancy rate ($y_t \in [0,1]$) of 440 SF Bay Area freeways aggregated on an hourly level.
- **Watershed:**[3] This multivariate dataset contains hydrological streamflow responses of ten watershed sites, aggregated on a 15 min level.

Regarding our choices of datasets, we select the traffic and electricity datasets that have been extensively used by a significant amount of research papers for modeling and evaluation [11,18,20,25,33]. We are also working with collaborators who are interested in modeling real-world stream chemistry for the watershed dataset. We use 160,000 samples for each dataset, each sample including historical observations of one week (168 h) for the traffic and electricity datasets and 42 (168 quarter) hours for the watershed dataset. We generate predictions for 24 and 48 future horizons on all datasets. After zero-mean normalization, we partition each dataset into three parts, 80% training set for the learning procedure, 10% validation set for hyperparameter optimization, and 10% hold-out test set for performance evaluation.

5.2   Evaluation Metrics

Models are evaluated by two standard metrics, including root mean squared error (RMSE): $\sqrt{\frac{1}{n}\sum_{i=1}^{n}(y-\hat{y})^2}$ and mean absolute error (MAE): $\frac{1}{n}\sum_{i=1}^{n}|y-\hat{y}|$. MAE is a linear score that equally weighs the errors, where RMSE is a quadratic score that assigns higher weights to larger errors.

---

[1] https://archive.ics.uci.edu/ml/machine-learning-databases/00321/LD2011-2014.

[2] https://archive.ics.uci.edu/ml/machine-learning-databases/00204.

[3] https://github.com/a1992/Context-Aware-Transformer/data/watershed.

5.3   Baselines

We compare a single layer architecture of our proposed ACAT model to the following methods. ARIMA is only applicable to univariate datatsets (traffic and electricity).

1. **ARIMA** [3]: Auto-regressive integrated moving average.
2. **LSTM** [13]: A single layer encoder-decoder Long Short Term Memory.
3. **Transformer** [30]: A single layer transformer equivalent to our approach with the basic multi-head attention.
4. **Trans-multi** [30]: A three encoder layer and one decoder layer transformer with multi-head basic attention.
5. **CNN-trans** [18]: A single layer transformer with convolutional multi-head attention.

Table 1. Results summary in RMSE and MAE of all methods on three datasets. Lower RMSE and MAE indicate a more accurate forecast. Best results are highlighted in boldface.

Dataset	Horizon	Metric	ARIMA	LSTM	Transformer	Trans-multi	CNN-trans	ACAT (Ours)
Traffic	24	RMSE	0.81 ± 0.00	0.50 ± 0.02	0.48 ± 0.00	0.59 ± 0.09	0.47 ± 0.00	**0.38 ± 0.00**
		MAE	0.56 ± 0.00	0.28 ± 0.02	0.25 ± 0.00	0.35 ± 0.09	0.24 ± 0.00	**0.16 ± 0.00**
	48	RMSE	0.79 ± 0.00	0.49 ± 0.00	0.46 ± 0.00	0.68 ± 0.09	0.46 ± 0.00	**0.35 ± 0.00**
		MAE	0.56 ± 0.00	0.26 ± 0.00	0.24 ± 0.00	0.45 ± 0,09	0.23 ± 0.00	**0.16 ± 0.00**
Electricity	24	RMSE	3.98 ± 0.00	1.29 ± 0.03	1.29 ± 0.07	1.48 ± 0.08	1.27 ± 0.08	**0.64 ± 0.02**
		MAE	0.41 ± 0.00	0.13 ± 0.01	0.15 ± 0.01	0.16 ± 0.00	0.14 ± 0.00	**0.08 ± 0.00**
	48	RMSE	4.06 ± 0.00	1.40 ± 0.07	1.47 ± 0.02	1.56 ± 0.14	1.26 ± 0.04	**0.84 ± 0.03**
		MAE	0.41 ± 0.00	0.14 ± 0.00	0.16 ± 0.00	0.17 ± 0.00	0.14 ± 0.00	**0.09 ± 0.00**
Watershed	24	RMSE	–	0.35 ± 0.05	0.33 ± 0.01	0.35 ± 0.01	0.34 ± 0.00	**0.28 ± 0.01**
		MAE		0.20 ± 0.03	0.19 ± 0.01	0.21 ± 0.01	0.20 ± 0.00	**0.16 ± 0.01**
	48	RMSE	–	0.42 ± 0.04	0.36 ± 0.01	0.35 ± 0.01	0.35 ± 0.01	**0.31 ± 0.01**
		MAE		0.25 ± 0.01	0.21 ± 0.03	0.20 ± 0.01	0.20 ± 0.01	**0.16 ± 0.01**

5.4   Model Training and Hyperprarameters

Training Procedure. All neural network methods are trained and evaluated multiple times. We use grid search for hyperparameter tuning. The model size is chosen from $\{16, 32\}$ for all neural network methods. The number of heads is set to 8 for all transformer-based models. The kernel size for convolutional processing layer of CNN-trans is chosen from $\{1, 3, 6, 9\}$. The mini batch-size is set to 256 for all datasets. We use the Adam optimizer [16] with $\beta_1 = 0.9$, $\beta_2 = 0.98$ and $\epsilon = 10^{-9}$, we update the learning rate and use `warmup_steps` $= 4000$ according to the basic transformer [30]:

$$\texttt{lrate} = d_{\texttt{model}}^{-0.5} \cdot \min(\texttt{step\_num}^{-0.5}, \texttt{step\_num}.\texttt{warmup\_steps}^{1.5})$$

The total number of epochs is 50 with early stopping set to five iterations.

Loss Function. For all methods, we choose the mean squared error (MSE) loss function to calculate the loss of generated predictions compared to the target sequence in the training procedure. The loss is back-propagated from the decoder's outputs to the entire model.

Hardware and Computational Cost. All models were trained on a single NVIDIA Titan XP GPU with 12 GB of memory. For our proposed ACAT model with $\mathcal{L} = \{1, 3, 6, 9\}$, it takes 0.3 s to finish one training step and each epoch takes 150 s.

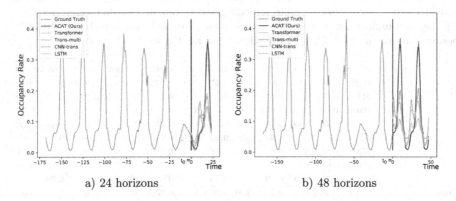

a) 24 horizons   b) 48 horizons

Fig. 5. Forecasted predictions of one sample of hold-out test set on the traffic dataset of neural network models. Predictions are generated for a) 24 and b) 48 horizons given the previous 168 input samples. The predictions generated by our ACAT model are exhibiting a higher accuracy than other baselines.

5.5 Results and Discussion

Results are reported as mean and standard error of RMSE and MAE scores for the total number of three experimental runs for neural networks and one experimental run for the ARIMA model.

Table 1 summarizes the evaluation results of all methods on three datasets when generating predictions for 24 and 48 forecasting horizons. Across all datasets we observe that ACAT outperforms other methods. The significant improvements of our ACAT model over other methods stem from our proposed adjustable context-aware attention. The difference in performance to CNN-trans demonstrates the gain when providing the model with the flexibility to choose the right context length adaptively. Regarding baselines, the performance of the Trans-multi model indicates that even a multi-layer transformer is ineffective in recovering from the point-wise attention. The performance of the CNN-trans model is relatively similar to the basic transformer. This indicates that integrating a temporal context with a fixed length cannot enhance the forecasting quality considerably if the model is not able to adjust the context length.

Figure 5 displays forecasted predictions of all neural network methods including our ACAT on one example from traffic dataset over 24 and 48 forecasting horizon. The predictions generated by ACAT are aligning closely with the ground truth, while the generated predictions of other neural network baselines exhibit larger errors and fail to resemble the temporal behaviour.

Table 2. Comparison of different subsampling rates. As a result of increasing the subsampling rate (maximum context size $\max(\mathcal{L})$) more keys are skipped. Lower RMSE and MAE indicate a more accurate forecast. Best results are highlighted in boldface. The last row indicates how many times this configuration obtained the best result. The performance of our ACAT model is resilient towards the subsampling rate.

Dataset	Horizon	Metric	$\max(\mathcal{L}) = 9$	$\max(\mathcal{L}) = 12$	$\max(\mathcal{L}) = 15$	$\max(\mathcal{L}) = 18$	$\max(\mathcal{L}) = 21$	$\max(\mathcal{L}) = 24$
Traffic	24	RMSE	0.38 ± 0.00	0.38 ± 0.00	$\mathbf{0.37} \pm 0.00$	$\mathbf{0.37} \pm 0.00$	0.37 ± 0.00	0.38 ± 0.00
		MAE	0.16 ± 0.00	0.16 ± 0.00	0.16 ± 0.00	$\mathbf{0.15} \pm 0.00$	0.16 ± 0.00	$\mathbf{0.15} \pm 0.00$
	48	RMSE	$\mathbf{0.35} \pm 0.00$	0.36 ± 0.00	0.36 ± 0.00	0.37 ± 0.00	0.37 ± 0.00	0.37 ± 0.00
		MAE	$\mathbf{0.16} \pm 0.00$	$\mathbf{0.16} \pm 0.00$	$\mathbf{0.16} \pm 0.00$	0.17 ± 0.00	0.17 ± 0.00	$\mathbf{0.16} \pm 0.00$
Electricity	24	RMSE	0.64 ± 0.02	0.66 ± 0.02	$\mathbf{0.63} \pm 0.02$	0.67 ± 0.03	0.73 ± 0.03	0.72 ± 0.05
		MAE	$\mathbf{0.08} \pm 0.00$	$\mathbf{0.08} \pm 0.00$	$\mathbf{0.08} \pm 0.00$	$\mathbf{0.08} \pm 0.00$	$\mathbf{0.08} \pm 0.00$	0.09 ± 0.00
	48	RMSE	0.84 ± 0.03	0.84 ± 0.01	0.83 ± 0.03	$\mathbf{0.80} \pm 0.09$	0.83 ± 0.06	0.83 ± 0.01
		MAE	$\mathbf{0.09} \pm 0.00$	$\mathbf{0.09} \pm 0.00$	$\mathbf{0.09} \pm 0.00$	$\mathbf{0.09} \pm 0.01$	$\mathbf{0.09} \pm 0.00$	$\mathbf{0.09} \pm 0.00$
Watershed	24	RMSE	0.28 ± 0.01	$\mathbf{0.25} \pm 0.00$	0.28 ± 0.01	0.27 ± 0.00	0.27 ± 0.00	0.28 ± 0.02
		MAE	0.16 ± 0.01	$\mathbf{0.13} \pm 0.00$	0.15 ± 0.01	0.14 ± 0.00	0.16 ± 0.00	0.15 ± 0.00
	48	RMSE	0.31 ± 0.01	0.30 ± 0.01	0.31 ± 0.02	0.30 ± 0.01	$\mathbf{0.29} \pm 0.00$	0.30 ± 0.01
		MAE	$\mathbf{0.16} \pm 0.00$	0.17 ± 0.01	0.17 ± 0.01	$\mathbf{0.16} \pm 0.01$	$\mathbf{0.16} \pm 0.00$	$\mathbf{0.16} \pm 0.01$
Total Wins			5	5	5	6	5	4

Ablation Study: The Impact of Subsampling Rate. To demonstrate that the performance of our ACAT model is resilient towards how many keys are skipped during subsampling, we conduct an ablation study by increasing the subsampling rate. As a result of choosing the subsampling rate as the maximum context size $\max(\mathcal{L})$, we skip more keys by increasing the value of the maximum context size. Table 2 demonstrates the results of this ablation study, it is observed that the performance of our model is resilient towards the subsampling rate. In contrast, increasing the subsampling rate allows us to include a longer history into the forecasting while adjusting the temporal context length, which leads to a better performance in some cases.

6   Conclusion

In this paper, we study the multi-horizon time series forecasting problem and introduce ACAT, the Adjustable Context-aware Transformer, which automatically selects the ideal context size to obtain the best forecasting results. We demonstrate the effectiveness of our approach on three real-world datasets in comparison with the classical forecasting method ARIMA, the RNN-based encoder-decoder LSTM, transformers based with basic and CNN attention, as well as multi-layer transformers. Our extensive analyses show that our ACAT model obtains performance improvements over state-of-the-art temporal attention approaches, including those based on the convolutional attention models. This indicates that incorporating the ideal context length in the query-key similarity of the attention mechanism can improve the forecasting quality.

In the introduction we hypothesized that the structure of the basic attention mechanism presents an impediment for the original transformer architecture when applied to temporal analyses, even when including multiple layers. Experimentally we verify this claim, and demonstrate that our ACAT model addresses its shortcoming even with a single layer.

Lastly, our ACAT model can benefit any application domain where accurate forecasts are important. For example in the watershed domain, natural scientists base their analysis on forecasting models. Incorrect forecasts can lead to false models of natural processes. Another example are forecasts on traffic or electricity consumption, which, if inaccurate, have severe negative effects on our society. Our work demonstrates significant improvements in all these three domains.

References

1. Alaa, A.M., van der Schaar, M.: Attentive state-space modeling of disease progression. In: Wallach, H., et al. (eds.) Advances in Neural Information Processing Systems, vol. 32. Curran Associates Inc. (2019). https://proceedings.neurips.cc/paper/2019/file/1d0932d7f57ce74d9d9931a2c6db8a06-Paper.pdf
2. Arik, S.Ö., Pfister, T.: TabNet: attentive interpretable tabular learning. In: Proceedings of the AAAI Conference on Artificial Intelligence, vol. 35, no. 8, pp. 6679–6687 (2021). https://ojs.aaai.org/index.php/AAAI/article/view/16826
3. Box, G.E.P., Jenkins, G.M.: Some recent advances in forecasting and control. J. R. Stat. Soc. Ser. C **17**(2), 91–109 (1968). https://doi.org/10.2307/2985674. https://ideas.repec.org/a/bla/jorssc/v17y1968i2p91-109.html
4. Capistrán, C., Constandse, C., Ramos-Francia, M.: Multi-horizon inflation forecasts using disaggregated data. Econ. Model. **27**(3), 666–677 (2010). https://ideas.repec.org/a/eee/ecmode/v27y2010i3p666-677.html
5. Chen, Y., et al.: Event extraction via dynamic multi-pooling convolutional neural networks. In: Proceedings of the 53rd Annual Meeting of the Association for Computational Linguistics and the 7th International Joint Conference on Natural Language Processing (Volume 1: Long Papers), Beijing, China, pp. 167–176. Association for Computational Linguistics (2015). https://doi.org/10.3115/v1/P15-1017. https://aclanthology.org/P15-1017
6. Choi, E., et al.: RETAIN: an interpretable predictive model for healthcare using reverse time attention mechanism. In: Proceedings of the 30th International Conference on Neural Information Processing Systems, NIPS 2016, Barcelona, Spain, pp. 3512–3520. Curran Associates Inc. (2016). ISBN 9781510838819
7. Courty, P., Li, H.: Timing of seasonal sales. J. Bus. **72**(4), 545–572 (1999). https://doi.org/10.1086/209627. https://ideas.repec.org/a/ucp/jnlbus/v72y1999i4p545-72.html

8. Durbin, J., Koopman, S.J.: Time Series Analysis by State Space Methods. OUP Catalogue 9780198523543. Oxford University Press (2001). https://ideas.repec.org/b/oxp/obooks/9780198523543.html. ISBN: ARRAY(0x4eed11c8)

9. Fan, C., et al.: Multi-horizon time series forecasting with temporal attention learning. In: Proceedings of the 25th ACM SIGKDD International Conference on Knowledge Discovery Data Mining, KDD 2019, Anchorage, AK, USA, pp. 2527–2535. Association for Computing Machinery (2019). https://doi.org/10.1145/3292500.3330662. ISBN 9781450362016

10. Graves, A.: Generating sequences with recurrent neural networks. CoRR abs/1308.0850 (2013). http://dblp.uni-trier.de/db/journals/corr/corr1308.html#Graves13

11. Wu, H., et al.: Autoformer: decomposition transformers with auto-correlation for long-term series forecasting. In: Ranzato, M., et al. (eds.) Advances in Neural Information Processing Systems, vol. 34, pp. 22419–22430. Curran Associates Inc. (2021). https://proceedings.neurips.cc/paper/2021/file/bcc0d400288793e8bdcd7c19a8ac0c2b-Paper.pdf

12. Hochreiter, S., Schmidhuber, J.: Long short-term memory. Neural Comput. $9(8)$, 1735–1780 (1997). https://doi.org/10.1162/neco.1997.9.8.1735. ISSN 0899-7667

13. Hochreiter, S., Schmidhuber, J.: Long short-term memory. Neural Comput. 9, 1735–1780 (1997). https://doi.org/10.1162/neco.1997.9.8.1735

14. Huang, C.-Z.A., et al.: Music transformer: generating music with long-term structure. In: ICLR (2019)

15. Khandelwal, U., et al.: Sharp nearby, fuzzy far away: how neural language models use context. In: Proceedings of the 56th Annual Meeting of the Association for Computational Linguistics (Volume 1: Long Papers) Melbourne, Australia, pp. 284–294. Association for Computational Linguistics (2018). https://doi.org/10.18653/v1/P18-1027. https://aclanthology.org/P18-1027

16. Kingma, D.P., Ba, J.: Adam: a method for stochastic optimization. CoRR abs/1412.6980 (2015)

17. LeCun, Y., Bengio, Y.: Convolutional networks for images, speech, and time series. In: The Handbook of Brain Theory and Neural Networks, pp. 255–258. MIT Press, Cambridge (1998). ISBN 0262511029

18. Li, S., et al.: Enhancing the locality and breaking the memory bottleneck of transformer on time series forecasting. In: Proceedings of the 33rd International Conference on Neural Information Processing Systems. Curran Associates Inc., Red Hook (2019)

19. Lim, B.: Forecasting treatment responses over time using recurrent marginal structural networks. In: Bengio, S., et al. (eds.) Advances in Neural Information Processing Systems, vol. 31. Curran Associates Inc. (2018). https://proceedings.neurips.cc/paper/2018/file/56e6a93212e4482d99c84a639d254b67-Paper.pdf

20. Lim, B., et al.: Temporal fusion transformers for interpretable multihorizon time series forecasting. Int. J. Forecast. $37(4)$, 1748–1764 (2021). https://doi.org/10.1016/j.ijforecast.2021.03.012. www.sciencedirect.com/science/article/pii/S0169207021000637. ISSN 0169-2070

21. Ma, J., et al.: CDSA: cross-dimensional self-attention for multivariate, geo-tagged time series imputation (2019). arXiv:1905.09904 [cs.LG]

22. Makridakis, S., Spiliotis, E., Assimakopoulos, V.: The M4 competition: 100,000 time series and 61 forecasting methods. Int. J. Forecast. $36(1)$, 54–74 (2020). https://EconPapers.repec.org/RePEc:eee:intfor:v:36:y:2020:i:1:p:54-74

23. Papadimitriou, S., Yu, P.: Optimal multi-scale patterns in time series streams, pp. 647–658 (2006). https://doi.org/10.1145/1142473.1142545

24. Rangapuram, S.S., et al.: Deep state space models for time series forecasting. In: Bengio, S., et al. (eds.) Advances in Neural Information Processing Systems, vol. 31. Curran Associates Inc. (2018). https://proceedings.neurips.cc/paper/2018/file/5cf68969fb67aa6082363a6d4e6468e2-Paper.pdf

25. Salinas, D., et al.: DeepAR: probabilistic forecasting with autoregressive recurrent networks. Int. J. Forecast. **36**(3), 1181–1191 (2020). https://doi.org/10.1016/j.ijforecast.2019.07.001. https://www.sciencedirect.com/science/article/pii/S0169207019301888. ISSN 0169-2070

26. Shih, S.-Y., Sun, F.-K., Lee, H.: Temporal pattern attention for multivariate time series forecasting. Mach. Learn. **108** (2019). https://doi.org/10.1007/s10994-019-05815-0

27. Song, H., et al.: Attend and diagnose: clinical time series analysis using attention models. In: AAAI Press (2018). ISBN 978-1-57735-800-8

28. Tang, P., et al.: Channel attention-based temporal convolutional network for satellite image time series classification. IEEE Geo-sci. Remote Sens. Lett. **19**, 1–5 (2022). https://doi.org/10.1109/LGRS.2021.3095505

29. Taylor, S., Letham, B.: Forecasting at scale (2017). https://doi.org/10.7287/peerj.preprints.3190v2

30. Vaswani, A., et al.: Attention is all you need. In: Guyon, I., et al. (eds.) Advances in Neural Information Processing Systems, vol. 30. Curran Associates Inc. (2017). https://proceedings.neurips.cc/paper/2017/file/3f5ee243547dee91fbd053c1c4a845aa-Paper.pdf

31. Wang, F., et al.: Residual attention network for image classification. In: 2017 IEEE Conference on Computer Vision and Pattern Recognition (CVPR), pp. 6450–6458 (2017). https://doi.org/10.1109/CVPR.2017.683

32. Wen, R., et al.: A multi-horizon quantile recurrent forecaster. In: NeurIPS 2017 (2017). https://www.amazon.science/publications/a-multi-horizon-quantile-recurrent-forecaster

33. Zhou, H., et al.: Informer: beyond efficient transformer for long sequence time-series forecasting. In: AAAI (2021)

34. Zhu, Y., Shasha, D.: StatStream: statistical monitoring of thousands of data streams in real time. In: Proceedings of the 28th International Conference on Very Large Data Bases, VLDB 2002, Hong Kong, China: VLDB Endowment, pp. 358–369 (2002)

Clustering of Time Series Based on Forecasting Performance of Global Models

Ángel López-Oriona[1]([✉]) [iD], Pablo Montero-Manso[2][iD], and José A. Vilar[1][iD]

[1] Research Group MODES, Research Center for Information and Communication Technologies (CITIC), University of A Coruña, 15071 A Coruña, Spain
{a.oriona,jose.vilarf}@udc.es
[2] The University of Sydney Business School, Sydney, Australia
pablo.monteromanso@sydney.edu

Abstract. This article proposes a new procedure to perform clustering of time series. The approach relies on the classical K-means clustering method and is based on two iterative steps: (i) K global forecasting models are fitted via pooling by using the series belonging to each group and (ii) each series is assigned to the cluster associated with the model yielding the best forecasts in accordance with a specific criterion. The resulting clustering solution includes groups which are optimal in terms of overall prediction error, and thus the procedure is able to detect the different forecasting patterns existing in a given dataset. Some simulation experiments show that our method outperforms several alternative techniques in terms of both clustering accuracy and forecasting error. The procedure is also applied to carry out clustering in three real time series databases.

Keywords: Time series · Clustering · Global forecasting models · Prediction error · K-means

1 Introduction

Time series clustering (TSC) is a fundamental problem in machine learning with applications in many fields, including geology, finance, computer science or psychology, among others. The task consists of splitting a large collection of unlabelled time series realizations into homogeneous groups so that similar series are located together in the same group and dissimilar series are placed in different clusters. As result, each group can be characterized by a specific temporal pattern, which allows to address key issues as discovering hidden dynamic structures, identifying anomalies or forecasting future behaviours. A comprehensive overview on the topic is provided in [10].

A crucial point in cluster analysis is to establish the dissimilarity notion since it determines the nature of the resulting clustering partition. Several distance measures have been proposed in the literature, each one of them associated with

T. Guyet et al. (Eds.): AALTD 2022, LNAI 13812, pp. 18–33, 2023.
https://doi.org/10.1007/978-3-031-24378-3_2

a different objective. If the goal is to discriminate between geometric profiles of the time series, then a shape-based dissimilarity is suitable. For instance, the well-known dynamic time warping (DTW) distance has been used in several works to perform TSC [3]. On the contrary, a structure-based dissimilarity is desirable if the target is to compare underlying dependence models. Examples of this type of distances are metrics comparing the autocorrelations [5] or the wavelet coefficients [4] of two time series. Additional types of dissimilarities are based on estimated model coefficients [2].

The goal of this work is to construct a TSC algorithm capable of returning a partition which is optimal in terms of overall forecasting accuracy. To that aim, we introduce the notion of dissimilarity between a time series and a given model (e.g., ARIMA) as the average prediction error produced when iteratively obtaining the point forecasts of the time series with respect to the corresponding model. It is worth highlighting that, although there are a few TSC methods based on forecast densities [14], to the best of our knowledge, nobody has employed the concept of similarity previously exposed to perform clustering in time series databases. Specifically, our clustering approach makes use of the so-called global models to minimize the average prediction error. Global models are constructed in the following way [12]: (i) each series in a set is lag-embedded into a matrix at a given AR order, l, fixed beforehand, (ii) these matrices are stacked together to form one big matrix, achieving data pooling and (iii) a classical regression model (e.g., linear regression, random forest etc.) is fitted to the resulting matrix.

Global models have been shown to outperform local models in terms of forecasting accuracy in several datasets [12]. In other words, when a single model is fitted to all the time series in the database, and used to obtain the corresponding predictions, a lower average forecasting error is produced than in the case where each time series is predicted by considering a different local model. Moreover, global models do not need any assumption about similarity of the time series in the collection, and need far fewer parameters than the simplest of local methods.

Although the global model approach produces outstanding results, it has one important drawback: it ignores the possible existence of homogeneous groups of series in terms of prediction patterns. For instance, a database could contain two groups of series in such a way that the series within each group are helpful to each other for obtaining accurate predictions (e.g., think of several countries whose behaviour concerning monthly economic growth is very similar), but totally use-less for the series in the remaining group. In the previous situation, it would be desirable to fit a global method for each distinct set of time series. Then the predictions would be computed for a given series by using its associated global model. In order to detect groups of series sharing similar forecasting structures, we propose a novel clustering method which is based on the traditional K-means algorithm. The technique relies on the following iterative process: (i) K global models (centroids) are fitted by taking into account the series pertaining to each cluster independently and (ii) each time series is assigned to the group associated with the centroid producing the lowest forecasting error according to a specific metric.

It is worth emphasizing that, by construction, the proposed algorithm produces a partition which is optimal in terms of overall prediction effectiveness. In fact, the objective function of the pseudo K-means method can be seen as a sum of forecasting errors (see Sect. 2), which is expected to decrease with each iteration of the two-step procedure described above. Therefore, the clustering algorithm is specifically designed to allocate the different time series in such a way that the corresponding global models represent in the best possible manner the existing prediction patterns. There are only a few works in the literature combining clustering and global methods in a single technique. For instance, [1] proposed an approach particularly devised to improve the forecasting accuracy of global models. First, the set of series is partitioned into different groups by using a specific clustering method. Then, global models are fitted by considering the series within each cluster. Although successful, the method of [1] splits the set of series by using a feature-based TSC clustering method so that there is not guarantee that the resulting partition is optimal in terms of total prediction accuracy. Note that our approach circumvents this limitation by adapting the objective function to the specific purpose of forecasting error reduction.

Some simulation experiments are carried out in the paper to assess the performance of the proposed algorithm in terms of both clustering effectiveness and forecasting accuracy. In all cases, synthetic partitions where the groups are characterized by different generating processes are considered, and the approach is compared with several alternative methods, as one procedure based on local models or the technique of [1]. The method is also applied to perform clustering in some well-known datasets. Overall, the algorithm exhibits a great behaviour when dealing with both synthetic and real data.

The remainder of this paper is organized as follows. Section 2 describes the clustering algorithm based on prediction accuracy of global forecasting models. The approach is analysed in Sect. 3 by means of a simulation study where different scenarios are taken into account. In Sect. 4, we apply the proposed method to real datasets of time series. Section 5 contains some concluding remarks.

2   A Clustering Algorithm Based on Prediction Accuracy of Global Forecasting Models

Consider a set of n time series, $\mathcal{S} = \left\{ \boldsymbol{X}_t^{(1)}, \ldots, \boldsymbol{X}_t^{(n)} \right\}$, where each $\boldsymbol{X}_t^{(i)} = \left(X_1^{(i)}, \ldots, X_{L_i}^{(i)} \right)$ is a series of length L_i, $i = 1, \ldots, n$. We assume that each series $\boldsymbol{X}_t^{(i)}$ contains training and a validation periods of lengths $r(i)$ and $s(i)$, denoted by $\boldsymbol{T}^{(i)} = (t_1^i, \ldots, t_{r(i)}^i)$ and $\boldsymbol{V}^{(i)} = (v_1^i, \ldots, v_{s(i)}^i)$, respectively, such that

- Both $\boldsymbol{T}^{(i)}$ and $\boldsymbol{V}^{(i)}$ are formed by consecutive observations and t_1^i has a position equal to or less than the position of v_1^i, considering both t_1^i and v_1^i as elements of the vector $\boldsymbol{X}_t^{(i)}$,
- $mset(\boldsymbol{T}^{(i)}) \subseteq mset(\boldsymbol{X}_t^{(i)})$ and $mset(\boldsymbol{V}^{(i)}) \subseteq mset(\boldsymbol{X}_t^{(i)})$ (both periods are included in the original series),

- $mset(\boldsymbol{X}_t^{(i)}) \subsetneq mset(\boldsymbol{T}^{(i)}) + mset(\boldsymbol{V}^{(i)})$ (both periods form a cover of the original series),

where the operator $mset(\boldsymbol{z}) = [z_1, \ldots, z_n]$ for the vector $\boldsymbol{z} = (z_1, \ldots, z_n)$, denoting $[\cdot]$ a multiset, i.e., a generalization of the traditional set in which each element can appear multiple times. Note that, by virtue of the previous three conditions, the training and validation periods may contain common observations. This general feature allows to consider traditional validation measures as the in-sample error.

The sets $\mathcal{T} = \{\boldsymbol{T}^{(1)}, \ldots, \boldsymbol{T}^{(n)}\}$ and $\mathcal{V} = \{\boldsymbol{V}^{(1)}, \ldots, \boldsymbol{V}^{(n)}\}$ are called the training and the validation set, respectively. We wish to perform clustering on the elements of $\mathcal{S}$ in such a way that the groups are associated with global models minimizing the overall forecasting error with respect to the validation set. The method we propose is a K-means-based algorithm having the classical two stages: (i) constructing a prototype for each cluster, usually referred to as centroid and (ii) assigning every series to a group. The assignment step often relies on the distance from the series to the prototypes. In this work, we propose to consider global models as prototypes for each group. Specifically, the prototype of kth cluster is a global model which is fitted to the series pertaining to kth cluster.

Assume there are n_k series in the kth cluster C_k, i.e., $C_k = \left\{\boldsymbol{X}_{t,k}^{(1)}, \ldots, \boldsymbol{X}_{t,k}^{(n_k)}\right\}$, with $k = 1, \ldots, K$. A global model $\mathcal{M}_k$ is fitted in cluster C_k by considering the training periods associated to $\boldsymbol{X}_{t,k}^{(j)}$, $j = 1, \ldots, n_k$. It is expected that the predictive ability of model $\mathcal{M}_k$ with respect to the series in cluster C_k is better the more related the series in the group are. In sum, the set of clusters $\boldsymbol{C} = \{C_1, \ldots, C_K\}$ produce the prototypes $\mathcal{M} = \{\mathcal{M}_1, \ldots, \mathcal{M}_K\}$.

Once the global models $\mathcal{M}_1, \ldots, \mathcal{M}_K$ have been constructed, each series is assigned to the cluster whose prototype gives rise to the minimal value for the mean absolute error (MAE) by considering the validation period. Specifically, series $\boldsymbol{X}_t^{(i)}$, $i = 1, \ldots, n$, is assigned to cluster k' such that

$$k' = \arg\min_{k=1,\ldots,K} d_{\text{MAE}}\left(\boldsymbol{X}_t^{(i)}, \mathcal{M}_k\right) = \arg\min_{k=1,\ldots,K} \frac{1}{s(i)} \sum_{j=1}^{s(i)} |v_j^i - F_{j,k}^{(i)}|, \qquad (1)$$

where $F_{j,k}^{(i)}$ is the prediction of v_j^i by considering the global model $\mathcal{M}_k$. Note that considering the MAE in (1) is appropriate because we are evaluating the forecasting effectiveness of K global models with respect to the ith series independently. Therefore, each assignation is only influenced by the units of the corresponding series so that no scaling issues arise. In fact, the simplicity of the MAE makes it a recommended error metric for assessing accuracy on a single series [9].

Both steps the computation of prototypes and the reassignment of series are iterated until convergence or a maximum number of iterations is reached. The corresponding clustering algorithm is described in Algorithm 1. Below we provide some remarks concerning the proposed method.

Algorithm 1. pseudo-K-means clustering algorithm based on prediction accuracy of global forecasting models

---
1: Fix K, l and *max.iter*
2: Set *iter* $= 1$
3: Randomly divide the n series into K clusters
4: Compute the initial set of l-lagged global models $\mathcal{M} = \{\mathcal{M}_1, \ldots, \mathcal{M}_K\} = \mathcal{M}^{(1)}$
5: **repeat**
6:     Set $\mathcal{M}_{\text{OLD}} = \mathcal{M}$ {Store the current prototypes}
7:     Assign each series to the cluster associated with its nearest prototype according to the rule in (1)
8:     Compute the new collection of prototypes by fitting a l-lagged global model to the training periods of the series in kth cluster, $k = 1, \ldots, K$. {Update the set of prototypes}
9:     *iter* $\leftarrow$ *iter* $+ 1$
10: **until** $\mathcal{M} = \mathcal{M}_{\text{OLD}}$ or *iter* $=$ *max.iter*

Remark 1 (*Interpretation of objective function*). Note that the objective function in Algorithm 1 can be written as

$$J(\boldsymbol{C}) = \sum_{k=1}^{K} \sum_{\substack{i=1: \\ \boldsymbol{X}_t^{(i)} \in C_k}}^{n} d_{MAE}(\boldsymbol{X}_t^{(i)}, \mathcal{M}_k), \tag{2}$$

which is a sum of prediction errors with respect to the validation periods. In particular, each series is forecasted by using the global model associated with the cluster it pertains. In this regard, the value of the objective function returned when Algorithm 1 stops, say J_{OPT}, can be regarded as the total optimal (minimal) prediction error when K groups are assumed to exist in the dataset. In the same way, the quantity J_{OPT}/n can be interpreted as the average optimal prediction error. In sum, the objective function of the proposed K-means clustering algorithm is very interpretable from a forecasting perspective.

Remark 2 (*Assessment of the resulting partition in terms of prediction error*). Although the quantity J_{OPT}/n can be seen as the average optimal prediction error, this value is not an appropriate metric to assess the predictive ability of the resulting clustering partition. Note that the two-step procedure described in Algorithm 1 attempts to find the partition minimizing the average prediction error with respect to the validation periods. Therefore, J_{OPT}/n is likely to underestimate the prediction error computed over future periods of the series which are not involved in the optimization process. In this regard, a proper error metric could be obtained through the following steps:

1. Given a prediction horizon $h \in \mathbb{N}$, divide each series into two periods. The first period contains all but the last h observations of the series. The second period, referred to as test period, contains the last h observations. The first periods constitute the set $\mathcal{S} = \left\{ \boldsymbol{X}_t^{(1)}, \ldots, \boldsymbol{X}_t^{(n)} \right\}$ introduced above, whereas

the second periods constitute the set $\mathcal{S}^* = \left\{ \boldsymbol{X}_t^{(1)*}, \ldots, \boldsymbol{X}_t^{(n)*} \right\}$, where each $\boldsymbol{X}_t^{(i)*} = (X_1^{(i)*}, \ldots, X_h^{(i)*})$ is a series of length h. The set $\mathcal{S}^*$ is called the test set.

2. Run Algorithm 1 using the set $\mathcal{S}$ as input, obtaining the clustering solution.
3. Given the clustering solution computed in Step 2, and for $k = 1, \ldots, K$, fit a l-lagged global model to the set of series in the kth cluster by considering both training and validation periods. This produces the set of global models $\overline{\mathcal{M}} = \{\overline{\mathcal{M}}_1, \ldots, \overline{\mathcal{M}}_K\}$.
4. Compute the average prediction error with respect to the test set as

$$\frac{1}{n} \sum_{k=1}^{K} \sum_{\substack{i=1: \\ \boldsymbol{X}_t^{(i)} \in C_k}}^{n} d^*\left(\boldsymbol{X}_t^{(i)*}, \overline{\mathcal{M}}_k\right), \tag{3}$$

where d^* is any function measuring discrepancy between the actual values of $\boldsymbol{X}_t^{(i)*}$ and their predictions according to model $\overline{\mathcal{M}}_k$. Note that these predictions are computed starting from the series $\boldsymbol{X}_t^{(i)}$ and in a recursive manner. As an example, if the MAE is chosen as the error metric, then (3) becomes

$$\frac{1}{n} \sum_{k=1}^{K} \sum_{\substack{i=1: \\ \boldsymbol{X}_t^{(i)} \in C_k}}^{n} d^*_{\mathrm{MAE}}\left(\boldsymbol{X}_t^{(i)*}, \overline{\mathcal{M}}_k\right) = \frac{1}{n} \sum_{k=1}^{K} \sum_{\substack{i=1: \\ \boldsymbol{X}_t^{(i)} \in C_k}}^{n} \frac{1}{h} \sum_{j=1}^{h} \left| X_j^{(i)*} - \overline{F}_{j,k}^{(i)*} \right|, \tag{4}$$

where $\overline{F}_{j,k}^{(i)*}$ is the prediction of $X_j^{(i)*}$ according to the global model $\overline{\mathcal{M}}_k$. The R code used for the implementation of Algorithm (1) is available at https://anloor//clustering_procedure.

3   Simulation Study

In this section we carry out a set of simulations with the aim of assessing the performance of the proposed approach in different scenarios. Firstly we describe the simulation mechanism, then we explain how the evaluation of the method was done and finally we show the results of the simulation study.

3.1   Experimental Design

Two specific scenarios were constructed, both of them including linear processes. Specifically, the first and second scenario involve short memory and long memory models, respectively. In this way, the proposed method is analysed under different degrees of serial dependence. Both scenarios contain three distinct generating processes. The particular generating models are given below.

Scenario 1. Consider the AR(p) process given by

$$X_t = \sum_{i=1}^{p} \varphi_i X_{t-i} + \epsilon_t, \tag{5}$$

where ϵ_t is a process formed by independent elements following the standard Gaussian distribution. We fix $p = 4$. The vector of coefficients $\varphi_4 = (\varphi_1, \varphi_2, \varphi_3, \varphi_4)$ is set as indicated below.

Process 1: $\varphi_4 = (0.1, 0.2, -0.4, 0.3)$.
Process 2: $\varphi_4 = (0.2, -0.5, 0.3, -0.3)$.
Process 3: $\varphi_4 = (-0.3, 0.4, 0.6, -0.2)$.

Scenario 2. Consider the AR(p) process given in (5). We fix $p = 12$. The vector of coefficients $\varphi_{12} = (\varphi_1, \varphi_2, \ldots, \varphi_{12})$ is set as

$(0.9, -0.5, -0.3, 0.3, 0.1, -0.3, 0.2, -0.3, 0.5, -0.5, 0.3, -0.3)$,
$(0.2, 0.3, -0.2, -0.2, 0.4, 0.2, -0.1, 0.2, 0.1, -0.2, -0.3, 0.5)$,
$(-0.3, -0.1, 0.3, -0.1, -0.2, -0.1, -0.4, -0.2, -0.3, 0.4, 0.1, 0.2)$,

for Processes 1, 2 and 3, respectively. It is worth emphasizing that, in both Scenarios 1 and 2, the vectors of coefficients were randomly selected with the only requirement of fulfilling the standard stationary condition for AR processes.

The simulation study was carried out as follows. For each scenario, N time series of length T were generated from each process. Several values of N and T were taken into account to analyse the effect of those parameters (see Sect. 3.3). The test set was constructed by considering the last $h = 2l_{\mathrm{SIG}}$ observations of each series, where l_{SIG} is the number of significant lags existing in each scenario (e.g., $l_{\mathrm{SIG}} = 4$ in Scenario 1). The training period was set to the first $(T - h)$ observations of each series. The validation period was set to observations from $(l + 1)$ to $(T - h)$. Note that this choice implies that the reassignation step in Algorithm 1 is carried out by considering the in-sample error (see (1)). The simulation procedure was repeated 200 times for each pair (T, N).

3.2 Alternative Approaches and Assessment Criteria

To throw light on the behaviour of the proposed algorithm, which we will refer to as *Clustering based on Prediction Accuracy of Global Models* (CPAGM), we decided to compare it with the alternative approaches described below.

- *Local Models* (LM). Specifically, a local model (e.g., an AR model) is fitted to each of the series in the collection (by jointly considering training and validation periods) and used to obtain the predictions with respect to the test period. In this way, each local model gives rise to an error metric measuring its forecasting accuracy. The average of these quantities can be seen as the overall error associated to the LM approach. Note that the LM method was already used by [12] to show the benefits of global models for forecasting purposes.

- *Global Models by considering an Arbitrary Partition* (GMAP). This procedure is based on 2 steps: (i) the original set of series S is randomly partitioned into K groups and (ii) for each group, a global model is fitted by considering the series pertaining to that cluster. The assessment task is carried out as indicated in Step 4 of Remark 2. It is worth highlighting that global models fitted to random groups of series have been shown to improve the forecasting accuracy of one global model fitted to all the series in some datasets (see, e.g., Fig. 4 in [12]). The approach GMAP can be seen as a meaningful benchmark for the proposed method, since it is expected that the groups produced by Algorithm 1 improve the forecasting effectiveness of global models in comparison with a random partition.
- *Global models by considering Feature-Based Clustering* (GMFBC). Particularly, the technique proposed by [1], which relies on two steps: (i) the original collection of series is splitted into K groups by using a clustering algorithm based on the feature extraction procedure described in [8] and (ii) K global models are constructed according to the resulting partition. This approach is evaluated in a similar way that GMAP. Note that, like CPAGM, GMFBC also tries to exploit the notion of similarity between time series in order to decrease the overall prediction error. However, GMFBC considers a specific clustering algorithm before fitting the global models, while CPAGM iterates until achieving the optimal clustering partition in terms of forecasting effectiveness.

The number of clusters was set to $K = 3$, since all scenarios contain 3 different generating processes. For approaches CPAGM, GMAP and GMFBC, the number of lags l to fit the global models was set to $l = l_{\text{SIG}}$. The considered global models were standard linear regression models adjusted by least squares. As for the method LM, a linear local model was fitted to each series by using the function **auto.arima** in the forecast R package [7], which contains classical linear regression as a particular case. Model selection was performed by means of AICc criterion. Note that classical linear models are important as a benchmark because they do not include any advanced machine learning technique and overlap the model class with ARIMA model (a common local approach). Therefore, they are ideal to isolate the effect of globality [12].

The quality of the procedures was evaluated by comparing the clustering solution given by the algorithms with the true partition, usually referred to as ground truth. Approaches CPAGM and GMFBC automatically provide a clustering partition. For method LM, each series was first described by means of the vector of estimated model coefficients returned by **auto.arima** function (all vectors were padded with zeros until reaching the length of the longest vector). Next, a standard K-means algorithm was executed by using these feature vectors as input. Experimental and true partitions were compared by considering the adjusted Rand index (ARI) [6], which is bounded between -1 and 1. Values of ARI close to 0 indicate a noninformative clustering solution, while the closer to 1 the index, the better the partition.

Note that, although CPAGM is a clustering method, it could be used as a tool to perform forecasting in a given set of series, since the iterative process outlined in Algorithm (1) attempts to minimize the total prediction error. In this regard, the forecasting accuracy of methods CPAGM, GMAP and GMFBC was assessed by recording the average MAE as indicated in (4). The MAE associated with each local model computed with respect to the test set was stored for LM and the average of those quantities was calculated as the error metric. Note that, since all series within a given scenario are measured in the same scale, the MAE is a proper measure to evaluate the overall prediction error.

In each simulation trial and given a pair (N, T), the proposed technique CPAGM was executed 5 times and the partition associated with the minimum value of $J(C)$ (see (2) in Remark 1) was stored. This way, we tried to avoid the well-known issue of local optima related to K-means-based procedures. A similar strategy was employed in the feature-based clustering of GMAP and GMFBC. The overall MAE produced by GMAP was approximated via Monte Carlo (i.e., by considering several random partitions).

3.3 Results and Discussion

Average values of ARI and MAE attained by the different techniques in Scenario 1 are provided in Tables 1 and 2, respectively. In order to perform rigorous comparisons, pairwise paired t-tests were carried out by taking into account the 200 simulation trials. In all cases, the alternative hypotheses stated that the mean ARI (MAE) value of a given method is greater (less) than the mean ARI (MAE) value of its counterpart. As asterisk was incorporated in Tables 1 and 2 if the corresponding method resulted significantly more effective than the remaining ones for a significance level 0.01. The results associated with running the approach CPAGM with $K = 1$ (only one global model) were incorporated to Table 2 by indicating "$(K = 1)$".

According to Table 1, the proposed method CPAGM achieved significantly greater ARI values than the alternative approaches in most of the cases. The only exceptions were $(T, N) = (400, 5)$ and $(T, N) = (400, 20)$, where CPAGM and LM showed a similar performance. What happens here is that, as long series are considered, the models coefficients are very accurately estimated and the clustering partition returned by the LM approach is quite similar to the ground truth. An increasing in the number of series per cluster was clearly beneficial for the proposed method when short series were considered ($T \in \{20, 50\}$), but it had little impact when $T > 50$. In some way, more series per cluster has a similar effect on CPAGM than longer lengths, since both phenomena result in better estimated global models. The approach GMFBC showed a steady improvement when increasing the series length, but it was still far from a perfect partition for $T = 400$. Due to a reviewer's suggestion, Table 1 also contains the results associated with a standard K-means approach based on the DTW distance and with the method of [13], denoted by KS, which relies on a normalized version

Table 1. Average ARI in Scenario 1. The best result is shown in bold. An asterisk indicates that a given method is better than the rest at level 0.01.

(T, N)	LM	CPAGM	GMFBC	DTW	KS
(20, 5)	0.027	**0.352***	0.094	−0.016	0.308
(20, 10)	0.032	**0.459***	0.090	0.023	0.270
(20, 20)	0.029	**0.556***	0.092	0.004	0.254
(20, 50)	0.026	**0.612***	0.076	0.019	0.308
(50, 5)	0.305	**0.914***	0.243	0.031	0.625
(50, 10)	0.336	**0.956***	0.222	0.021	0.777
(50, 20)	0.331	**0.988***	0.216	0.016	0.758
(50, 50)	0.331	**0.981***	0.195	0.026	0.864
(100, 5)	0.747	**0.946***	0.379	0.042	0.717
(100, 10)	0.740	**0.954***	0.380	0.028	0.870
(100, 20)	0.743	**0.961***	0.334	0.026	0.818
(100, 50)	0.740	**0.956***	0.311	0.025	0.799
(200, 5)	0.876	**0.906***	0.581	0.046	0.831
(200, 10)	0.854	**0.919**	0.561	0.040	0.873
(200, 20)	0.820	**0.921***	0.516	0.025	0.813
(200, 50)	0.800	**0.926***	0.488	0.030	0.817
(400, 5)	0.897	**0.908**	0.719	0.010	0.825
(400, 10)	0.848	**0.900***	0.725	0.022	0.769
(400, 20)	0.877	**0.881**	0.732	0.036	0.841
(400, 50)	0.803	**0.872***	0.726	0.034	0.688

Table 2. Average MAE in Scenario 1. The best result is shown in bold. An asterisk indicates that a given method is better than the rest at level 0.01.

(T, N)	LM	CPAGM ($K = 1$)	GMFBC	GMAP
(20, 5)	1.066	**1.043*** (1.069)	1.072	1.078
(20, 10)	1.068	**0.997*** (1.075)	1.046	1.080
(20, 20)	1.070	**0.964*** (1.076)	1.036	1.052
(20, 50)	1.073	**0.942*** (1.075)	1.034	1.046
(50, 5)	1.019	**0.921*** (1.065)	1.011	1.100
(50, 10)	1.023	**0.913*** (1.073)	1.021	1.044
(50, 20)	1.024	**0.910*** (1.082)	1.024	1.072
(50, 50)	1.016	**0.907*** (1.074)	1.020	1.042
(100, 5)	0.976	**0.919*** (1.072)	0.994	1.225
(100, 10)	0.978	**0.913*** (1.075)	0.996	1.148
(100, 20)	0.976	**0.911*** (1.076)	1.003	1.067
(100, 50)	0.977	**0.911*** (1.079)	1.009	1.061
(200, 5)	0.929	**0.911*** (1.062)	0.949	1.025
(200, 10)	0.942	**0.918*** (1.083)	0.968	1.058
(200, 20)	0.938	**0.912*** (1.070)	0.969	1.062
(200, 50)	0.942	**0.916*** (1.073)	0.978	1.090
(400, 5)	0.920	**0.915** (1.069)	0.937	1.092
(400, 10)	0.920	**0.916** (1.076)	0.937	1.069
(400, 20)	0.929	**0.926** (1.080)	0.949	1.071
(400, 50)	0.925	**0.925** (1.076)	0.944	1.101

of the cross-correlation. Both methods exhibited worse overall behaviour than the proposed approach, although KS obtained large values for the ARI index in many settings.

The results in terms of MAE (see Table 2) are very similar to those in Table 1, with the proposed method outperforming the remaining approaches in most of the settings. Specifically, Table 2 indicates that the forecasting accuracy of local models is as good as that of global models for $T = 400$, but significantly worse for shorter lengths. Note that CPAGM obtained substantially better results than fitting one global model to all the series in the collection ($K = 1$) and GMAP, which is expected since these approaches do not take into account the underlying generating processes.

Average results for Scenario 2 concerning ARI and MAE are displayed in Tables 3 and 4, respectively. The proposed approach showed a similar behaviour than in Scenario 1 in terms of both clustering effectiveness and predictive accuracy, but the difference with respect to the remaining techniques was more marked in Scenario 2. The long memory patterns arising in the processes of this scenario negatively affected both methods LM and GMFBC. In fact, the LM approach was not able to exhibit forecasting and clustering accuracies similar to CPAGM even when very long series ($T = 1000$) were considered. Method KS displayed a similar performance than CPAGM in this scenario. In short, the iterative procedure of Algorithm 1 takes advantage of the excellent accuracy of global models to properly estimate the complex forecasting patterns arising in the long-memory processes of Scenario 2.

Table 3. Average ARI in Scenario 2. The best result is shown in bold. An asterisk indicates that a given method is better than the rest at level 0.01.

(T, N)	LM	CPAGM	GMFBC	DTW	KS
$(50, 5)$	0.243	0.584	0.238	0.107	**0.765***
$(50, 10)$	0.259	**0.853***	0.222	0.135	0.789
$(50, 20)$	0.250	**0.956***	0.219	0.144	0.723
$(50, 50)$	0.256	**0.980***	0.205	0.155	0.767
$(100, 5)$	0.386	**0.933***	0.278	0.198	0.869
$(100, 10)$	0.387	**0.937***	0.274	0.122	0.907
$(100, 20)$	0.410	**0.979**	0.277	0.144	0.968
$(100, 50)$	0.412	**0.986***	0.286	0.158	0.927
$(200, 5)$	0.453	0.907	0.302	0.123	**0.934**
$(200, 10)$	0.478	**0.937***	0.317	0.174	0.897
$(200, 20)$	0.468	**0.959**	0.306	0.152	0.937
$(200, 50)$	0.477	**0.972***	0.303	0.128	0.920
$(400, 5)$	0.517	0.898	0.383	0.165	**0.955***
$(400, 10)$	0.510	0.918	0.382	0.160	**0.921**
$(400, 20)$	0.507	**0.926***	0.368	0.169	0.883
$(400, 50)$	0.487	0.921	0.365	0.131	**0.983***
$(1000, 5)$	0.571	0.846	0.497	0.184	**0.935***
$(1000, 10)$	0.556	0.841	0.456	0.249	**0.878**
$(1000, 20)$	0.552	**0.867**	0.453	0.272	0.863
$(1000, 50)$	0.532	0.877	0.457	0.273	**0.923***

Table 4. Average MAE in Scenario 2. The best result is shown in bold. An asterisk indicates that a given method is better than the rest at level 0.01.

(T, N)	LM	CPAGM ($K = 1$)	GMFBC	GMAP
$(50, 5)$	1.854	**1.375*** (1.871)	1.657	1.902
$(50, 10)$	1.855	**1.333*** (1.885)	1.616	1.888
$(50, 20)$	1.856	**1.183*** (1.905)	1.625	1.838
$(50, 50)$	1.857	**1.153*** (1.901)	1.647	1.898
$(100, 5)$	1.670	**1.185*** (1.871)	1.492	1.756
$(100, 10)$	1.665	**1.173*** (1.891)	1.553	1.667
$(100, 20)$	1.683	**1.148*** (1.898)	1.578	1.890
$(100, 50)$	1.683	**1.147*** (1.903)	1.590	1.884
$(200, 5)$	1.615	**1.191*** (1.884)	1.507	1.613
$(200, 10)$	1.628	**1.168*** (1.899)	1.558	1.772
$(200, 20)$	1.635	**1.156*** (1.902)	1.591	1.852
$(200, 50)$	1.631	**1.152*** (1.906)	1.624	1.866
$(400, 5)$	1.566	**1.197*** (1.906)	1.483	1.743
$(400, 10)$	1.574	**1.177*** (1.898)	1.526	1.729
$(400, 20)$	1.561	**1.177*** (1.900)	1.573	1.885
$(400, 50)$	1.563	**1.181*** (1.904)	1.596	1.916
$(1000, 5)$	1.486	**1.219*** (1.885)	1.394	1.898
$(1000, 10)$	1.513	**1.231*** (1.899)	1.473	1.887
$(1000, 20)$	1.516	**1.210*** (1.908)	1.497	1.892
$(1000, 50)$	1.505	**1.205*** (1.902)	1.516	1.881

4   Application to Real Data

In this section we apply the proposed algorithm to perform clustering in 3 well-known datasets. They have been used in many peer-reviewed publications as standard benchmarks, from local models to recent literature for global models. Specifically, [12] employed these databases to show the advantages of global methods over local methods in terms of forecasting accuracy. The datasets pertain in turn to the data collection M1, used in a forecasting competition [11]. It contains 1001 series subdivided in yearly (181), quarterly (203) and monthly (617) periodicity. These three subsets define precisely the three considered databases.

Method CPAGM and the alternative approaches studied in Sect. 3 were executed in each of the three datasets. No data preprocessing was performed, since there is not a clear agreement about the benefits of preprocessing when fitting global models [12]. Note that, unlike in the simulation study, there is no way of objectively assessing the quality of the clustering partition in these databases, since no information about the ground truth is available. Hence, our analyses focus on the predictive effectiveness of the evaluated techniques. Procedures CPAGM, GMFBC and GMAP were run for several values of K, namely $K \in \{1, 2, 3, 4, 5, 7, 10\}$ and l. Note that the range of l is limited by the minimum series length existing in a given database.

To measure the forecasting accuracy, we considered the symmetric Mean Absolute Percentage Error (sMAPE). Using a percentage error is desirable here because, unlike in the numerical experiments of Sect. 3, some databases contain series which are recorded in very different scales. Thus, employing the MAE could have resulted in the average forecasting error being corrupted by the higher influence of the series in the largest scales. Note that, by considering the sMAPE metric, the average prediction error in (3) takes the form

$$
\frac{1}{n} \sum_{k=1}^{K} \sum_{\substack{i=1: \\ \boldsymbol{X}_t^{(i)} \in C_k}}^{n} d_{\text{sMAPE}}^{*}\left(\boldsymbol{X}_t^{(i)*}, \overline{\mathcal{M}}_k\right) = \frac{1}{n} \sum_{k=1}^{K} \sum_{\substack{i=1: \\ \boldsymbol{X}_t^{(i)} \in C_k}}^{n} \frac{200}{h} \sum_{j=1}^{h} \left(\frac{\left| X_j^{(i)*} - \overline{F}_{j,k}^{(i)*} \right|}{\left| X_j^{(i)*} \right| + \left| \overline{F}_{j,k}^{(i)*} \right|} \right).
$$
(6)

Concerning the proposed algorithm CPAGM, the test sets were constructed by considering the last $h = 5$ observations of each time series. As in the simulations of Sect. 3, the in-sample error was used to assign each series to its closest cluster in the iterative mechanism of Algorithm 1. Traditional least squares linear regression was considered to fit the global models.

Figures 1, 2 and 3 contain the results for yearly, quarterly and monthly datasets, respectively. Left, middle and right panels refer to the approaches CPAGM, GMFBC and GMAP, respectively. Curves of average sMAPE are depicted as a function of the number of lags, l. Each colour corresponds to a different value of the number of clusters, K. In all cases, the proposed algorithm CPAGM attains a substantially lower average error than the alternative methods GMFBC and GMAP for a large number of pairs (K, l). Specifically, the differences by taking into account the minimum average errors (those associated with the optimal pair for each method) are dramatic in some cases. For instance, in dataset M1 Quarterly, procedures GMFBC and GMAP obtain a minimum average error two times and three times higher, respectively, than the one associated with CPAGM. In addition, considering a number of clusters of $K > 1$ is advantageous in the three datasets, as the red curve is significantly above the remaining curves in all of the settings. This suggests that M1 databases contain groups of series sharing common forecasting patterns, and thus fitting a global model to the series within each group is beneficial in terms of forecasting effectiveness.

It is worth highlighting that, for the proposed approach, there is usually at least one nonoptimal pair (K, l) for which the average sMAPE is not significantly different from that of the optimal one. For example, in dataset M1 Quarterly, pairs $(10, 10)$ and $(7, 6)$ produce almost the same average error. In such a case, selecting the latter could be more appropriate for performing further data mining tasks, as it would result in better interpretability of centroids (fewer parameters) and lower computational complexity.

Optimal pairs (K, l) for each method in Figs. 1, 2 and 3 are summarized in Table 5 along with the corresponding forecasting errors. Average sMAPE attained by the local-based approach LM in each dataset is also shown. It is clear that the method CPAGM outperforms all alternative approaches in the three cases.

In short, the application of this section shows the advantages of the proposed algorithm CPAGM when performing forecasting in time series databases. It is

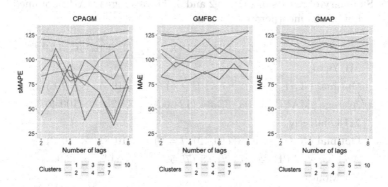

Fig. 1. Average sMAPE as a function of the number of lags in dataset M1 Yearly. Each colour corresponds to a different value of the number of clusters, K.

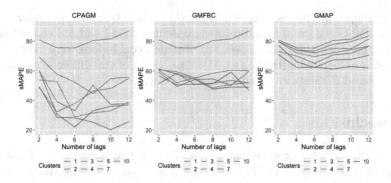

Fig. 2. Average sMAPE as a function of the number of lags in dataset M1 Quarterly. Each colour corresponds to a different value of the number of clusters, K.

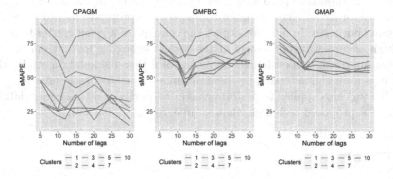

Fig. 3. Average sMAPE as a function of the number of lags in dataset M1 Monthly. Each colour corresponds to a different value of the number of clusters, K.

Table 5. Summary of results of Figs. 1, 2 and 3. The average sMAPE obtained by the LM approach was also incorporated.

	LM	CPAGM ($K = 1$)	GMFBC	GMAP
M1 Yearly				
Optimal (K, l)	–	$(7, 7)$ $(l = 4)$	$(10, 3)$	$(10, 6)$
Average sMAPE	39.08	**33.34** (124.00)	78.28	100.40
M1 Quarterly				
Optimal (K, l)	–	$(10, 10)$ $(l = 6)$	$(10, 8)$	$(10, 8)$
Average sMAPE	26.27	**20.18** (75.52)	61.40	47.00
M1 Monthly				
Optimal (K, l)	–	$(7, 30)$ $(l = 12)$	$(4, 12)$	$(10, 20)$
Average sMAPE	18.51	**14.22** (64.78)	42.95	52.20

worth highlighting that the proposed algorithm was also applied to perform clustering in additional databases from several domains (M3 and M4 competitions, medicine, finance...). In most cases, the obtained conclusions were very similar to the ones associated with dataset M1. The scores of the different methods in the considered datasets are available under request.

5   Conclusions

In this work, a clustering algorithm based on prediction accuracy of global forecasting models was introduced. The procedure is based on the traditional K-means method and relies on a two-step iterative process: (i) K global models (centroids) are fitted by considering the series belonging to each cluster and (ii) each time series is assigned to the group associated with the centroid yielding the lowest forecasting error according to the MAE metric. Although the main goal of the method is to produce a meaningful clustering partition, the nature of the iterative process makes the algorithm also an appropriate tool to be used for forecasting purposes. In fact, we expect the centroid of a given cluster to predict with high accuracy future values of the series belonging to that cluster. The proposed approach was evaluated by means of a broad simulation study where the groups were characterized by different underlying stochastic processes. The algorithm was also applied to perform clustering in classical time series datasets. Overall, the proposed technique showed an excellent performance.

References

1. Bandara, K., Bergmeir, C., Smyl, S.: Forecasting across time series databases using recurrent neural networks on groups of similar series: a clustering approach. Expert Syst. Appl. **140**, 112896 (2020)

2. D'Urso, P., De Giovanni, L., Massari, R.: Garch-based robust clustering of time series. Fuzzy Sets Syst. **305**, 1–28 (2016)
3. D'Urso, P., De Giovanni, L., Massari, R.: Trimmed fuzzy clustering of financial time series based on dynamic time warping. Ann. Oper. Res. **299**(1), 1379–1395 (2021)
4. D'Urso, P., De Giovanni, L., Massari, R., D'Ecclesia, R.L., Maharaj, E.A.: Cepstral-based clustering of financial time series. Expert Syst. Appl. **161**, 113705 (2020)
5. D'Urso, P., Maharaj, E.A.: Autocorrelation-based fuzzy clustering of time series. Fuzzy Sets Syst. **160**(24), 3565–3589 (2009)
6. Hubert, L., Arabie, P.: Comparing partitions. J. Classif. **2**(1), 193–218 (1985)
7. Hyndman, R., et al.: Forecasting functions for time series and linear models. R package version 6 (2015)
8. Hyndman, R.J., Wang, E., Laptev, N.: Large-scale unusual time series detection. In: 2015 IEEE International Conference on Data Mining Workshop (ICDMW), pp. 1616–1619. IEEE (2015)
9. Hyndman, R.J., et al.: Another look at forecast-accuracy metrics for intermittent demand. Foresight Int. J. Appl. Forecast. **4**(4), 43–46 (2006)
10. Liao, T.W.: Clustering of time series data: a survey. Pattern Recogn. **38**(11), 1857–1874 (2005)
11. Makridakis, S., et al.: The accuracy of extrapolation (time series) methods: results of a forecasting competition. J. Forecast. **1**(2), 111–153 (1982)
12. Montero-Manso, P., Hyndman, R.J.: Principles and algorithms for forecasting groups of time series: locality and globality. Int. J. Forecast. **37**(4), 1632–1653 (2021)
13. Paparrizos, J., Gravano, L.: K-shape: efficient and accurate clustering of time series. In: Proceedings of the 2015 ACM SIGMOD International Conference on Management of Data, pp. 1855–1870 (2015)
14. Vilar, J.A., Alonso, A.M., Vilar, J.M.: Non-linear time series clustering based on non-parametric forecast densities. Comput. Stat. Data Anal. **54**(11), 2850–2865 (2010)

Experimental Study of Time Series Forecasting Methods for Groundwater Level Prediction

Michael Franklin Mbouopda[1(✉)], Thomas Guyet[2], Nicolas Labroche[3], and Abel Henriot[4]

[1] University Clermont Auvergne, Clermont Auvergne INP, CNRS, Mines Saint-Etienne, LIMOS, Clermont-Ferrand, France
michael.mbouopda@uca.fr
[2] Inria – Centre Inria de Lyon, Villeurbanne, France
[3] Université de Tours, Tours, France
[4] BRGM, Orléans, France

Abstract. Groundwater level prediction is an applied time series forecasting task with important social impacts to optimize water management as well as preventing some natural disasters: for instance, floods or severe droughts. Machine learning methods have been reported in the literature to achieve this task, but they are only focused on the forecast of the groundwater level at a single location. A global forecasting method aims at exploiting the groundwater level time series from a wide range of locations to produce predictions at a single place or at several places at a time. Given the recent success of global forecasting methods in prestigious competitions, it is meaningful to assess them on groundwater level prediction and see how they are compared to local methods. In this work, we created a dataset of 1026 groundwater level time series. Each time series is made of daily measurements of groundwater levels and two exogenous variables, rainfall and evapotranspiration. This dataset is made available to the communities for reproducibility and further evaluation. To identify the best configuration to effectively predict groundwater level for the complete set of time series, we compared different predictors including local and global time series forecasting methods. We assessed the impact of exogenous variables. Our result analysis shows that the best predictions are obtained by training a global method on past groundwater levels and rainfall data.

Keywords: Time series · Forecasting · Groundwater · Local and global forecasting · Benchmark

1 Introduction

Groundwaters are water bodies entrapped in soils and rocks, representing storage of significant volumes of water, usually preserved from pollutants. Generally

T. Guyet et al. (Eds.): AALTD 2022, LNAI 13812, pp. 34–49, 2023.
https://doi.org/10.1007/978-3-031-24378-3_3

speaking, rainfall would penetrate through soils, rocks and tends to increase the volume of groundwater, whereas drainage by springs or rivers, or water abstraction by pumping would decrease the volume of available groundwater in a given reservoir. Wells and boreholes are the devices capable of monitoring the level of water in the reservoir, and are more generally designated under the term of *piezometers*. Forecasting groundwater levels contributes to the responsible management of an essential resource for different uses—human consumption (two-thirds of the water supplies for human consumption come from underground sources), irrigation, industrial uses (cooling, washing, etc.) – but also to watercourse flow management [21,22].

This article is focused on comparing local and global forecasting methods for predicting the evolution of groundwater levels at single or multiple locations. In France, groundwater levels records are stored in a publicly available database (ADES) operated by BRGM[1]. Data can be requested using public API's through the Hub'Eau portal http://hubeau.eaufrance.fr/. The database stores a network of approximately twenty thousand wells with at least one measure, but for more than a thousand of those piezometers, several years of continuous data are available, with only a few missing data. The prediction horizon was set to about three months (90 days). This corresponds to a forecast of the medium-term evolution of the groundwater levels. In terms of water management, this length of time corresponds to the needs of drought anticipation, usually performed in the late spring after the winter recharge period. In general terms, this timescale corresponds to the vast majority of the needs of applied water management.

The prediction of these levels is a true challenge given the complexity of the hydrological mechanisms at play [5]. Many numerical models have been developed for this purpose. Certain models are based on physical groundwater modelling. Physical models require their parameters to be adjusted to each situation [19]. They offer an accurate prediction solution but are generally difficult to generalize on a large scale. For more systematic prediction, the use of past groundwater level time series has been viewed for years as an essential tool for water resource planning [14]. Many machine learning models have therefore been developed to predict groundwater levels. For instance, Brédy et al. [5] put forward a modelling approach for groundwater level forecasting based on two decision-tree-based models, namely Random Forest (RF) and Extreme Gradient Boosting (XGB). Rahman et al. [21] combined wavelet transform with random forest and gradient boosting trees to predict groundwater level at scale in the city of Kumamoto in Japan. Osman et al. [12] also evaluated an XGB model but also support vector regression (SVR) and neural networks. In these studies, data includes past groundwater level values as well as rainfall and evapotranspiration data. With this information, two natural groundwater inflows and outflows are taken into account. Note that we do not have information about water usage that is difficult to collect from open resources.

Among the many state-of-the-art models, it is difficult to identify the best one for predicting the evolution of groundwater levels. Therefore, it turns out

---

[1] BRGM: Bureau des Recherches Géologiques et Minières (French geological survey).

to be relevant to explore various models designed to predict the evolution of time series for the specific data provided and compare them to identify the best model.

In this article, we focus specifically on the following question: "*Is it preferable to train a model on measurements from a single sensor (local model) or to train a global model to forecast the evolution of piezometric levels?*". The usual time series forecasting approaches are designed to train models to predict future measurements from a sensor based on past measurements by the same sensor. However, a model trained on each piezometer would require a large volume of past data for each device. Such an approach would rapidly fail as the amount of available data is limited. This is also not the case for the installation of new sensors for example, and more generally it means that the model has low robustness to changes in the functioning of the hydrological system measured. The use of models trained on several piezometers can ensure greater robustness and less training effort for new piezometers. Recently, global forecasting methods (GFM) has shown astonishing results by achieving the best score on distinguished sales prediction competitions [16,17], however no prior work on groundwater level forecasting has considered these approaches yet. In aquifers, groundwater level fluctuations are not completely independent since water flows from high to low altitudes, along flow paths that depend on the aquifer geometry, porosity (the amount of connected void in the soils and rocks) and thus types of rocks, geometry of the recharge area, or discharge area, unsaturated zone thickness, etc. Inside a given aquifer, it is then expected that groundwater levels at close locations or best, along a same flow path, would have a strong co-linearity, whereas this similarity would fade with increasing distance. For distinct aquifers, it is expected that a similar groundwater level signal could be observed when input signals (rainfall, effective rainfall) are similar or close, with a certain proportion of divergence due to distinct aquifers properties. In simpler words, a proportion of redundant signal can be found along all the groundwater level records, the remaining signal being site specific. These reasons make us hypothesize that GFM would be more effective on groundwater level forecasting than local forecasting methods (LFM). Our exploration of models designed to predict the evolution of groundwater level is therefore structured around the goal of comparing two modelling strategies: local vs global methods.

For each of these types of modelling, we put forward several possible implementations and compared them with respect to the root mean squared scaled error. The rest of this paper is organized as follows: The data used in this study are described in Sect. 2. Section 3 presents the formalization of the studied problem and the resolution methods. The conducted experiment and the results are detailed in Sect. 4. This work is finally concluded in Sect. 6.

2   Data Collection

For this study, we compiled a dataset for the period from January 2015 to January 2021 (2,221 days) for a subset of 1,026 piezometers in the French mainland.

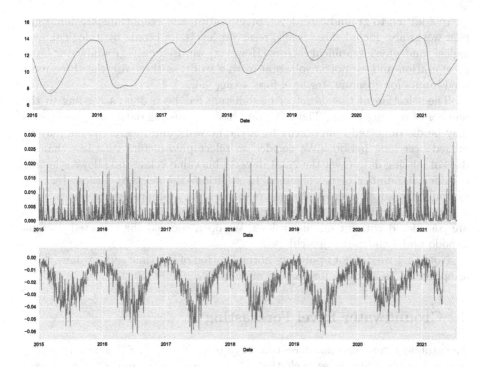

Fig. 1. From top to down, daily groundwater level, rainfall and evapotranspiration time series for the piezometer BSS000EBLL.

In the following, we explain the selection of the subset of piezometers. Each piezometer corresponds to a multivariate time series. The multivariate time series has three variables: the groundwater level and two exogenous weather variables: rainfall and evapotranspiration (ETO). These latter values have been collected from ERA5 archives using the Climate Data Store (CDS) API [10] at the location of the piezometer. This simple approach has been considered accurate enough in the context of this work, even if a more realistic approach had considered the recharge area. Nevertheless, considering a weather variable computed at the scale of each recharge area would have led to a significant increase in the complexity of the models. In addition, weather variables considered at this spatial resolution do not vary significantly with small distances, then the value at the location of the piezometer seems to be an accurate approximation. CDS provides daily weather variable measurements with a spatial resolution of 0.25° for rain and 0.1° for ETO. Hence, the three variables (groundwater level, rainfall and evapotranspiration) are available daily for each piezometer. Figure 1 shows the data for the piezometer BSS000EBLL installed in the city of *Senlis-le-Sec*. It illustrates a time series that is regular: the range of values remains between $7m$ and $16m$ all over the period, and we can identify a yearly seasonality. This is not the case for all the piezometers. Some of them do not have such seasonality and exhibit brutal changes at some dates.

In addition to groundwater level, precipitation and evapotranspiration, some past works also included sea levels, reservoir levels, and some hydrological, geological, and physiographical factors. However, we used only groundwater level, precipitation and evapotranspiration in this study as these are the three most used inputs for groundwater level forecasting [24].

The selection of the subset of piezometers has been done according to the number of missing values. The CDS data have no missing data, but piezometers may be disconnected temporarily from the network and measurements may be missed over long periods. We decided to select piezometers with less than 50 days of missing data (over the 2,221 days). This value is low and allows selecting a sufficient number of piezometers. In addition, the selected piezometers are spatially spread all over the French mainland. As a preprocessing, the missing values were attributed by linear interpolation. Thus, in the sequel, time series are considered without missing values. We open sourced the collected data on Zenodo under the name FrenchPiezo[2].

Note that we did not apply any normalization of the time series values. They are provided as it to the forecasting methods.

3   Groundwater Level Forecasting

The groundwater levels database is a set of pairs $\mathcal{Y} = \langle Y^k, \mathbf{Z}^k \rangle$ where $Y^k : y_{1...t}^k$ is a univariate time series such that $y_i^k \in \mathbb{R}$ for any i, and $Z^k : \mathbf{z}_{1..\infty}^k$ is a multivariate time series, so-called exogenous time series data ($Z : \mathbf{z}_i^k \in \mathbb{R}^m$, where m is the number of exogenous time series), known as far as date t but also beyond. Time series Y^k is the groundwater level series for piezometer k, while the exogenous data series corresponds to rainfall and evapotranspiration associated to this piezometer (thus $m = 2$ in this study).

The prediction of a time series Y^k for forecast horizon h consists in estimating $y_{t+1...t+h}^k$. For this time series prediction task, the conventional data analysis approach is to construct an autoregressive model. Such a method constructs a function for the prediction of the value at date t_0 from the r latest observations of Y and $\mathbf{Z}$. Such a function for the prediction of the next value in the series is denoted $\varphi : \mathbb{R}^{r \times (m+1)} \mapsto \mathbb{R}$. φ can thus be seen as a regressor: it predicts a real value from the input characteristics.

Classical autoregressive models assume that φ is a linear regression (AR model), but φ can be modelled by any trainable regression function. We denote such methods as a **generalized** autoregressive model. Notice that the classical AR model is a special case of the generalized autoregressive model which assures a linear relationship between the variables.

To produce a forecast for horizon h, the prediction function is recursively applied h times. We note that it is assumed that the exogenous time series are known in the future. This problem is therefore different from that of forecasting a multivariate time series for which the prediction function outputs the value

---

[2] FrenchPiezo dataset https://zenodo.org/record/7193812.

of the target series together with the values of the exogenous series. In our problem, we hypothesize that rainfall and evapotranspiration were similar from one year to the next. Consequently, forecasts can be obtained in the future by taking the mean daily values of past years. The approximation error made by this hypothesis is preferable to that of the cumulative errors of a medium-term multivariate recursive prediction.

There exists many methods for constructing the φ function in the state-of-the-art and one goal of this work is to compare the most classical on groundwater level forecasting. The second goal is to decide whether it is better to use a local or a global method.

3.1   Local Versus Global Time Series Forecasting

Given a set of time series, we denote by "local" the approaches that consider each time series as an independent dataset and build an individual model to forecast the future values of each time series. Local time series forecasting has been the de facto approach for time series forecasting. However, nowadays, many companies are collecting a large set of time series from similar sources routinely, and training a single model for each individual series is time-consuming, costly, and difficult to maintain; furthermore, possible relationships between these time series are not taken into account by local approaches. For these reasons, a new forecasting paradigm called global forecasting has emerged. A Global Forecasting Model (GFM) [13] is trained on a set of time series and is then used to forecast future values of each time series. In other words, a GFM learns to predict future values given historic values regardless of the sources of data. Global forecasting is obtaining astonishing results today, by winning prestigious competitions such as the M4 and M5 challenges [16,17] and competitions held recently on the Kaggle platform [4]. Former works on global time series forecasting claimed that time series need to be related. However, Montero-Manso and Hyndman [18] shown theoretically that whatever the heterogeneity of time series, there always exists a GFM that is as good as, or even better than any collection of local models. This result has been further supported by an experimental study [11]. Since global method has shown good results, especially in forecasting time series of sales, we are wondering if this is also the case for forecasting time series of groundwater level.

3.2   Considered Methods

We explored four versions of the generalized autoregressive forecasting method (see above) as well as recent state-of-the-art neural network methods in the field. More specifically, we considered:

- Linear regression. This is the standard method for regression problems. This method is equivalent to using an AR model of order r.
- SVR [2]. Support vector regression (SVR) models address high-dimensional problems and propose non-linear models. We also used Gaussian kernels. After a few experiments, we set parameter $C = 100$.

- Random Forest [6]. This is a bagging method. We opted for a forest of 100 trees.
- Extreme Gradient Boosting [7]. This is a tree-based method which uses optimization techniques to improve the calculation efficiency of machine learning. It can thus process large datasets.
- DeepAR [23]. This is a probabilistic forecasting method based on autoregressive recurrent neural networks.
- Prophet [25]. A modular regression model with parameters that are intuitive for analysts and that can be easily adjusted using domain knowledge. Prophet is a decomposable model with three components which are trending to model non-periodic changes in the values of time series, seasonality to model periodic changes (weekly, yearly, etc.) and holidays to represent the effect of holidays on the time series values.
- NeuralProphet [26]. This is a neural network-based implementation of the Prophet model with some enhancements. In addition to the trend, seasonality and holidays components, NeuralProphet considers three additional regression components: auto-regression effect on past observations, regression effect of exogenous variables, and regression effect of lagged observations of exogenous variables. By using neural networks to learn each component, activation functions can be used to learn non-linear behaviours in the time series.

4   Experimental Settings

This section presents our experimental settings. We start by presenting in detail the experiments and then give the comparison metrics.

4.1   Setup

We organized our experiments by grouping the considered forecasting models in three categories and by following a naming convention to make things easier to follow. The three categories are generalized autoregressive models, DeepAR-based models, and Prophet-based models.

Generalized autoregressive models which contains traditional models not necessarily specifically designed for forecasting: eXtreme Gradient Boosting (XGB), Linear regression (LM), Random Forest (RF), and Support Vector Machine (SVR). These regression models consider a vector as input and output a real value. Therefore, we create a dataset by sliding a window of length $r + h$ over our time series. Each position of the sliding window is a sample in our dataset with the first r values (the history) being the input and the last h (the horizon or the forecast) being the output. In the experiments, we fixed the horizon h to 93 (three months), and did not put any constraint on r, however r is generally required to be greater than h in order to expect good forecasting. We tested values from 40 to 140 and found that the best value is 100 or 110 in average – this result is in accordance with the results from [15] which suggests that a history length $1.25 \times h$ leads to the best forecasting.

DeepAR-based models composed of two models as `DeepAR` [23] is a global forecasting method. `DeepAR-L` is the `DeepAR` model trained locally, meaning that for each individual time series, a new instance of the model is trained on this time series to forecast future values of this individual time series only. On the contrary, `DeepAR-G` is a `DeepAR` model trained once on every time series to predict future values of all the time series simultaneously.

Prophet-based models made of `Prophet` [25] and `NeuralProphet` [26]. NeuralProphet is by default a local forecasting model, but can be configured to run as a global method. Therefore, we considered `NeuralProphet-L` (for the local version of NeuralProphet) and `NeuralProphet-G` (for the global version). Prophet can only be used as a local forecasting method.

`DeepAR`, `Prophet`, and `NeuralProphet` are specifically designed for time series forecasting: they take as input a time series and predict the user-defined number of values in the future (93 in our case). Unlike the generalized autoregressive models which use a fixed-length history, `DeepAR`, `Prophet`, and `NeuralProphet` learn from the whole past observations of the time series to make predictions.

For each forecasting method, we considered two configurations and defined a naming convention to make things easier to understand:

- the first configuration uses only historic groundwater levels in order to forecast the future levels: exogenous data are not used. This configuration is named using the forecaster name. For instance, this configuration is named `NeuralProphet-L` and `XGB` when the models used are `NeuralProphet-L` and XGBoost respectively.
- the second configuration does not use only historic groundwater levels to predict the future, but also historic rain and/or evapotranspiration (ETO) data as the dynamic of their corresponding phenomenons could have a significant impact on groundwater level. This configuration is named as `[forecaster]+rain`, `[forecaster]+eto` and `[forecaster]+rain+eto` depending on the exogenous variables used: respectively, rain data, evapotranspiration data, or both. For instance, the configuration that uses `Random Forest (RF)` to forecast the piezometric level using historic groundwater levels and rain data is named `RF+rain`. These exogenous variables are times series that made the Z variable.

The experiment source code is written in the Python programming language using open source libraries. For `DeepAR`, we use the implementation provided in the GluonTS library [1]; for `Prophet` and `NeuralProphet` we use the implementation provided by the authors; we use the official implementation of the eXtreme Gradient Boosting model[3]; and for the remaining models we use Scikit-learn [20]. The source code is available as supplementary material and is available on a public repository[4].

---

[3] Source code and supplementary material: https://github.com/dmlc/xgboost.
[4] Source code: https://github.com/frankl1/piezoforecast.

4.2   Comparison Metrics

The methods are compared with respect to their ability to predict the next three months of daily values. More specifically, we analysed the root mean squared scaled error (RMSSE) of the methods over the period from the 15th of October 2021 to the 15th of January 2022, corresponding to a horizon of 93 days (roughly three months). This period is not used during the training phase of the methods. Indeed, predictions may be easier or more difficult to perform depending on the period of the year. For instance, during dry periods, groundwater is less affected by rainfall, for example. However, we focused on these three months horizon as it corresponds to the needs of drought anticipation and is also used in the literature [21]. For a time series of length n and a forecasting horizon h, the RMSSE is defined as follows:

$$RMSSE = \sqrt{\frac{\frac{1}{h} \sum_{t=n+1}^{n+h} \left(y_t - \hat{y}_t\right)^2}{\frac{1}{n-1} \sum_{t=2}^{n} \left(y_t - y_{t-1}\right)^2}} \tag{1}$$

In addition to the RMSSE, we assess the significance of the difference between the methods. This evaluation is summarized using critical difference diagrams [8] by rejecting the null hypothesis using the Friedman test followed by a pairwise post-hoc analysis as recommended by Benavoli et al. [3]. The critical difference diagrams are drawn using the source code made public by Fawaz et al. [9]. Elsewhere, we also use box plots to summarize our results. Detailed results are available in the accompanying repository of this paper (See footnote 4).

5   Results

5.1   Generalized Autoregressive Models Results

The performance achieved by the generalized autoregressive models are summarized on Fig. 2 and the significance of the difference between each pair of models is depicted on Fig. 3.

It can be observed that the best performing configurations use either only evapotranspiration as exogenous data, or no exogenous data at all. These configurations are made of linear models (see LM and LM+eto) and random forests (see RF and RF+eto). Although the difference is not significant, LM+eto performs better than LM. On the contrary, RF performs better than RF+eto. When there are no exogenous data, LM is the best model.

SVR, SVR+rain and SVR+rain+eto have very similar RMSSE in average, meaning that the impact of exogenous data is not significant for SVR-based configurations. On the contrary, exogenous data have a significant negative impact on tree-based configurations (RF and XGB) since XGB+rain and XGB+rain+eto, RF+rain, and RF+rain+eto achieve the highest RMSSE while XGB and RF are among the top four best configurations.

It is observed that the left part of Fig. 3 is mainly made of configurations that use exogenous data, while the right part is mainly composed of a mix

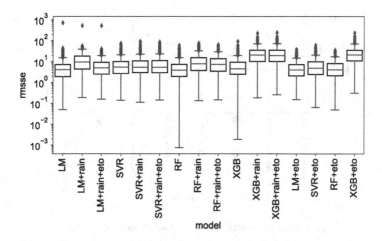

Fig. 2. RMSSE of the generalized autoregressive models.

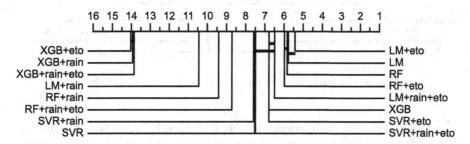

Fig. 3. Critical difference diagram of the generalized autoregressive models.

of configurations that use or do not use exogenous data. Using exogenous data decreases the performance of LM, XGB (XGB+eto, XGB+rain, and XGB+rain+eto are the worst configurations), RF, but increases performances of SVR (see SVR+eto and SVR+rain+eto). Therefore, using exogenous data makes the forecast better or worse, depending on the used forecaster and its ability to capture complex relationships.

5.2   DeepAR-Based Models Results

The results obtained using DeepAR as local method as well as a global method are shown in Fig. 4 and Fig. 5.

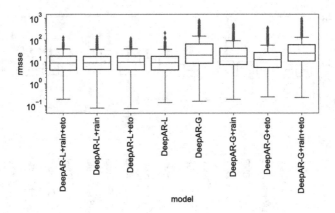

Fig. 4. Box plots summary of `DeepAR` models results.

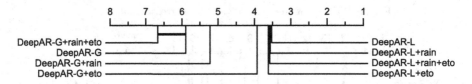

Fig. 5. Critical difference diagram of `DeepAR`-based models.

`DeepAR-L` produces predictions that are significantly better than predictions of `DeepAR-G`, and this regardless of using exogenous data or not. This suggests that a local training strategy for `DeepAR` is better than a global one for groundwater level prediction.

Although `DeepAR` is naturally designed to take advantage of exogenous data when available, it can be observed that rain and/or evapotranspiration have negative, yet insignificant impact on `DeepAR-L`'s predictions. On the contrary, exogenous data significantly improve `DeepAR-G`'s predictions, except when rain and evapotranspiration are used simultaneously.

5.3   Prophet-Based Models Results

The comparison of `Prophet` and `NeuralProphet`-based configurations are displayed in Fig. 6 and Fig. 7.

Unexpectedly, `NeuralProphet-G` produces forecasts that are worse than those obtained by any other `NeuralProphet` or `Prophet`-based configurations. However, using exogenous data (rain and/or evapotranspiration) makes `Neural-Prophet-G` the best forecaster, particularly `NeuralProphet-G+rain`. This result suggests that training a global `NeuralProphet` model for groundwater forecasting achieves more reliable predictions when exogenous data are used.

Unlike `DeepAR`, `NeuralPhophet` works better when executed globally than locally, in particular when exogenous data are used. Furthermore, using

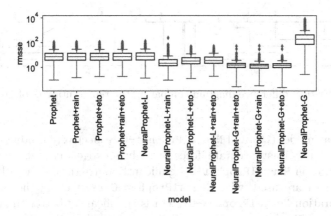

Fig. 6. Box plots summary of `Prophet` and `NeuralProphet` results.

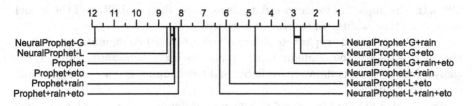

Fig. 7. Critical difference diagram of `Prophet`-based models.

exogenous data has a positive impact on `Prophet`, `NeuralProphet-L`, and `NeuralProphet-G`. This impact is not significant for `Prophet`, but it is for `NeuralProphet`.

In the absence of exogenous data, `Prophet` significantly outperforms `Neural-Prophet` at predicting the future values of groundwater levels.

5.4   Comparing the Three Groups of Models

The previous section discussed the performances of the three groups of models separately. It compares them to each other. For the sake of readability, we selected some "representative" methods from each group. However, an exhaustive comparison is available as supplementary material (See footnote 4). The representative models for each category are the two best and the two worst configurations. Also, we make sure that predictions of the selected methods are significantly different from each other regarding the critical difference diagram of the corresponding group. The comparison of the representatives methods is depicted in Fig. 8.

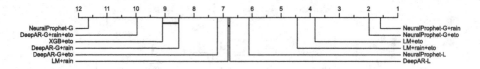

Fig. 8. Critical difference diagram comparing the representatives of groups.

The linear model (LM) and NeuralProphet-G respectively produce the most accurate and the least accurate forecasts when exogenous data are absent. The configuration NeuralProphet-G significantly outperforms the others when exogenous data are used, with NeuralProphet-G+rain being the best of all. The configuration NeuralProphet-G+rain is significantly better than the configuration NeuralProphet-G+eto, suggesting that precipitations impact groundwater level more than evapotranspiration does. However, as LM+eto outperforms LM+rain, the impact of exogenous data depends on the capabilities of the model to exploit these additional sources of knowledge.

Except for NeuralProphet-G, NeuralProphet-based configurations are better than DeepAR-based configurations at forecasting groundwater levels, especially when exogenous data are available and the training is done on every time series (i.e. globally).

DeepAR-L and LM+rain are not significantly different from each other in terms of RMSSE. The same observation is true for XGB+rain+eto and DeepAR-G+rain. This result suggests that no long-term dependency is lost by using a history of length 100. In other words, the time dependency in groundwater level data is not longer than 100 time steps when focused on the prediction at a horizon of 90 time steps.

Figure 9 shows predictions obtained with NeuralProphet-G+rain for some piezometers. We observe that forecasts are very close to ground truth groundwater levels.

5.5   Discussion

We have compared a set of state-of-the-art forecasting methods for groundwater level prediction in order to come up with the best method. We have considered local forecasting methods as well as global methods and we evaluated the impact of using exogenous data. Our finding is that selection of the best model is highly dataset dependent. When no exogenous data are considered, LM models perform better than more complex models. Nevertheless, these models do not appear as the more useful, as they cannot efficiently afford any prediction given a set of weather prediction (drought/flood). They can still be used when no rain or evapotranspiration data are available at a given location. When considering exogenous data, NeuralProphet-G+rain has been found to be the best model among the set we tested. In this particular case, the global model tends to outperform local models. It catches useful information in the redundancy found in the different piezometers. Our intuition is that complex processes are at play on

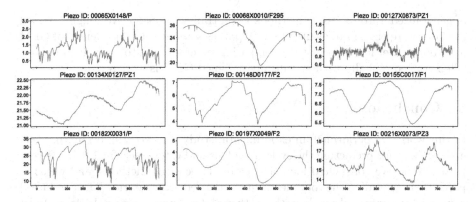

Fig. 9. Some forecasts obtained using the configuration NeuralProphet-G+rain.

groundwater levels (trends, seasonality). They have to be taken into account in forecasting models, for instance with NeuralProphet models. In addition, this type of model is rather simple to implement and could be easily extended or enhanced for a larger dataset. Nonetheless, this training strategy does not work with all the forecaster, e.g. with DeepAR.

We did not consider a couple of aspects of this study and that could improve groundwater level predictions.

The first limitation is related to the choice of the methods compared and the datasets. On the one hand, we acknowledge that there exist many more forecasting methods in the literature in addition to what we considered in this study. But as we wanted to evaluate the performance of global methods trained on a large collection of groundwater level time series, we selected the most effective forecasting methods in the literature. On the other hand, the dataset used in this study is only representative of the French groundwater levels – there is no guarantee that our results generalize to a different country. Keeping this in mind, we made our source public to allow our work to be extended easily. Nevertheless, as global methods achieved the best performance, we believe that they will generalize at least as well as any local method.

The second limitation is that we did not search for the optimal hyperparameter values for each method. Instead, we used the default parameters of the implementation used. Although we could have fixed this limitation using techniques such as a grid search and Bayesian optimization. We chose a simple approach with the default values because performing hyperparameter tuning for such a large number of datasets (1,026 multiplied by the number of methods) would require a lot of time and resources. However, knowing how methods are compared to each other without hyperparameters tuning could be seen as a measure of the effort required by methods to be effective; in other words, how many are methods "plug-and-playable".

Finally, global forecasting methods we evaluated in this work have been specifically designed for global forecasting. We have not assessed the capabilities of generalized autoregressive methods when trained globally. Although assessed methods were enough to evaluate our hypothesis about the effectiveness of GFM for groundwater level forecasting, comparing generalized autoregressive methods when trained globally with specifically designed GFM is worthy.

6 Conclusion

In this work, we performed an experimental study consisting of evaluating several methods for predicting the evolution of groundwater levels for 1,026 different piezometers. We considered local and global forecasting methods, and we compared them regarding the root mean squared scaled error metrics. The conducted experiments confirmed our hypothesis that global forecasting methods could be more effective than local ones for groundwater level prediction. In particular, global `NeuralProphet` achieved the best predictions when using past groundwater levels and rainfall as input. However, when only past groundwater levels are available (no rainfall and no evapotranspiration) local methods and particularly the linear regression model achieve the best predictions. As mentioned in the discussion section, this work could be improved. In particular, we are planning to assess the performance of generalized autoregressive methods (XGB, RF, LM, SVR, etc.) when they are trained globally and comparing them to specifically designed global methods.

References

1. Alexandrov, A., et al.: GluonTS: probabilistic and neural time series modeling in Python. J. Mach. Learn. Res. **21**(116), 1–6 (2020)
2. Awad, M., Khanna, R.: Support vector regression. In: Efficient Learning Machines, chap. 4, pp. 67–80. APress (2015)
3. Benavoli, A., Corani, G., Mangili, F.: Should we really use post-hoc tests based on mean-ranks? J. Mach. Learn. Res. **17**(1), 152–161 (2016)
4. Bojer, C.S., Meldgaard, J.P.: Kaggle forecasting competitions: an overlooked learning opportunity. Int. J. Forecast. **37**, 587–603 (2021)
5. Brédy, J., Gallichand, J., Celicourt, P., Gumiere, S.J.: Water table depth forecasting in cranberry fields using two decision-tree-modeling approaches. Agric. Water Manag. **233**, 106090 (2020)
6. Breiman, L.: Random forests. Mach. Learn. **45**(1), 5–32 (2001)
7. Chen, T., Guestrin, C.: XGBoost: a scalable tree boosting system. In: Proceedings of the International Conference on Knowledge Discovery and Data Mining (SIGKDD), pp. 785–794 (2016)
8. Demšar, J.: Statistical comparisons of classifiers over multiple data sets. J. Mach. Learn. Res. **7**(1), 1–30 (2006)
9. Ismail Fawaz, H., Forestier, G., Weber, J., Idoumghar, L., Muller, P.-A.: Deep learning for time series classification: a review. Data Min. Knowl. Disc. **33**(4), 917–963 (2019). https://doi.org/10.1007/s10618-019-00619-1
10. Hersbach, H., et al.: ERA5 hourly data on single levels from 1979 to present. Copernicus Climate Change Service (C3S) Climate Data Store (CDS), vol. 10 (2018)

11. Hewamalage, H., Bergmeir, C., Bandara, K.: Global models for time series forecasting: A simulation study. Pattern Recogn. **124**, 108441 (2022)
12. Osman, A.I.A., Ahmed, A.N., Chow, M.F., Huang, Y.F., El-Shafie, A.: Extreme gradient boosting (XGBoost) model to predict the groundwater levels in Selangor Malaysia. Ain Shams Eng. J. **12**(2), 1545–1556 (2021)
13. Januschowski, T., et al.: Criteria for classifying forecasting methods. Int. J. Forecast. **36**, 167–177 (2020)
14. Kisi, O., Shiri, J., Nikoofar, B.: Forecasting daily lake levels using artificial intelligence approaches. Comput. Geosci. **41**, 169–180 (2012)
15. Lara-Benítez, P., Carranza-García, M., Riquelme, J.C.: An experimental review on deep learning architectures for time series forecasting. Int. J. Neural Syst. **31**, 2130001 (2021)
16. Makridakis, S., Spiliotis, E., Assimakopoulos, V.: The M4 competition: 100,000 time series and 61 forecasting methods. Int. J. Forecast. **36**, 54–74 (2020)
17. Makridakis, S., Spiliotis, E., Assimakopoulos, V.: M5 accuracy competition: results, findings, and conclusions. Int. J. Forecast. (2022). In press
18. Montero-Manso, P., Hyndman, R.J.: Principles and algorithms for forecasting groups of time series: locality and globality. Int. J. Forecast. **37**, 1632–1653 (2021)
19. Nayak, P.C., Rao, Y.S., Sudheer, K.: Groundwater level forecasting in a shallow aquifer using artificial neural network approach. Water Resour. Manage **20**(1), 77–90 (2006)
20. Pedregosa, F., et al.: Scikit-learn: machine learning in Python. J. Mach. Learn. Res. **12**, 2825–2830 (2011)
21. Rahman, A.S., Hosono, T., Quilty, J.M., Das, J., Basak, A.: Multiscale groundwater level forecasting: coupling new machine learning approaches with wavelet transforms. Adv. Water Resour. **141**, 103595 (2020)
22. Rodriguez-Galiano, V., Mendes, M.P., Garcia-Soldado, M.J., Chica-Olmo, M., Ribeiro, L.: Predictive modeling of groundwater nitrate pollution using random forest and multisource variables related to intrinsic and specific vulnerability: a case study in an agricultural setting (southern Spain). Sci. Total Environ. **476**, 189–206 (2014)
23. Salinas, D., Flunkert, V., Gasthaus, J., Januschowski, T.: DeepAR: probabilistic forecasting with autoregressive recurrent networks. Int. J. Forecast. **36**, 1181–1191 (2017)
24. Tao, H., et al.: Groundwater level prediction using machine learning models: a comprehensive review. Neurocomputing **489**(C), 271–308 (2022)
25. Taylor, S.J., Letham, B.: Forecasting at scale. PeerJ Preprints (2017)
26. Triebe, O., Hewamalage, H., Pilyugina, P., Laptev, N., Bergmeir, C., Rajagopal, R.: NeuralProphet: explainable forecasting at scale. arXiv:2111.15397v1 (2021)

Fast Time Series Classification with Random Symbolic Subsequences

Thach Le Nguyen[✉] and Georgiana Ifrim

School of Computer Science, University College Dublin, Dublin, Ireland
{thach.lenguyen,georgiana.ifrim}@ucd.ie

Abstract. Symbolic representations of time series have proven to be effective for time series classification, with many recent approaches including BOSS, WEASEL, and MrSEQL. These classifiers use various elaborate methods to select discriminative features from symbolic representations of time series. As a result, although they have competitive results regarding accuracy, their classification models are relatively expensive to train. Most if not all of these approaches have missed an important research question: are these elaborate feature selection methods actually necessary? ROCKET, a state-of-the-art time series classifier, outperforms all of them without utilizing any feature selection techniques. In this paper, we answer this question by contrasting these classifiers with a very simple method, named MrSQM. This method samples random subsequences from symbolic representations of time series. Our experiments on 112 datasets of the UEA/UCR benchmark demonstrate that MrSQM can quickly extract useful features and learn accurate classifiers with the logistic regression algorithm. MrSQM completes training and prediction on 112 datasets in 1.5 h for an accuracy comparable to existing efficient state-of-the-art methods, e.g., MrSEQL (10 h) and ROCKET (2.5 h). Furthermore, MrSQM enables the user to trade-off accuracy and speed by controlling the type and number of symbolic representations, thus further reducing the total runtime to 20 min for a similar level of accuracy. With these results, we show that random subsequences extracted from symbolic transformations can be as effective as the more sophisticated and expensive feature selection methods proposed in previous works. We propose MrSQM as a strong baseline for future research in time series classification, especially for approaches based on symbolic representations of time series.

1 Introduction

Symbolic representations of time series are a family of techniques to transform numerical time series to sequences of symbols, and were shown to be more robust to noise and useful for building effective time series classifiers. Two of the most prominent symbolic representations are Symbolic Aggregate Approximation (SAX) [18] and Symbolic Fourier Approximation (SFA) [26]. SAX-based classifiers include BOP [18,19], FastShapelets [23], SAX-VSM [28]; SFA-based

T. Guyet et al. (Eds.): AALTD 2022, LNAI 13812, pp. 50–65, 2023.
https://doi.org/10.1007/978-3-031-24378-3_4

classifiers include BOSS [24], BOSS VS [25] and WEASEL [27]. MrSEQL [17] is a symbolic classifier which utilizes both SAX and SFA transformations, which further improved the accuracy and speed of classification. Several state-of-the-art ensemble methods, e.g., HIVE-COTE [2, 3, 20] and TS-CHIEF [29], incorporate symbolic representations for their constituent classifiers and are the current state-of-the-art with regard to accuracy.

Symbolic representations of time series enable the adoption of techniques developed for text mining. For example, SAX-VSM, BOSS VS and WEASEL make use of tf-idf vectors and vector space models [25, 28], while MrSEQL is based on a sequence learning algorithm developed for text classification [15]. These apparently different approaches can be summarized as methods of extracting discriminative features from symbolic representations of time series, coupled with a classifier. While achieving high accuracy, the key challenge for symbolic classifiers is to efficiently select good features from a large feature space. For example, even with fixed parameters, a SAX bag-of-words can contain as many as α^w unique words, in which α is the size of the alphabet (the number of distinct symbols) and w is the length of the words. Even for moderate alphabet and word sizes, this feature space grows quickly, e.g., for typical SAX parameters $\alpha = 4, w = 16$, there can be 4 billion unique SAX words. SAX-VSM works with a single optimized SAX representation, but the process for optimizing the SAX parameters is expensive. WEASEL has high accuracy by using SFA unigrams and bigrams but a high memory demand, due to needing to store all the SFA words before applying feature selection. MrSEQL uses the feature space of all subsequences in the training data, in order to find useful features inside SAX or SFA words. It employs greedy feature selection and a gradient bound to quickly prune unpromising features. Despite these computational challenges, these methods are still vastly faster and less resource demanding than most state-of-the-art classifiers, in particular ensembles, e.g., HIVE-COTE, TS-CHIEF, and deep learning models, e.g., InceptionTime [10].

Recently, these symbolic classifiers had been outperformed by ROCKET [6] and MiniROCKET [7], a family of methods that uses random kernels to extract features from raw time series. Rather than finding the most discriminative features, ROCKET generates 10,000 random kernels regardless of their discriminative strength. As a result, while they also combine large feature spaces with linear classifiers, the ROCKET methods are faster and more accurate than the existing symbolic classifiers. This intriguing observation raises a simple question: are the expensive feature selection techniques employed by the previous symbolic classifiers (e.g., SAX-VSM, BOSS, WEASEL, MrSEQL) necessary? This question has inspired us to re-examine fast symbolic transformations, feature selection and linear classifiers for working with symbolic representations of time series. We thus propose MrSQM, a simple time series classifier which samples random subsequences from symbolic representations of time series. Our experiments on the UEA/UCR benchmark show that, even without any feature selection method, a large enough number of random symbolic subsequences can be as effective for learning accurate classifiers. More importantly, the method is significantly faster than most of its counterparts: it can complete training and prediction on 112 datasets in 1.5 h, for an accuracy comparable to existing efficient state-of-the-art methods, e.g., MrSEQL (10 h) and ROCKET (2.5 h). Furthermore, MrSQM enables the user to trade-off accuracy and speed by controlling the type and number of symbolic representations.

Our main contributions in this paper are as follows:

– We propose **Multiple Representations Sequence Miner (MrSQM)**, a new symbolic time series classifier which builds on multiple symbolic representations, random sequence mining and a linear classifier, to achieve high accuracy with reduced computational cost.
– We present an extensive empirical study comparing the accuracy and runtime of MrSQM to recent state-of-the-art time series classifiers on 112 datasets of the new UEA/UCR TSC benchmark [1]. Our study demonstrates that random subsequences can be as effective as complex feature selection methods proposed in previous works on symbolic approaches.
– All our code and data is publicly available to enable reproducibility of our results[1]. Our code is implemented in Python and C++ (in Python wrappers) and a Python Jupyter Notebook with detailed examples to make the implementation more widely accessible.

The rest of the paper is organised as follows. In Sect. 2 we discuss the state-of-the-art in time series classification research. In Sect. 3 we describe our research methodology. In Sect. 4 we present an empirical study with a detailed sensitivity analysis for our methods and a comparison to state-of-the-art time series classifiers. We conclude in Sect. 5.

2   Related Work

The state-of-the-art in time series classification (TSC) has evolved rapidly with many different approaches contributing to improvements in accuracy and speed. The main baseline for TSC is 1NN-DTW [3], a one Nearest-Neighbor classifier with Dynamic Time Warping as distance measure. While this baseline is at times preferred for its simplicity, it is not very robust to noise and has been significantly outperformed in accuracy by more recent methods. Some of the most successful TSC approaches typically fall into the following three groups.

Ensemble Classifiers aggregate the predictions of many independent classifiers. Each classifier is trained with different data representations and feature spaces, and the individual predictions are weighted based on the quality of the classifier on validation data. HIVE-COTE [20] is the most popular example of such an approach. It is an evolution of the COTE [3] ensemble and it is still currently the most accurate TSC approach. While being very accurate, this method's runtime is bound to the slowest of its component classifiers. Recent work [2,21] has proposed techniques to make this approach more usable by

---

[1] https://github.com/mlgig/mrsqm.

improving its runtime, but it still requires more than two weeks to train on the new UEA/UCR benchmark which has a moderate size of about 300Mb. TS-CHIEF [29] is another recent ensemble which only uses decision tree classifiers. It was proposed as a more scalable alternative to HIVE-COTE, but still takes weeks to train on the UEA/UCR benchmark. This makes the reproducibility of results with these methods challenging.

Deep Learning Classifiers were recently proposed for time series data and analysed in an extensive empirical survey [16]. Methods such as Fully Convolutional Networks (FCN) and Residual Networks (Resnet) were found to be highly effective and achieve accuracy comparable to HIVE-COTE. One issue with such approaches is their tendency to overfit with small training data and to have a high variance in accuracy. In order to create a more stable approach Inception-Time [10] was proposed to ensemble five deep learning classifiers. InceptionTime achieves an accuracy comparable to HIVE-COTE, but requires vast computational resources and requires days to train on the same benchmark [2,10].

Linear Classifiers were recently shown to work well for time series classification. Given a large feature space, the need for further feature expansion and learning non-linear classifiers is reduced. This idea was incorporated very successfully for large scale classification in libraries such as LIBLINEAR [9]. In the context of TSC, this idea was first incorporated by classifiers such as WEASEL [27], which creates a large SFA-words feature space, filters it with Chi-square feature selection, then learns a logistic regression classifier. Another linear classifier, MrSEQL [17], uses a large feature space of SAX and SFA subwords, which is filtered using greedy gradient descent and logistic regression. A recent classifier ROCKET [6] generates many random convolutional kernels and uses max pooling and a feature called *ppv* to capture good features from the time series. ROCKET uses a large feature space of 20,000 features (default settings) associated with the kernels, and a linear classifier (logistic regression or ridge regression). MiniROCKET [7] is a recent extension of ROCKET with comparable accuracy and faster runtime. These approaches were shown to be as accurate as ensembles and deep learning for TSC, but are orders of magnitude faster to train [6,17,21]. MrSEQL can train on the UEA/UCR benchmark in 10h, while ROCKET has further reduced this time to 2.5h. Another advantage of these methods is their conceptual simplicity, since the method can be broken down into three stages: (1) transformation (e.g., symbolic for WEASEL and MrSEQL, or convolutional kernels for ROCKET), (2) feature selection and (3) linear classifier. Intuitively, these methods extract many shapelet-like features from the training data, and use the linear classifier to learn weights to filter out the useful features from the rest. While there is a vast literature on shapelet-learning techniques, e.g., [2,3,14,23,30] these recent linear classification methods were shown to be more accurate and faster than other shapelet-based approaches. In particular, the SFA transform does not require data normalisation (which may harm accuracy for some problems), it was shown to be robust to noise [24], and has very fast implementations which build on the past 20 years of work on speeding up the computation of Discrete Fourier Transform [11,12].

Based on these observations and the success of symbolic transforms and linear classifiers, we focus our work on designing and evaluating new TSC methods built on large symbolic feature spaces and efficient linear classifiers.

3 Proposed Method

The MrSQM time series classifier has three main building blocks: (1) **symbolic transformation**, (2) **feature transformation** and (3) **learning algorithm** for training a classifier. In the first stage, we transform the numerical time series to multiple symbolic representations using either SAX or SFA transforms. We carefully analyse the impact of parameter selection for the symbolic transform, as well as integrate fast transform implementations, especially for the Discrete Fourier Transform in SFA. For the second stage, random subsequences are sampled from the symbolic representations. Each subsequence then becomes a feature for model training. The value of the feature is a binary value: 1 if the subsequence can be found in the symbolic representation of the sample and 0 if not. The output of this stage is transformed data in tabular form. For the third stage, we employ an efficient linear classifier based on logistic regression. While the choice of the learning algorithm does not depend on the previous two stages, we select logistic regression for its scalability, accuracy and the benefit of model transparency and calibrated prediction probabilities, which can benefit some follow up steps such as classifier interpretation. For example, as done in the MrSEQL approach [17], the symbolic features selected by the logistic regression model can be mapped back to the time series to compute a saliency map explanation for the classifier prediction. A schematic representation of the MrSQM approach is given in Fig. 1.

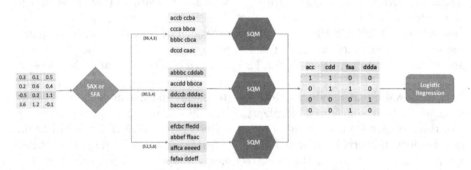

Fig. 1. Workflow for the MrSQM time series classifier with 3 stages: 1. symbolic transform, 2. feature transform, 3. classifier learning.

3.1 Symbolic Representations of Time Series

While SAX and SFA are two different techniques to transform time series data to symbolic representations, both can be summarized in three steps:

- Use a sliding window to extract segments of time series (parameter l: window size).
- Approximate each segment with a vector of smaller or equal length (parameter w: word size).
- Discretise the approximation to obtain a symbolic word (e.g., *abbacc*; parameter α: alphabet size).

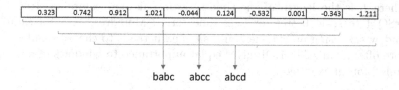

Fig. 2. Example symbolic transform using a sliding window over the time series.

As a result, the output of transforming a time series is a sequence of symbolic words (e.g., *abbacc aaccdd bbacda aacbbc*). Figure 2 shows an example symbolic transform applied to a time series, and the resulting sequence of symbolic words.

The main differences between SAX and SFA are the approximation and discretisation techniques, which are summarized in Table 1. The SAX transform works directly on the raw numeric time series, in the time domain, using an approximation called Piecewise Aggregate Approximation (PAA). The SFA transform builds on the Discrete Fourier Transform (DFT), followed by discretisation in the frequency domain. Hence these two symbolic transforms should capture different types of information about the time series structure. Each transform results in a different symbolic representation, for a fixed set of parameters (l, w, α). This means that for a given type of symbolic transform (e.g., SAX), we can obtain multiple symbolic representations by varying these parameters. This helps in capturing the time series structure at different granularity, e.g., by varying the window size l the symbolic words capture more detailed or higher level information about the time series.

MrSQM generates $k \times log(L)$ representations by randomly sampling values for (l, w, α) from a range of values, as shown in Table 2. Parameter $k \in \mathbb{N}, k > 0$ is a controlling parameter that can be set by the user. In comparison, the MrSEQL classifier creates approximately $\sqrt{L}$ symbolic representations for each time series

Table 1. Steps for SAX and SFA symbolic transforms. N is the number of time series and L is the length of time series. Piecewise Aggregate Approximation (PAA) is used in SAX and Discrete Fourier Transform (DFT) is used in SFA.

	SAX	SFA
Approximation	PAA	DFT
Discretisation	Equi-probability bins	Equi-depth bins
Complexity	$\mathcal{O}(NL)$	$\mathcal{O}(NL\log L)$

Table 2. An example of parameter sampling for a dataset of time series length $L = 64$.

	MrSQM	MrSEQL
Window size	$2^{3+i/k}$ for i in $(0, 1, \ldots log(L))$	16, 24, 32, 40, 48, 54, 60, 64
Word length	6, 8, 10, 12, 14, 16	16
Alphabet size	3, 4, 5, 6	4

(where L is the length of the time series). This new sampling strategy helps MrSQM to scale better for long time series. Moreover, MrSQM samples the window size using an exponential scale, i.e., it tends to choose smaller windows more often, while MrSEQL gives equal importance to windows of all sizes (see Table 2 for an example).

3.2   MrSQM Variants

We create two variants for MrSQM. The first variant (MrSQM-R) is the base variant with three stages of transforming and learning as described in Fig. 1. The second variant (MrSQM-RS) includes an extra step of feature selection. After the features are extracted from each representation, a feature selection module (*SelectKBest* from the *sklearn* library) ranks the features according to their importance. Only the most important features are kept for the later stage. While the number of features per representation is also configurable, in our experiments we set it so both variants produce 500 features from each representation for learning.

Time Complexity. All our classifier variants have a time complexity dominated by the symbolic transform time complexity. In our case, the SFA transform, which is $\mathcal{O}(NL \log L)$ is the dominant factor. This is repeated $\mathcal{O}(\log L)$ times (the number of symbolic representations being generated) hence the overall time complexity of MrSQM is $\mathcal{O}(NL(\log L)^2)$. Although SFA has a time complexity of $\mathcal{O}(NL \log L)$, we build our SFA implementation using the latest advances for efficiently computing the Discrete Fourier Transform[2], which results in significant time savings as compared to older SFA implementations.

4   Evaluation

4.1   Experiment Setup

We ran experiments on 108 fixed-length univariate time series classification datasets from the new UEA/UCR TSC Archive. MrSQM also works with variable-length time series, without any additional steps being required (i.e., once it is supported by the input file format). Since the majority of state-of-the-art TSC implementations only support fixed-length time series, for comparison, we have restricted our experiments to fixed-length datasets.

---

[2] FFTW is an open source C library for efficiently computing the Discrete Fourier Transform (DFT): https://www.fftw.org.

MrSQM is implemented in Python and C++ (wrapped with Cython). For our experiments we use a Linux workstation with an Intel Core i7-7700 Processor and 32 GB memory. To support the reproducibility of results, we have a Github repository[3] with all the code and results. All the datasets used for experiments are available from the UEA/UCR TSC Archive website[4]. We also obtained the accuracy results for some of the existing classifiers from the same website. For the classifiers that we ran ourselves, we have used the implementation provided in the sktime library[5].

For accuracy comparison of multiple classifiers, we follow the recommendation in [4,8,13]. The accuracy gain is evaluated using a Wilcoxon signed-rank test with Holm correction and visualised with the critical difference (CD) diagram. The CD shows the ranking of methods with respect to their average accuracy rank computed across multiple datasets. For computing the CD we use the R library scmamp[6] [5]. While CDs are a useful visualization tool, they do not tell the full story since minor differences in accuracy can lead to different ranks. We thus supplement the CDs with tables and pairwise scatter plots for a closer look at the accuracy and runtime performance.

4.2 Sensitivity Analysis

Comparing MrSQM Variants. Here, we investigate the two variants of MrSQM (R and RS) in relation to the symbolic transformation (i.e., SAX and SFA). Figure 3 compares four different combinations of MrSQM.

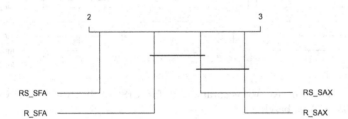

Fig. 3. Comparison of combinations between two variants of MrSQM and two symbolic representations.

Table 3. Time (minutes) comparison for SAX versus SFA combined with different feature selection strategies with $k = 1$.

Symbolic transform	MrSQM-R	MrSQM-RS
SAX	27	28
SFA	17	22

[3] https://github.com/mlgig/mrsqm.
[4] https://timeseriesclassification.com.
[5] https://www.sktime.org/en/stable/get_started.html.
[6] https://github.com/b0rxa/scmamp.

It is clear from this experiment (Fig. 3) that the SFA symbolic transform is generally superior to SAX. On the other hand, feature selection (R versus RS) appears to be useful with minimal cost (Table 3). All of these variants are very fast, totaling less than 30 min for training and predicting on the entire 108 datasets. Since the RS-SFA combination is more accurate than the others, from this point onward it is our default choice for the experiments unless stated otherwise.

Parameter Sampling for the Symbolic Transform. In this set of experiments, we study the impact of the symbolic transformation in terms of both quality and quantity of representations. Figure 4 shows results comparing different numbers of SFA representations (with k varying from 1 to 8), when using the RS feature selection strategy for MrSQM. It also includes a comparison to the MrSEQL classifier restricted to only using SFA features, in order to directly compare the accuracy and speed, using the same type of representation. The results show that adding more symbolic representations by varying the control parameter k can benefit MrSQM, albeit with the cost of extra computation reflected in the runtime. In addition, MrSQM at $k = 3$ is already significantly more accurate than MrSEQL, while still being four times faster.

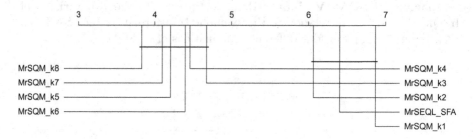

Fig. 4. Comparison of average accuracy rank for MrSQM-SFA variants at variable k and MrSEQL-SFA as baseline.

Figure 5 shows a comparison of the accuracy and runtime of MrSQM (for different values for k) and the MrSEQL classifier. Overall, the MrSQM variant with $k = 5$ seems to achieve a good trade-off between accuracy and speed, taking slightly over 100 min total time.

Combining SAX and SFA Features. Next we explore the option of combining SAX and SFA feature spaces. The work of [17] found that the combination of SAX and SFA features (with a 1:1 ratio) is very effective for the MrSEQL classifier. For MrSQM, we do not find the same behaviour when combining the two types of representations. Figure 6 shows that the MrSQM variant that only uses the SFA transform is as effective as when using combinations of SAX and SFA representations in different ratios. These results suggest that, to maximise accuracy and speed, the recommended choice of symbolic transformation for MrSQM

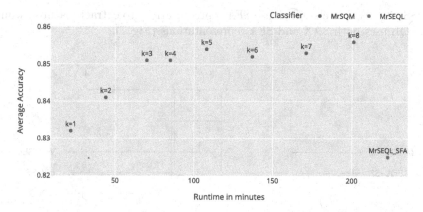

Fig. 5. Comparison of average accuracy and total training and prediction time (minutes) for MrSQM-SFA variants at varying k and MrSEQL variants as baseline.

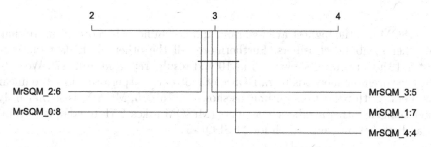

Fig. 6. Comparison between variants of MrSQM with different ratios of SAX and SFA representations. $k_1 : k_2$ means MrSQM generates $k_1 \times log(L)$ SAX representations and $k_2 \times log(L)$ SFA representations.

is SFA. However, it is worth noting that in practice this choice can depend on the requirements of the application. Across the 108 datasets coming from a wide variety of domains, SFA seems to be outperforming the SAX transform in both accuracy and speed. Nevertheless, for many datasets, SAX and SFA models have similar accuracy. Furthermore, like MrSEQL, the MrSQM classifier can produce a saliency map for each time series, from models trained with SAX features. This can be valuable in some scenarios where classifier interpretability is desirable. MrSQM enables the user to select the transform (type and number) that best fits their application scenario.

4.3 MrSQM Versus State-of-the-Art Symbolic Time Series Classifiers

We compare the best classifier variant for MrSQM (MrSQM_k5 has a good accuracy-time trade-off as shown in Fig. 5) with state-of-the-art symbolic time series classifiers. This group includes WEASEL, MrSEQL, BOSS and cBOSS [22]. All five classifiers use SFA representations to extract features, while MrSEQL uses both SAX and SFA representations (Fig. 7).

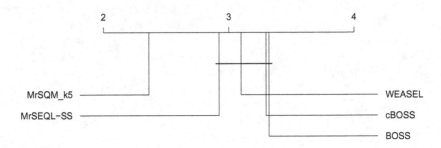

Fig. 7. Comparison of state-of-the-art symbolic time series classifiers across 108 UEA/UCR TSC datasets. The leftmost method has the best average rank.

MrSQM has the highest average rank and is significantly more accurate than the other symbolic classifiers. Furthermore, all the other methods require at least 5–12 h to train, as shown in Fig. 10 and results reported in [2,17]. We note that the ensemble methods (e.g., BOSS, cBOSS) are outperformed by the linear classifiers. With regard to runtime, as shown in Table 5, MrSQM is significantly faster than the other symbolic classifiers (MrSQM takes 1.5 h to complete training and prediction, versus 10 h for MrSEQL-SS).

4.4   MrSQM Versus Other State-of-the-Art Time Series Classifiers

The group of the most accurate time series classifiers that have been published to date include HIVE-COTE, TS-CHIEF, ROCKET (and its extension MiniROCKET), and InceptionTime. With the exception of the ROCKET family, these classifiers are very demanding in terms of computing resources. Running them on 108 UEA/UCR TSC datasets takes days and even weeks to complete training and prediction [2,21].

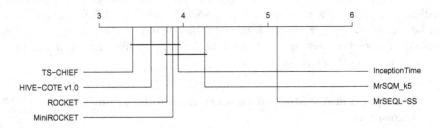

Fig. 8. Comparison with state-of-the-art time series classifiers across 108 UEA/UCR TSC datasets. The leftmost method has the best average rank.

Figure 8 shows the accuracy rank comparison between these methods and MrSQM. Among the methods compared, only TS-CHIEF and HIVE-COTE were found to have a statistically significant difference in accuracy when compared to MrSQM. Nevertheless, these methods require more than 100 h to complete training [2], for a relatively small gain in average accuracy, typically of about 2% (see Table 4). In this diagram, MrSQM is in the same accuracy group as Inception-Time, MiniROCKET and ROCKET. In terms of runtime, MrSQM is in a group with ROCKET: MrSQM takes 100 min to complete training and prediction on 108 datasets, while ROCKET, in our run on the same machine, takes 150 min (see more details on runtime in Table 5 and Fig. 10). The MrSQM-k1 variant takes only 20 min and for many datasets this variant is enough to achieve high accuracy. This variant is comparable in accuracy and runtime to the MiniROCKET classifier. In Fig. 10 we show a comparison of some of these methods with regards to the accuracy versus runtime (we only include the methods that we ran ourselves on the same machine).

Figure 9 shows the pairwise-comparison of accuracy between these methods and MrSQM. Each dot in the plot represents one dataset from the benchmark. MrSQM is more accurate above the diagonal line and highly similar methods cluster along the line. We note that the accuracy across datasets is similar for MrSQM versus ROCKET or MiniROCKET, the only other two methods in the same runtime category.

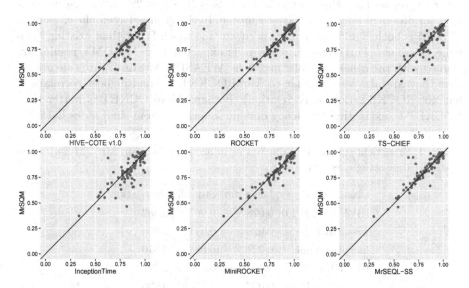

Fig. 9. Pairwise comparison between state-of-the-art time series classifiers and MrSQM with regard to accuracy across 108 UEA/UCR TSC datasets.

In Table 4, we summarize the accuracy differences between MrSQM and the other classifiers. For context, in Table 5 we also provide the runtime for all the

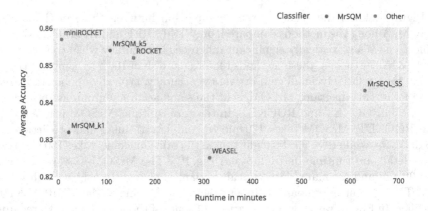

Fig. 10. Comparison of accuracy and total time (minutes) trade-off for MrSQM variants and state-of-the-art methods that complete training within 12 h.

methods. We observe that when taken together, the average difference in accuracy and the total time to complete training and prediction over the 108 datasets, we see a clear grouping of methods. If we focus on fast methods that can complete training and prediction in a couple of hours, only the ROCKET/MiniROCKET methods and MrSQM can achieve this. If we look at the average difference in accuracy versus the other methods, there is only about 2% difference in accuracy, for orders of magnitude faster runtime. In the group of symbolic classifiers, MrSQM is both significantly more accurate and much faster than existing symbolic classifiers. Furthermore, while it is expected that MrSQM's results are aligned with the other symbolic methods (WEASEL, MrSEQL), it is surprising that they are also very similar to MiniROCKET (second-highest correlation) but not ROCKET (lowest correlation). Perhaps MiniROCKET is better than ROCKET at extracting frequency domain knowledge from time series data.

Table 4. Statistical summary of differences in accuracy between MrSQM and state-of-the-art time series classifiers.

Classifiers	Mean diff	Std diff	Correlation
HIVE COTE 1.0	0.028	0.067	0.882
TS-CHIEF	0.026	0.071	0.866
InceptionTime	0.021	0.084	0.816
ROCKET	0.002	0.099	0.797
MiniROCKET	0.007	0.052	0.936
WEASEL	−0.025	0.069	0.91
MrSEQL-SS	−0.011	0.055	0.927
MrSQM_K1	−0.021	0.038	0.97

Table 5. Runtime of state-of-the-art classifiers for training and prediction over 108 datasets. For HIVE-COTE1.0 and TS-CHIEF the time is taken directly from [2].

Classifier	Total (hours)
MiniROCKET	0.1
MrSQM_K1	0.3
MrSQM_K5	1.5
ROCKET	2.5
WEASEL	5
MrSEQL-SS	10
HIVE-COTE1.0	400
TS-CHIEF	600

5   Conclusion

In this paper we have presented MrSQM, a new symbolic time series classifier which works with multiple symbolic representations of time series, fast feature selection for symbolic sequences and a linear classifier. We showed that while conceptually very simple, MrSQM achieves state-of-the-art accuracy on the new UEA/UCR time series classification benchmark, and can complete training and prediction in under two hours on a regular computer. This compares very favorably to existing methods such as HIVE-COTE, TS-CHIEF and InceptionTime, which achieve only slightly better accuracy, but require days to train on the same datasets and require advanced compute infrastructure. MrSQM is comparable to the recent classifier ROCKET, in regard of both accuracy and speed. This work has shown again that methods from the group of linear classifiers working in large feature spaces are very effective for the time series classification task. For future work we intend to study methods to further reduce the computational complexity of symbolic transformations and extend MrSQM to work on multivariate time series classification.

Acknowledgments. This publication has emanated from research supported in part by a grant from Science Foundation Ireland through the VistaMilk SFI Research Centre (SFI/16/RC/3835) and the Insight Centre for Data Analytics (12/RC/2289_P2).

References

1. Bagnall, A., et al.: The UEA multivariate time series classification archive. arXiv preprint arXiv:1811.00075 (2018)
2. Bagnall, A., Flynn, M., Large, J., Lines, J., Middlehurst, M.: On the usage and performance of the hierarchical vote collective of transformation-based ensembles version 1.0 (HIVE-COTE v1.0). In: Lemaire, V., Malinowski, S., Bagnall, A., Guyet, T., Tavenard, R., Ifrim, G. (eds.) AALTD 2020. LNCS (LNAI), vol. 12588, pp. 3–18. Springer, Cham (2020). https://doi.org/10.1007/978-3-030-65742-0_1

3. Bagnall, A., Lines, J., Bostrom, A., Large, J., Keogh, E.: The great time series classification bake off: a review and experimental evaluation of recent algorithmic advances. Data Min. Knowl. Disc. **31**(3), 606–660 (2016). https://doi.org/10.1007/s10618-016-0483-9

4. Benavoli, A., Corani, G., Mangili, F.: Should we really use post-hoc tests based on mean-ranks? J. Mach. Learn. Res. **17**(5), 1–10 (2016). http://jmlr.org/papers/v17/benavoli16a.html

5. Calvo, B., Santafé, G.: scmamp: statistical comparison of multiple algorithms in multiple problems. R J. **8**(1), 248–256 (2016). https://doi.org/10.32614/RJ-2016-017

6. Dempster, A., Petitjean, F., Webb, G.I.: ROCKET: exceptionally fast and accurate time series classification using random convolutional kernels. Data Min. Knowl. Disc. **34**(5), 1454–1495 (2020). https://doi.org/10.1007/s10618-020-00701-z

7. Dempster, A., Schmidt, D.F., Webb, G.I.: MINIROCKET: a very fast (almost) deterministic transform for time series classification. In: Zhu, F., Ooi, B.C., Miao, C. (eds.) KDD 2021: The 27th ACM SIGKDD Conference on Knowledge Discovery and Data Mining, Virtual Event, Singapore, 14–18 August 2021, pp. 248–257. ACM (2021). https://doi.org/10.1145/3447548.3467231

8. Demšar, J.: Statistical comparisons of classifiers over multiple data sets. J. Mach. Learn. Res. **7**, 1–30 (2006). http://dl.acm.org/citation.cfm?id=1248547.1248548

9. Fan, R.E., Chang, K.W., Hsieh, C.J., Wang, X.R., Lin, C.J.: LIBLINEAR: a library for large linear classification. J. Mach. Learn. Res. **9**, 1871–1874 (2008)

10. Ismail Fawaz, H., et al.: InceptionTime: finding AlexNet for time series classification. Data Min. Knowl. Disc. **34**(6), 1936–1962 (2020). https://doi.org/10.1007/s10618-020-00710-y

11. Frigo, M., Johnson, S.G.: The design and implementation of FFTW3. Proc. IEEE **93**(2), 216–231 (2005). Special issue on "Program Generation, Optimization, and Platform Adaptation"

12. Frigo, M., Johnson, S.G.: Fastest Fourier transform in the west (2021). https://www.fftw.org

13. Garcia, S., Herrera, F.: An extension on "statistical comparisons of classifiers over multiple data sets" for all pairwise comparisons. J. Mach. Learn. Res. **9**, 2677–2694 (2008)

14. Grabocka, J., Schilling, N., Wistuba, M., Schmidt-Thieme, L.: Learning time-series shapelets. In: Proceedings of the 20th ACM SIGKDD International Conference on Knowledge Discovery and Data Mining, KDD 2014, pp. 392–401. ACM, New York (2014). https://doi.org/10.1145/2623330.2623613, http://doi.acm.org/10.1145/2623330.2623613

15. Ifrim, G., Wiuf, C.: Bounded coordinate-descent for biological sequence classification in high dimensional predictor space. In: Proceedings of the 17th ACM SIGKDD International Conference on Knowledge Discovery and Data Mining, KDD 2011, pp. 708–716. ACM, New York (2011). https://doi.org/10.1145/2020408.2020519, http://doi.acm.org/10.1145/2020408.2020519

16. Ismail Fawaz, H., Forestier, G., Weber, J., Idoumghar, L., Muller, P.-A.: Deep learning for time series classification: a review. Data Min. Knowl. Disc. **33**(4), 917–963 (2019). https://doi.org/10.1007/s10618-019-00619-1

17. Le Nguyen, T., Gsponer, S., Ilie, I., O'Reilly, M., Ifrim, G.: Interpretable time series classification using linear models and multi-resolution multi-domain symbolic representations. Data Min. Knowl. Disc. **33**(4), 1183–1222 (2019). https://doi.org/10.1007/s10618-019-00633-3

18. Lin, J., Keogh, E., Wei, L., Lonardi, S.: Experiencing SAX: a novel symbolic representation of time series. Data Min. Knowl. Discov. **15**(2), 107–144 (2007). https://doi.org/10.1007/s10618-007-0064-z
19. Lin, J., Khade, R., Li, Y.: Rotation-invariant similarity in time series using bag-of-patterns representation. J. Intell. Inf. Syst. **39**(2), 287–315 (2012). https://doi.org/10.1007/s10844-012-0196-5
20. Lines, J., Taylor, S., Bagnall, A.: HIVE-COTE: the hierarchical vote collective of transformation-based ensembles for time series classification. In: 2016 IEEE 16th International Conference on Data Mining (ICDM), pp. 1041–1046 (2016). https://doi.org/10.1109/ICDM.2016.0133
21. Middlehurst, M., Large, J., Flynn, M., Lines, J., Bostrom, A., Bagnall, A.J.: HIVE-COTE 2.0: a new meta ensemble for time series classification. Mach. Learn. **110**(11), 3211–3243 (2021). https://doi.org/10.1007/s10994-021-06057-9
22. Middlehurst, M., Vickers, W., Bagnall, A.: Scalable dictionary classifiers for time series classification. In: Yin, H., Camacho, D., Tino, P., Tallón-Ballesteros, A.J., Menezes, R., Allmendinger, R. (eds.) IDEAL 2019. LNCS, vol. 11871, pp. 11–19. Springer, Cham (2019). https://doi.org/10.1007/978-3-030-33607-3_2
23. Rakthanmanon, T., Keogh, E.: Fast shapelets: a scalable algorithm for discovering time series shapelets. In: Proceedings of the thirteenth SIAM conference on data mining (SDM), pp. 668–676. SIAM (2013)
24. Schäfer, P.: The boss is concerned with time series classification in the presence of noise. Data Min. Knowl. Disc. **29**(6), 1505–1530 (2015)
25. Schäfer, P.: Scalable time series classification. Data Min. Knowl. Disc. **30**(5), 1273–1298 (2015). https://doi.org/10.1007/s10618-015-0441-y
26. Schäfer, P., Högqvist, M.: SFA: a symbolic Fourier approximation and index for similarity search in high dimensional datasets. In: Proceedings of the 15th International Conference on Extending Database Technology, EDBT 2012, pp. 516–527. ACM, New York (2012). https://doi.org/10.1145/2247596.2247656, http://doi.acm.org/10.1145/2247596.2247656
27. Schäfer, P., Leser, U.: Fast and accurate time series classification with weasel. In: Proceedings of the 2017 ACM on Conference on Information and Knowledge Management, CIKM 2017, pp. 637–646. ACM, New York (2017). https://doi.org/10.1145/3132847.3132980, http://doi.acm.org/10.1145/3132847.3132980
28. Senin, P., Malinchik, S.: SAX-VSM: interpretable time series classification using sax and vector space model. In: 2013 IEEE 13th International Conference on Data Mining (ICDM), pp. 1175–1180 (2013). https://doi.org/10.1109/ICDM.2013.52
29. Shifaz, A., Pelletier, C., Petitjean, F., Webb, G.: TS-CHIEF: a scalable and accurate forest algorithm for time series classification. Data Min. Knowl. Disc. **34**, 742–775 (2020)
30. Ye, L., Keogh, E.: Time series shapelets: a new primitive for data mining. In: Proceedings of the 15th ACM SIGKDD International Conference on Knowledge Discovery and Data Mining, pp. 947–956. ACM (2009)

RESIST: Robust Transformer for Unsupervised Time Series Anomaly Detection

Naji Najari[1,2,3], Samuel Berlemont[1(✉)], Grégoire Lefebvre[1], Stefan Duffner[2,3], and Christophe Garcia[2,3]

[1] Orange Innovation, Meylan, France
{naji.najari,samuel.berlemont,gregoire.lefebvre}@orange.com
[2] LIRIS UMR 5205 CNRS, Villeurbanne, France
{naji.najari,stefan.duffner,christophe.garcia}@liris.cnrs.fr
[3] INSA Lyon, Villeurbanne, France

Abstract. In the last decades, Internet of Things objects have been increasingly integrated into smart environments. Nevertheless, new issues emerge due to numerous reasons such as fraudulent attacks, inconsistent sensor behaviours, and network congestion. These anomalies can have a drastic impact on the global Quality of Service in the Local Area Network. Consequently, contextual anomaly detection using network traffic metadata has received a growing interest among the scientific community. The detection of temporal anomalies helps network administrators anticipate and prevent such failures. In this paper, we propose RESIST, a Robust transformEr developed for unSupervised tIme Series anomaly deTection. We introduce a robust learning strategy that trains a Transformer to model the nominal behaviour of the network activity. Unlike competing methods, our approach does not require the availability of an anomaly-free training subset. Relying on a contrastive learning-based robust loss function, RESIST automatically downweights atypical corrupted training data, to reduce their impact on the training optimization. Experiments on the CICIDS17 public benchmark dataset show an improved accuracy of our proposal in comparison to recent state-of-the-art methods.

Keywords: Unsupervised anomaly detection · Robust transformers · Self and Co-attention · Network traffic anomaly detection

1 Introduction

With the substantial increase of network anomalies in modern communication networks, anomaly detection has gained considerable interest over the last few years. The classical detectors, i.e., signature-based detectors, identify anomalies based on a predefined set of rules that models known attack signatures. These signatures must repeatedly be updated to integrate new attacks. Despite

T. Guyet et al. (Eds.): AALTD 2022, LNAI 13812, pp. 66–82, 2023.
https://doi.org/10.1007/978-3-031-24378-3_5

their effectiveness in identifying known threats, these systems fail to detect new emerging anomalies, e.g., zero-day attacks and non-malicious faults. To address these limitations, all the more present with the development of the Internet of Things (IoT), contextual anomaly detection becomes of big interest in the network analysis landscape.

Anomaly Detection (AD) in time series is a broad research field affecting numerous application domains such as network and object monitoring, medical data analysis, fraud detection, and network intrusion detection [8]. In such fields, detecting outliers mainly relies on the *temporal continuity* assumption, defined by Aggrawal [1] as "the fact that the patterns in the data are not expected to change abruptly unless there are abnormal processes at work." As such, a temporal outlier is an abrupt change in the data pattern, which results in a discontinuity of the data with its local context. This assumption makes temporal AD more challenging than the classical unsupervised punctual AD, since considering the ordinal causality between observations is of paramount importance.

Numerous extensive studies have been carried out in the field of temporal AD. Contributions have shifted their focus towards semi-supervision, a.k.a., One-Class Classification. Here, an algorithm is first trained to model the nominal patterns of the anomaly-free training data. Then, any deviation from the trained model is flagged as an outlier. Despite yielding encouraging results in some specific applications, these classical anomaly detectors generally assume the availability of anomaly-free training data, and their performance drastically declines in the presence of corrupted observations. Unfortunately, in real-world applications, the data collection process is prone to contamination, as the training data may be corrupted with an unknown fraction of outliers. For example, in network intrusion detection, diverse anomalies may occur during the collection of the training network trace, due to faulty sensors, traffic congestions, and security attacks. The manual filtering of training anomalies is laborious, because of increasing data volumes and the diversity of emergent anomalies. This motivates the development of robust unsupervised temporal anomaly detectors, insensitive to training contamination.

In this paper, we propose RESIST, a Robust transformEr designed for unSupervised tIme Series anomaly deTection. We introduce a novel training strategy that identifies and downweights the impact of contaminants. RESIST is trained to mine the common temporal correlations that link successive sliding windows. Only common patterns are modelled and instance-specific rare patterns are ignored, since they may be caused by training corrupted data. RESIST training optimizes the robust Geman-McClure loss function to reduce the impact of training outliers.

This paper is organized as follows: Sect. 2 introduces related work in temporal AD, and focuses particularly on Transformers for robust AD. Section 3 presents our contribution: RESIST. Section 4 depicts the datasets used in our experiments, the training protocols, and the experimental results. Finally, conclusions and perspectives are drawn.

2   Related Work

Time series AD is an active research field that has drawn increasing attention in the data mining and machine learning community [5, 8].

Time series AD mainly include four main families: density-based, clustering-based, prediction-based, and reconstruction-based methods. Density-based methods rely on a *local density* criterion to identify outliers. Observations that have few adjacent neighbours are considered anomalous. Density-based methods, such as Local Outlier Factor (LOF) [6] and Deep Autoencoding Gaussian Mixture Model (DAGMM) [32], are extensively used in non-temporal anomaly detection. Many works extend these classical methods to time series anomaly detection, by restricting the local density criterion to local sliding windows [2]. Cluster-based methods firstly determine the optimal set of clusters that model the nominal data. Then, these clusters are used as a reference for normality: the anomaly score is defined as the distance to the closest cluster centre. The most common cluster-based anomaly detectors include Support Vector Data Description (SVDD) [22], and Deep-SVDD [16]. Similarly, numerous studies aimed to adapt such methods to temporal AD [2]. Prediction-based methods train a model to forecast a posterior observation using only past data. Anomalies are points that are different from their predictions. Various models were developed within this category, ranging from AutoRegressive Integrated Moving Average (ARIMA) [31], to Long Short-Term Memory recurrent neural networks [9]. Finally, reconstruction-based methods learn to compress the nominal data points into a low-dimensional representation and reconstruct the original data based on these compressed encodings. In other words, these methods learn to extract the most important information of the norm by mapping the data into a subspace of lower dimensionality, with the least reconstruction error. Since anomalies generally comprise non-representative features, it is harder to project them in this subspace without loss of information, which results in a larger reconstruction error. The most common reconstruction-based anomaly detectors are AutoEncoders. They are extensively used to identify non-temporal anomalies [13–15, 20]. To extend this approach to time series data, Su et al. [20] propose a hybrid method that combines a Variational AutoEncoder (VAE) and a Gated Recurrent Unit (GRU). While the GRU learns the temporal correlations of the input sequences, the VAE is trained to map the observations into a latent stochastic space. Similarly, Malhotra et al. [13] propose an LSTM-AE.

Within the reconstruction-based category, a series of recent studies has shown the advantage of using Transformers over classical methods [7]. Benefiting from the self-attention mechanism and parallel computations, Transformer-based anomaly detectors show a higher detection performance and a more efficient training process [26]. Some recent studies, e.g., TranAD [23] and MT-RVAE [25], propose combining the Transformer-based architecture with common generative models, Generative Adversarial Networks (GANs) and VAEs, to further improve the model performance and robustness to training contaminations.

Alternatively, Xu et al. [27] renovate the self-attention mechanism by introducing a new *AnomalyAttention* module, specifically tailored for unsupervised time series anomaly detection. Their method, called AnomalyTransformer, is based on the intuition that, due to the rarity of anomalies, it is harder to find an association spread over the whole sequence. The authors remark that the self-attentions of anomalous points generally tend to be located in their adjacent data points. Consequently, AnomalyTransformer leverages this *adjacent concentration bias* to make anomalous points more distinguishable. The authors formalize the *adjacent concentration bias* by defining the Association Discrepancy (AssDis) criterion. For each data point, the Association Discrepancy quantifies the disparity between the local attention relative to the adjacent points and the global attention with the whole series. As it is difficult to find a global mapping that links anomalous points with the whole sequence, both local and global self-attentions are mostly localized in the surrounding. As such, anomalies have smaller Association Discrepancy than nominal points.

After training, AnomalyTransformer is used to assess the anomalousness of new samples. For a test data matrix $\mathbf{X} \in \mathbb{R}^{T \times d}$, containing T consecutive data points of dimension d, and its reconstruction $\widehat{\mathbf{X}} \in \mathbb{R}^{T \times d}$, the anomaly score is computed as follows:

$$\text{AnomalyScore}(\mathbf{X}) = \text{Softmax}(-\text{AssDis}) \left\| \mathbf{X} - \widehat{\mathbf{X}} \right\|_2^2. \tag{1}$$

The classical reconstruction error is amplified with a term inversely proportional to the AssDis. Since anomalies have smaller AssDis than inliers, their reconstruction error is amplified, which improves anomaly detection performance.

AnomalyTransformer shows that encouraging global attention spread over the entire sequence improves Transformer anomaly detection performance. Despite being more robust than vanilla Transformers, AnomalyTransformer attention is still restricted to the input sequence and lacks longer-term dependencies extracted from historical sequences. In fact, time-series data are usually split into fixed-length consecutive segments using a sliding window. The reference of normality in AnomalyTransformer is bounded to a single segment and ignores all previous windows. Even though anomalies are rare, the same anomaly may occur twice in the same window. In this case, the adjacent concentration bias becomes invalid, as anomalous observation self-attention is no longer limited to its surroundings. This is why we propose RESIST, which addresses this limitation, by extending the adjacent concentration prior to accounting for historical long-range properties.

3 Method

Unlike AnomalyTransformer, we propose to extend the Transformer attention to cover the historical data, in order to reject unusual observations. We hypothesize that rejecting training contaminants requires building pairwise associations not only between data points of the same sequence but also with instances of previous segments. The main intuition is that nominal instances present a regular behaviour shared across multiple segments. That is, reconstructing nominal sequences using either self-information extracted from the current input (i.e., self-reconstruction) or using relevant information extracted from the history (i.e., cross-reconstruction) would lead to similar results. In contrast, since anomalies are rare and different, building inter-sequence associations (or similarities) is more difficult and less informative. Building on this insight, we propose RESIST, a Robust transformEr for unSupervISed Time-series anomaly detection. RESIST is trained to reconstruct input sequences using a hybrid representation that combines local intra-sequence information as well as global properties, shared between multiple segments. Firstly, we introduce a Siamese training strategy that ensures that the model pays equal attention to the input sequence as well as to the previous ones. Secondly, we train RESIST with a robust loss function to reduce the impact of large reconstruction errors caused by training outliers. In the following, we detail our contributions and the hypotheses that we will analyze in the experimental part. First, we depict a global architecture overview of RESIST to present its main building blocks. Then, we present each component separately. Finally, we present our hypotheses, the corresponding experimental protocols and results.

3.1   RESIST Architecture

RESIST presents an encoder-decoder architecture, comprised of four main components: a positional encoding and embedding layer, a siamese encoder, a fusion layer, and a decoder (cf. Fig. 1). Similar to vanilla Transformers [24], the original data is firstly encoded using the linear embedding and the positional encoding units. Both encoder and decoder are composed of stacked identical blocks, where each block contains a multi-head attention unit followed by a Feed-Forward Network (FFN) layer.

RESIST takes as input K non-overlapping sequences $\mathbf{X}_t^w = (\mathbf{x}_{t-K+1}^w, ..., \mathbf{x}_t^w)$: an input sequence $\mathbf{x}_t^w$ and its $K-1$ previous sequences. Here, each sequence is composed of w consecutive data points $\mathbf{x}_t^w = (\mathbf{x}_{t-w+1}, ..., \mathbf{x}_t)$, where $\mathbf{x_t} \in \mathbb{R}^d$ is an observation of dimension d, recorded at the timestamp t. In Fig. 1, we illustrate our method for $K = 2$. Firstly, the linear embedding and the positional encoding units encode the input sequences $(\mathbf{x}_{t-K+1}^w, ..., \mathbf{x}_t^w)$ and output the K embedded sequences $(\mathbf{e}_{t-K+1}^w, ..., \mathbf{e}_t^w)$. Secondly, the encoder extracts from each embedded sequence $\mathbf{e}_t^w$ a low-dimensional latent encoding $\mathbf{z}_t^w$. Then, the fusion layer aggregates these encodings into a single representation. The decoder maps the fusion encoding to the input space in order to reconstruct the original sequence $\mathbf{x}_t$. Finally, RESIST minimizes the Geman-McClure robust function between the reconstructed sequence $\widehat{\mathbf{x}_t^w}$ and the original one $\mathbf{x}_t^w$.

After presenting the global architecture of our method, we will thoroughly review each component in the following Sections.

Siamese Encoder. RESIST encoder, illustrated in Fig. 1, learns to project K consecutive sequences into K low-dimensional embeddings. The encoder receives a sequence $\mathbf{x}_t^w$ and its associated history, which contains the $K-1$ sequences preceding $\mathbf{x}_t^w$. It models the point-wise correlations between $\mathbf{x}_t^w$ and the history.

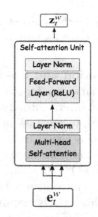

Fig. 2. Self-attention unit

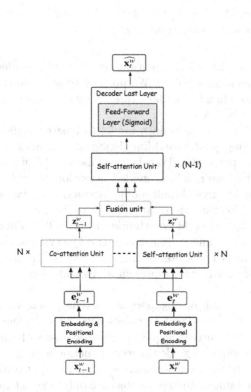

Fig. 1. RESIST architecture.

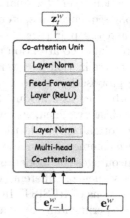

Fig. 3. Co-attention unit

Then, it learns to project these data into a common reduced space of dimension $d_{enc} \in \mathbb{N}^*$, where common data points share similar representations. This task is notoriously hard for anomalies, since they present non-representative uncommon patterns. For this reason, we propose an encoder with a Siamese architecture, with K identical sub-networks that share the same parameters. Input sequences are simultaneously processed using these networks. The sequences that share common proprieties have close encodings.

Unlike classical Siamese Neural Networks, our encoder is not trained to learn a similarity metric between input sequences. Its objective is to reduce the data dimensionality to only keep the most important information. Each siamese encoder sub-network is composed of a stack of $N = 2$ identical blocks. Each block comprises two sub-modules: a multi-head attention unit followed by a FFN layer (cf. Figs. 2 and 3). While the attention mines the temporal correlations in the data, the FFN layers are used for dimensionality reduction.

The Siamese encoder is a hybrid composition of both Self-Attention (SA) and Co-Attention (CA) units. While the SA units are used to extract the contextual properties of the current sequence, the CA unit is destined to extract inter-segment properties and only keep common relationships.

Self-attention and Co-attention Module. Attention modules are intended to mine pairwise interactions between data points. We propose to leverage the SA and CA layers, initially introduced in multimodal Visual Question Answering (VQA) [28], to our task of unsupervised AD.

VQA is a visual reasoning task where we train a model to answer a question concerning an image. Identifying joint visual-linguistic representations is crucial in VQA. In [28], Yu et al. propose a Transformer-based VQA model where they introduce a co-attention layer, a.k.a., guided attention layer (see Fig. 3). This layer is mainly designed to model multimodal interactions between a sentence and an image. The architecture of co-attention is the same as the self-attention layer. The main difference is that co-attention receives two different input sequences, a sentence and an image. It extracts the Query from the image and the pair (Key, Value) from the sentence. Recent studies [21] show the potential of co-attention to learn contextual representations and to improve model generalization performance.

We propose to extend CA to our task of unsupervised anomaly detection. CA can be seen as a module that filters similar data points between a sequence and the history. Then, it weights the current sequence observations with the relative normalized similarities. The aim is to guide the reconstruction with inter-sequence common information and to filter out sequence-specific rare patterns. This encourages the model to ignore unusual patterns that are only relevant for a single sequence. Different compositions of CA and SA may result in different configurations of RESIST. In Sect. 4.3, we will present these configurations and we will experimentally evaluate their impact on the AD performance.

Fusion Layer. We propose to leverage multiple data views for robust reconstruction. The fusion layer combines the multiple encodings extracted by RESIST encoder into a single vector representation. In this work, we propose an addition-based fusion. This module comprises a fusion layer, followed by a FFN layer. The RESIST additive fusion strategy is inspired from the well-known manifold *mixup* method [30]. The original *mixup* method was initially proposed for data augmentation in supervised learning. For two training inputs x_i and x_j, having two labels y_i and y_j, respectively, *mixup* generates a new training instance, $\hat{x}$, using a linear interpolation:

$$\hat{x} = \beta x_i + (1 - \beta)x_j \quad \text{and} \quad \hat{y} = \beta y_i + (1 - \beta)y_j. \tag{2}$$

$\hat{y}$ is the corresponding label of $\hat{x}$. The interpolation term $\beta \in [0, 1]$ is an hyper-parameter. In other words, *mixup* trains supervised classifiers to adapt a linear behaviour in the boundaries between training classes. *Mixup* reduces classifier regularization error and makes classifiers more robust to corrupted labels [30].

We extend the *mixup* method to robust unsupervised anomaly detection. Similar to the original *mixup* strategy, *mixup* fusion merges K instances into a single vector through linear interpolation. The merged representation of K encodings $(\mathbf{z}_{t-K+1}^w, ..., \mathbf{z}_t^w)$ is defined as follow:

$$\widehat{\mathbf{z}_t^w} = \frac{1}{K} \sum_{i=t-K+1}^{t} \mathbf{z}_i^w \tag{3}$$

We propose a uniform contribution of all encodings. For $K = 2$, we have $\widehat{\mathbf{z}_t^w} = 0.5\,\mathbf{z}_{t-1}^w + 0.5\,\mathbf{z}_t^w$. When the input sequence $\mathbf{x}_t^w$ presents common properties relative to its history, represented by $\mathbf{x}_{t-1}^w$, we expect that the siamese encoder extracts close latent representations $\mathbf{z}_t^w$ and $\mathbf{z}_{t-1}^w$. In this case, the fusion representation would be similar to the encoding of a vanilla Transformer, i.e., $\widehat{\mathbf{z}_t^w} \approx \mathbf{z}_{t-1}^w$. In contrast, when the current sequence comprises an uncommon pattern, the encoder self-attention and co-attention modules potentially extract different encodings. Therefore, the linear interpolation may generate an inconsistent sample and the reconstruction task become more difficult.

Finally, this compact representation $\widehat{\mathbf{z}_t^w}$ is forwarded to the FFN of the fusion module and the final output is:

$$\mathbf{F}_t^w(\mathbf{z}_{t-K+1}^w, ..., \mathbf{z}_t^w) = ReLU(\widehat{\mathbf{z}_t^w}\mathbf{W}_f + \mathbf{b}_f), \tag{4}$$

where $\mathbf{W}_f \in \mathbb{R}^{d_{enc} \times d_f}$ refers to the linear layer weights and $\mathbf{b}_f \in \mathbb{R}^{d_f}$ to the bias vector. d_{enc} is the dimension of the fusion module inputs and d_f is the dimension of the outputs. In all experiments, we use $d_f = d_{enc} = 16$.

RESIST Decoder. Finally, the RESIST decoder learns to reconstruct the last sequence of the input using the compact representation that is the output of the fusion module. It is composed of a stack of $N = 2$ identical blocks. Each block comprises two sub-modules: a multi-head self-attention unit followed by a FFN layer. While Rectified Linear Unit (ReLU) activation function is used in the first block, the last block is followed by a Sigmoid function to ensure that the output has the same range as the input $[0, 1]$.

3.2   Robust Training Loss

To hedge against training contaminants, we train RESIST using a robust loss function. Indeed, the commonly used Mean Squared Error (MSE) is sensitive to outliers, since squaring large deviations results in the dominance of anomalies during the training. In contrast, a robust loss can resist noise and anomalies by reducing the influence of their large reconstruction errors. There have been numerous studies to explore robust leaning in the presence of outliers. The robust function list includes Charbonnier loss, Cauchy loss, Geman-McClure loss, and Welsch loss. Recently, Barron [4] generalizes these common losses in a single parametric function, $\rho(x, \alpha, c)$, parameterized by the scale c and the robustness parameter α.

$$\rho(x,\alpha,c) = \begin{cases} \frac{1}{2}(\frac{x}{c})^2 & if\ \alpha = 2 \\ \log(\frac{1}{2}(\frac{x}{c})^2 + 1) & if\ \alpha = 0 \\ 1 - \exp(-\frac{1}{2}(\frac{x}{c})^2) & if\ \alpha = -\infty \\ \frac{|\alpha-2|}{\alpha}((\frac{(\frac{x}{c})^2}{|\alpha-2|} + 1)^{\frac{\alpha}{2}} - 1) & otherwise \end{cases} \quad (5)$$

Particular values of α define common robust losses: L2 loss ($\alpha = 2$), Charbonnier loss ($\alpha = 1$), Cauchy loss ($\alpha = 0$), Geman-McClure loss ($\alpha = -2$), and Welsch loss ($\alpha = -\infty$). These cases are visualized in Fig. 4, extracted from [4]. We refer the reader to [4] for a detailed description of these losses.

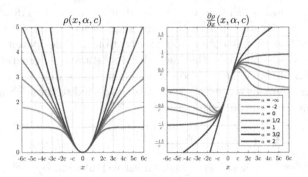

Fig. 4. The general robust loss function proposed in [4].

In particular, we propose to train RESIST by minimizing the Geman-McClure robust function, which reduces the influence of high reconstruction errors in gradient computations during training. The Geman-McClure function is:

$$L(x) = \rho(x, \alpha = -2, c) = 2\frac{(\frac{x}{c})^2}{4 + (\frac{x}{c})^2} \quad (6)$$

where c is a scale parameter that modulates the loss robustness range. In all our experiments, we set $x = \lambda$IQR, where IQR is the interquartile range and $\lambda = 0.1$.

3.3 Hypotheses

We synthesize our contributions into the following hypotheses:

- **Hypothesis 1 (H1)** *We conjecture that guiding the Transformer reconstruction with both intra-sequence properties, extracted using SA units, and inter-sequence pairwise interactions with the history, extracted with CA units, results in a more robust anomaly detector.*
- **Hypothesis 2 (H2)** *We hypothesize that training RESIST with a robust loss function, and particularly the Geman-McClure loss, reduces the impact of training noise and anomalies;*

4   Experiments and Results

In this section, we explore the validity of the assumed hypotheses on the benchmark dataset: the Canadian Institute of Cybersecurity Intrusion Detection System (CICIDS17) evaluation dataset [18]. In addition, we extensively compare our contribution against common unsupervised anomaly detectors. First, we provide an overview of the dataset. Then, we develop the training and testing protocols. Finally, we present and analyze the empirical results.

4.1   Dataset Description

CICIDS17 [18] is a recent public dataset developed by the Canadian Institute of Cybersecurity (CIC) for IDS evaluation. Overall, this dataset comprises about 3 million labelled network flows collected over 5 days, starting from July 3, 2017, and ending on Friday, July 7, 2017. 83% of this traffic is benign and the remaining 17% is anomalous. To collect the traffic, Sharafaldin et al. developed a testbed containing two networks: an Attack-Network and a Victim-Network. The Victim-Network comprises three servers, one firewall, two switches and ten interconnected PCs. One switch was configured to mirror all the traffic passing through the network. The Attack-Network is a separate network that runs network attacks on the Victim-Network.

CICIDS17 provides full packet capture of the collected data in *pcap* files. In addition, the raw data are processed using CICFlowMeter, a flow-based feature extractor, to extract metadata from the packet traces. Each flow record is represented by 85 features: a flow ID, 83 flow metadata features, and a class label. A detailed description of the 83 flow-based features is presented in [10]. CICIDS2017 comprises 15 classes: a nominal class and 14 attack types, including DoS, Distributed DoS (DDoS), Web attacks, and Infiltration attacks. This dataset was extensively used in many recent publications [10], since it covers various recent attacks and it comprises both punctual and collective anomalies.

4.2   Data Preprocessing

We follow the same preprocessing steps proposed in [11]. Since the original dataset is voluminous, we focus on the data subset that is collected during one day: Thursday, July 6 2017. This subset contains 170231 network flow and represents around 6% of the whole dataset. 98.7% of this traffic is benign and the remaining 1.3% is anomalous. We rescale numerical features to be in the range $[0, 1]$, using the min-max normalization method. Then, we randomly split the benign data into 40% for the training and 60% for testing.

4.3   Training and Testing Protocols

Protocol 1 (P1): Modular Composition of Co-attention and Self-attention Modules. RESIST encoder is composed of two attention-based components: the self-attention and the co-attention modules. Different combinations of these modules result in different variants. In this section, we study the performance of RESIST with three modular compositions of these units.

For ease of illustration, we only visualize the RESIST encoder part for the three configuration. The first variant, RESIST-SS (cf. Fig. 5), is the baseline. This first configuration does not consider the history for data reconstruction. In this case, only the input sequence flows through self-attention units to gradually extract the intra-properties of each sequence Then, RESIST-SS decoder is trained to reconstruct the sequence based only on this self-encoded representation. The second configuration, RESIST-SC (cf. Fig. 6), considers inter-sequence similarities between the input and the history. Indeed, both sequences are processed using a first self-attention unit to model intra-sequence relationships. Then, the encoded representation of the current sequence is processed using a self-attention unit, while the historical representations are fed into a co-attention unit to introduce pairwise similarities between consecutive sequences. Finally, the third variant is RESIST-CC (cf. Fig. 7). Here, the input sequence is encoded through cascaded self-attention units and adjacent sequences are encoded using co-attention units. The main difference between RESIST-SC and RESIST-CC is that the former encodes the history with a hybrid encoder that alternates CA and SA, while in the latter, only CA units are used to encode the previous segments.

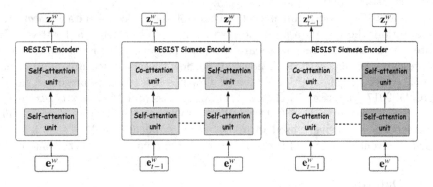

Fig. 5. RESIST-SS   **Fig. 6.** RESIST-SC   **Fig. 7.** RESIST-CC

Protocol 2 (P2): Robust Loss Function. In this section, we explore the importance of the robust loss function to reduce model sensitivity with respect to anomalies. As previously mentioned in Sect. 3.2, various robust losses are developed in the literature, such as Charbonnier loss, Cauchy loss, Geman-McClure loss, and Welsch loss. In particular, we compare three different training losses. The first function is the classical L2 loss. Here, we train this first variant of RESIST with the common L2 loss to study its sensitivity to training outliers, in the absence of a robust training loss. Then, we compare three common robust functions: Charbonnier loss, Cauchy loss, and Geman-McClure loss [4].

Protocol 3 (P3): Comparison with Competing Methods. Finally, we globally compare our contribution against common unsupervised time series anomaly detectors. In this experiment, we select the best performing configuration of RESIST: a siamese encoder that comprises a hybrid composition of self and co-attention units, and trained with the Geman-McClure loss. The baselines selected in our experiments belong to the different categories of unsupervised anomaly detection presented in Sect. 2. These baselines include one-class classifiers: IF [12], OSVM [22]; density-based methods: LOF [6]; reconstruction-based algorithms: OmniAnomaly [20], LSTM-AE [13], MSCRED [29], USAD [3], and vanilla Transformer [24]. In addition, we assess the performance of robust Transformers including TranAD [23] and AnomalyTransformer [27].

4.4   Training Parameter Settings and Evaluation Criteria

We follow the well-established protocol used by many recent papers [19]. We transform the input time series into consecutive sub-sequences using non-overlapped sliding windows of length $w = 100$. After preliminary tests, we use the same architecture for all autoencoder-based models. The autoencoders are a 5-layer MLP with 78-32-16-32-78 units. All latent layers are followed by ReLU activation function. The last layer is followed by a sigmoid function. We use the Adam optimizer to train all the neural networks, with an initial learning rate of 0.001, and a step-scheduler with a step of 0.5. All models are trained for 100 epochs, with a batch size of 64 in all experiments, and random parameter initialization. To limit the impact of random parameter initialization, we repeat each experiment five times and average the results over these five runs. Regarding Transformer-based anomaly detectors, we set the dimension of the embedding to 128 and we use 2-head attention units. In all our experiment, RESIST hyperparameter c is set as $c = 0.1$IQR (cf. Eq. 6). Similar to the validation protocol adapted by Ruff et al. [17], the competing methods hyperparameters are tuned on the predefined validation subset. To minimize hyperparameter selection problems, we select the optimal hyperparameters that maximize their validation Area Under the Curve of the Receiver Operating Characteristics (AUROC). This deliberately grants competing methods an advantage over RESIST. Lastly, all the experiments were run on a laptop equipped with a 12-core Intel i7-9850H CPU clocked at 2.6 GHz and with NVIDIA Quadro P2000 GPU.

4.5   Results

Protocol 1 (P1): Modular Composition of Co-attention and Self-attention Modules. For a fair comparison, the three variants have the same architecture and configuration. The three variants use the *mixup* fusion strategy and are trained with the same robust loss: Geman-McClure loss. The only difference between the three variants, is the modular composition of co-attention and self-attention units. The experimental results of these 3 variants are shown in Fig. 8. These first results highlight that the structure of RESIST encoder has a significant impact on the global performance, since varying the encoder composition of self and co-attention units is clearly reflected in the results.

Firstly, RESIST-SS, whose encoder is purely composed of a cascade of self-attention units, performs poorly compared to the other variants. Indeed, RESIST-SS is similar to a vanilla Transformer trained to reconstruct the input, using the robust Geman-McClure loss, and without considering the historical data. This variant shows the lowest AUROCs in this first set of experiments, with a mean equal to 76.6%, and with a large standard variation of 5%. The other two variants, which integrate intra and inter-sequence properties with co-attention units, globally show better results with reduced standard variations. This confirms our first hypothesis (H1), in the sense that guiding the Transformer reconstruction with both intra-sequence properties and inter-sequence pairwise interactions with the history results in a more robust anomaly detector.

Furthermore, we note that the hybrid RESIST-SC reports higher AUROC, $80.5\% \pm 0.9$, compared to RESIST-SS, $78.8\% \pm 0.3$. This advantage is statistically significant, according to Welch's test with p-value $= 0.05$. This observation reveals that encoding the history with both self-attention and co-attention units is better than using only co-attention units. In RESIST-SC, the self-attention unit firstly extracts the intra-dependencies of the history. Then this first representation, which considers the history local context, is combined with the intermediate representation of the input. In contrast, RESIST-CC neglects history intra-sequence context and focuses only on inter-sequence properties. This result is consistent with other works in VQA [28]. In the following, we will use RESIST-SC encoder architecture as the basis for all next RESIST variants.

Protocol 2 (P2): Robust Loss Function. Similar to the protocol followed previously, all the variants share the same configuration, except the training loss function. The three variants have a hybrid siamese encoder, similar to RESIST-SC encoder. The results are reported in Fig. 9. From this figure, we can see that the training loss function has a significant influence on the performance. We note that the results steadily improve when decreasing the robustness parameter α of the loss function $\rho(x, \alpha, c)$, defined in Sect. 3.2. Firstly, RESIST-MSE, trained with the common Euclidean distance, i.e., $\alpha = 2$, show the worst performance, with an AUROC around 74%. This result is in line with previous studies, which state that the mean-squared error is considerably influenced by outliers. Secondly, the Charbonnier loss, a.k.a, the pseudo-Huber loss, with $\alpha = 1$, does not improve the performance (cf. Fig. 9). As shown in Fig. 4 (left), even though the gradients of large error are reduced compared to the L2 loss, these gradients saturate to a non-zero value. That is, even though their contribution is slightly reduced, training contaminants still contribute to parameter optimization during the training. Nevertheless, when $\alpha \leq 0$, the gradient magnitude decreases and converges to 0, when the error is higher than the scale parameter c. As such, large errors are completely ignored and do not impact the training. The speed of converging to 0 clearly depends on the parameter α. The lower α, the higher

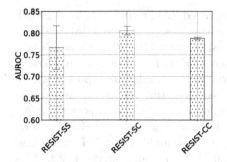

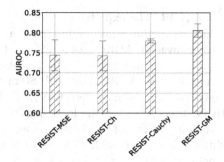

Fig. 8. Comparison between RESIST three variants: RESIST-SS, RESIST-SC, and RESIST-CC, on the CICIDS17.

Fig. 9. Experimental results for RESIST trained with different loss functions, on the CICIDS17 dataset.

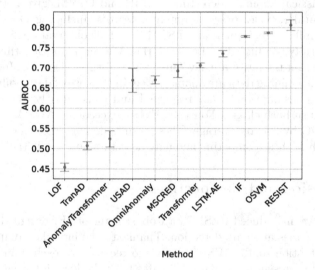

Fig. 10. Comparison between RESIST and the baselines on CICIDS17 dataset.

the decreasing speed of large error gradients. Our results confirm this interpretation, in the sense that RESIST-GM, trained with Geman-McClure loss ($\alpha = -2$), exceeds RESIST-Cauchy, trained with Cauchy loss ($\alpha = 0$), by 2.6% on average. We can conclude that the second hypothesis (H2) is validated. Training RESIST with the Geman-McClure loss significantly reduces the impact of anomalies.

Protocol 3 (P3): Comparison with Competing Methods. In this section, we compare RESIST performance against common unsupervised anomaly detectors, presented in Sect. 4.3. We aim to demonstrate that RESIST outperforms these competing methods. The RESIST configuration used in this part is composed of the default architectures: a hybrid siamese encoder, i.e., the encoder of RESIST-SC, the *mixup* fusion layer, and the robust Geman-McClure loss, with

$c = 0.1$IQR. The experiment results are reported in Fig. 10. Globally, RESIST achieves superior results compared to all the baselines, on the CICIDS17 dataset, with an average AUROC of 80.6% $\pm$ 1.3. First, we note that RESIST is substantially more robust than vanilla Transformers. RESIST improves vanilla Transformer average AUROC by 10%. Second, the lowest results are reported with a density-based anomaly detector: LOF. Indeed, detecting contextual and collective outliers based on the local density of high-dimensional data is challenging. Surprisingly, Transformer-based anomaly detectors show poor performance on this dataset, even with a careful tuning of these architectures. TranAD and AnomalyTranformer report AUROCs of 50.7% $\pm$ 1.0 and 52.4% $\pm$ 2.1. This implies that these methods are significantly sensitive to training outliers, on this network traffic dataset. It is however difficult to explain such poor results, despite the careful fine-tuning of the hyperparameter on the dedicated validation subset. Third, classical anomaly detectors, i.e., IF and OSVM, give better results than deep neural network-based anomaly detectors, including OmniAnomaly, MSCRED, Vanilla Transformer, and LSTM-AE. This observation ties well with the previous study conducted by Lai et al. [11]. We speculate that this might be due to the fact that the latter are developed for semi-supervised AD. Indeed, they assume that the training data are anomaly free. In the case of data pollution with anomalies, this assumption is not respected and consequently, these methods fail to distinguish both classes. Fourth, RESIST exceeds IF AUROC by 4% and OSVM AUROC by 3%, on average. These results demonstrate that RESIST is more robust than these competing anomaly detectors on the CICIDS17 dataset.

5 Conclusion and Perspectives

In this paper, we introduced RESIST, a Robust transformEr designed for unSupervised tIme Series anomaly detection. Thanks to the modular composition of self and co-attention units, RESIST learns to reconstruct each input sequence using a hybrid representation that aggregates both the local information that is specific to the current input and the global information shared with the history. Moreover, we proposed a robust training strategy that minimizes the Geman-McClure function, to reduce the impact of training contaminants. We extensively studied the contributions of RESIST components in the global performance, and the experimental evaluation on the CICIDS17 benchmark dataset confirmed that RESIST outperforms existing unsupervised anomaly detection.

References

1. Aggarwal, C.C.: Outlier Analysis. Springer, Cham (2017)
2. Angiulli, F., Fassetti, F.: Distance-based outlier queries in data streams: the novel task and algorithms. Data Min. Knowl. Discov. **20**, 290–324 (2009). https://doi.org/10.1007/s10618-009-0159-9
3. Audibert, J., Michiardi, P., Guyard, F., Marti, S., Zuluaga, M.A.: USAD: unsupervised anomaly detection on multivariate time series. In: SIGKDD (2020)

4. Barron, J.T.: A general and adaptive robust loss function. In: CVPR (2019)
5. Blázquez-García, A., Conde, A., Mori, U., Lozano, J.A.: A review on outlier/anomaly detection in time series data. ACM Comput. Surv. **54**(3), 1–33 (2021)
6. Breunig, M.M., Kriegel, H.P., Ng, R.T., Sander, J.: LOF: identifying density-based local outliers. In: Proceedings of the 2000 ACM SIGMOD International Conference on Management of Data, p. 12 (2000)
7. Chaudhari, S., Mithal, V., Polatkan, G., Ramanath, R.: An attentive survey of attention models. Trans. Intell. Syst. Technol. **12**(5), 1–32 (2021)
8. Choi, K., Yi, J., Park, C., Yoon, S.: Deep learning for anomaly detection in time-series data: review. Anal. Guidelines **9**, 120043–120065 (2021)
9. Hundman, K., Constantinou, V., Laporte, C., Colwell, I., Soderstrom, T.: Detecting spacecraft anomalies using LSTMs and nonparametric dynamic thresholding. In: ACM SIGKDD, pp. 387–395 (2018)
10. Stiawan, D., Idris, M.Y.B., Bamhdi, A.M., Budiarto, R.: CICIDS-2017 dataset feature analysis with information gain for anomaly detection. IEEE Access **8**, 132911–132921 (2020)
11. Lai, K.H., Zha, D., Zhao, Y., Wang, G., Xu, J., Hu, X.: Revisiting time series outlier detection: definitions and benchmarks. In: NeurIPS (2021)
12. Liu, F.T., Ting, K.M., Zhou, Z.H.: Isolation forest. In: ICDM (2008)
13. Malhotra, P., Ramakrishnan, A., Anand, G., Vig, L., Agarwal, P., Shroff, G.: LSTM-based encoder-decoder for multi-sensor anomaly detection. CoRR (2016)
14. Najari, N., Berlemont, S., Lefebvre, G., Duffner, S., Garcia, C.: Robust variational autoencoders and normalizing flows for unsupervised network anomaly detection. In: AINA (2022)
15. Najari, N., Berlemont, S., Lefebvre, G., Duffner, S., Garcia, C.: RADON: robust autoencoder for unsupervised anomaly detection. In: SIN, pp. 1–8 (2021)
16. Ruff, L., et al.: Deep one-class classification. In: International Conference on Machine Learning, vol. 80, pp. 4393–4402 (2018)
17. Ruff, L., et al.: Deep semi-supervised anomaly detection. In: ICLR (2020)
18. Sharafaldin, I., Lashkar, A.H., Ghorbani, A.: Intrusion Detection Evaluation Dataset (CICIDS2017), Canadian Institute for Cybersecurity (2017)
19. Shen, L., Li, Z., Kwok, J.T.: Timeseries anomaly detection using temporal hierarchical one-class network. In: NeurIPS (2020)
20. Su, Y., Zhao, Y., Niu, C., Liu, R., Sun, W., Pei, D.: Robust anomaly detection for multivariate time series through stochastic recurrent neural network. In: SIGKDD (2019)
21. Tan, H., Bansal, M.: LXMERT: learning cross-modality encoder representations from transformers. In: EMNLP-IJCNLP, pp. 5099–5110 (2019)
22. Tax, D.M., Duin, R.P.: Support vector data description. Mach. Learn. **54**(1), 45–66 (2004). https://doi.org/10.1023/B:MACH.0000008084.60811.49
23. Tuli, S., Casale, G., Jennings, N.R.: TranAD: deep transformer networks for anomaly detection in multivariate time series data. CoRR (2022)
24. Vaswani, A., et al.: Attention is all you need. In: NeurIPS, vol. 30 (2017)
25. Wang, X., Pi, D., Zhang, X., Liu, H., Guo, C.: Variational transformer-based anomaly detection approach for multivariate time series. Measurement **191**, 110791 (2022)
26. Wen, Q., et al.: Transformers in time series: a survey. CoRR (2022)
27. Xu, J., Wu, H., Wang, J., Long, M.: Anomaly transformer: time series anomaly detection with association discrepancy. In: ICLR, p. 20 (2022)
28. Yu, Z., Yu, J., Cui, Y., Tao, D., Tian, Q.: Deep modular co-attention networks for visual question answering. In: CVPR, pp. 6274–6283 (2019)

29. Zhang, C., et al.: A deep neural network for unsupervised anomaly detection and diagnosis in multivariate time series data. In: AAAI (2019)
30. Zhang, H., Cisse, M., Dauphin, Y.N., Lopez-Paz, D.: Mixup: beyond empirical risk minimization. In: ICLR, p. 13 (2018)
31. Zhang, Y., Hamm, N.A.S., Meratnia, N., Stein, A., van de Voort, M., Havinga, P.J.M.: Statistics-based outlier detection for wireless sensor networks. Int. J. Geogr. Inf. Sci. **26**, 1373–1392 (2012)
32. Zong, B., et al.: Deep autoencoding gaussian mixture model for unsupervised anomaly detection. In: ICLR (2018)

Window Size Selection in Unsupervised Time Series Analytics: A Review and Benchmark

Arik Ermshaus[✉], Patrick Schäfer, and Ulf Leser

Humboldt-Universität zu Berlin, Berlin, Germany
{ermshaua,patrick.schaefer,leser}@informatik.hu-berlin.de

Abstract. Time series (TS) are sequences of values ordered in time. Such TS have in common, that important insights from the data can be drawn by inspecting local substructures, and not the recordings as a whole. ECG recordings, for instance, are characterized by normal or anomalous heartbeats that repeat themselves often within a longer TS. As such, many state-of-the-art time series data mining (TSDM) methods characterize TS by inspecting local substructures. The window size for extracting such subsequences is a crucial hyper-parameter, and setting an inappropriate value results in poor TSDM results. Finding the *optimal* window size has remained to be one of the most challenging tasks in TSDM domains, where no domain-agnostic method is known for learning the window size. We provide, for the first time, a systematic survey and experimental study of 6 TS window size selection (WSS) algorithms on three diverse TSDM tasks, namely anomaly detection, segmentation and motif discovery, using state-of-the art TSDM algorithms and benchmarks. We found that WSS methods are competitive with or even surpass human annotations, if an interesting or anomalous pattern can be attributed to (changes in) the period. That is because current WSS methods aim at finding the period length of data sets. This assumption is mostly true for segmentation or anomaly detection, by definition. In the case of motif discovery, however, the results were mixed. Motifs can be independent of a period, but repeat themselves unusually often. In this domain, WSS fails and more research is needed.

Keywords: Time series · Unsupervised · Learning · Subsequences · Windows · Data mining · Motif discovery · Segmentation · Anomaly detection · Review · Benchmark

1 Introduction

Time series (TS) are sequences of real values ordered in time. Use cases include biological processes like ECG recordings of patient's heartbeats, EEG recordings collected from people taking a nap or physical processes like printer pressure pump sensor recordings from industrial printers. Such recordings have in common, that the main insights from the data can be drawn by inspecting local

T. Guyet et al. (Eds.): AALTD 2022, LNAI 13812, pp. 83–101, 2023.
https://doi.org/10.1007/978-3-031-24378-3_6

Fig. 1. The famous NYC taxi traffic data set contains anomalous as well as reoccurring local temporal patterns that can be analysed with TSDM techniques.

substructures, and not the recordings as a whole. As such, most state-of-the-art TS data mining (TSDM) algorithms are applied to local substructures, which are referred to as *windows*. However, setting the *right* window size is crucial for most of these tasks. When applied to production-ready systems, failure to provide an *optimal* window size may cause bad decision-making and thus monetary damage.

Many state-of-the-art unsupervised TSDM algorithms can be formulated as a self-join of all pairs of subsequences for a given window length. Examples include Matrix Profile I-XXV [20], ClaSP [14], EMMA [11], etc. With a poor choice of window length, these methods fail to give good results. While in a supervised setting, the window length can be learned by maximizing an evaluation metric, in an unsupervised setting, such as anomaly detection, segmentation or motif discovery, this is not possible by definition, and algorithms rely on human annotations. Using domain-agnostic methods to learn the window length for unsupervised TSDM is at the core of this experimental study.

Many window size selection (WSS) methods for finding the period length of a TS have been published. This is the first survey and experimental evaluation of WSS for TSDM tasks. We chose three common, yet diverse unsupervised TSDM tasks, namely motif discovery, anomaly detection and segmentation for analysis. We use the famous NYC taxi data set in Fig. 1 as an example to illustrate the different requirements of the TSDM tasks. It shows the hourly traffic in NYC throughout the year in 2015. It has a weakly pattern with increasing traffic throughout the weekdays and during rush hours. It has some known anomalies that can be attributed to events, marches or public holidays. The task of anomaly detection aims at finding anomalous structure in a periodic TS [1]. In the NYC taxi data set, this corresponds to anomalous (increased or decreased) traffic at Independence Day, Labor Day, etc. Such anomalies can be attributed to a deviation from the periodicity of the TS. The window size, used for anomaly detection, should thus roughly capture the length of an anomalous event, i.e. some hours or at most a day, or we may miss this anomalous event. The task of segmentation is the process of dividing a periodic TS into disjoint segments, e.g. based on detecting changes in periodicity [6]. In our example, we see a clear weekly or monthly pattern of taxi traffic that repeats throughout the year. These segments themselves are highly repetitive. A window size should thus roughly capture the weekly or monthly periodicity to identify relevant segments. The task of motif discovery aims at finding frequent, similar local patterns in a TS [11]. In our running example, this could be similar traffic on public holidays or on some weekdays, e.g. the first Monday in every month is similar. Other than in the former two use cases, the TS itself need not be periodic, but the window size should be set to discover repetitive local behaviour.

To sum up, the tasks have very diverse requirements for a WSS method: small vs large window sizes, associated with vs independent of the period. The survey and experimental evaluation of WSS techniques is the main focus of this study. The contributions of this paper are as follows:

1. We review 6 established and recent domain-agnostic WSS algorithms from the literature, including technical descriptions, computational complexity analyses and examples for illustration.
2. We benchmarked, for the first time, 6 WSS methods and compared these to human annotations on three diverse and challenging unsupervised TSDM tasks: anomaly detection, segmentation and motif discovery. For all of these tasks, we tested the state-of-the-art algorithms in their field in combination with all WSS methods on established benchmarks.
3. Overall, we find that if the analysed TS were periodic, as is the case for anomaly detection or segmentation, the WSS methods even surpassed human annotations. If the analysed TS were non-periodic, as for motif discovery, WSS fails.
4. In this work, we make a special effort to provide the sources codes and results on our website [15] to foster follow-up works and reproducibility. We provide a Python implementation of the used methods as well as Jupyter-Notebooks, visualizations and raw measurement sheets.

The remainder of this paper is structured as follows: Sect. 2 introduces related work, Sect. 3 reviews the WSS algorithms, Sect. 4 presents our experimental evaluation, and Sect. 5 explains our results and concludes the paper.

2   Background and Related Work

In this study, we assume that a TS is generated by observing some output of a physical process, that consists of one (or several) distinct states at arbitrary and a-priori unknown points in time, leading to different measurements [6] in the signal. Unsupervised TSDM algorithms are concerned with finding anomalous subsequences in such signals, detecting their segmentation or instances of similar substructures. We introduce these concepts and the related literature in the following subsections.

2.1   Definitions

Definition 1. *A time* series (TS) T *is a sequence of* $n \in \mathbb{N}$ *real values,* $T = (t_1, \ldots, t_n), t_i \in \mathbb{R}$ *that measures an observable output of a process. The values are also called data points.*

Definition 2. *Given a TS T, a subsequence (or* window*) $T_{s,e}$ of T with start offset s and end offset e consists of the contiguous values of T from position s to position e, i.e., $T_{s,e} = (t_s, \ldots, t_e)$ with $1 \leq s \leq e \leq n$. The length (or width) of $T_{s,e}$ is $\|T_{s,e}\| = e - s + 1$.*

Definition 3. *A periodic TS is one that approximately repeats a subsequence of values after a fixed length of time. We call such a subsequence a temporal pattern (or period) of a TS.*

The two tasks anomaly detection (Sect. 2.2) and segmentation (Sect. 2.3) are applied to periodic TS by definition. Still, local parts of a TS can nevertheless deviate from each other, e.g. in period length, shape or amplitude. This is typically due to anomalies, motifs, evolving patterns, or regime changes. In motif discovery (Sect. 2.4), data need not be periodic, however, but the pattern to be identified repeats unusually often.

2.2   Anomaly Detection

Time series anomaly detection (TSAD) aims to find erroneous or novel behaviour within expected observations. Such outliers are typically categorized as point or subsequence outliers. While the former is an unexpected high (low) data point, the latter is a deviation of the baseline temporal pattern (as consecutive observations). Blázquez-García et al. [1] formalize the TSAD problem and review techniques to tackle it. Model-based approaches like Isolation Forest (IF) and one-class support vector machine (SVM) learn the temporal dynamics from subsequences of a baseline TS to estimate the novelty of new incoming data points as a reconstruction score. Discord detection is another approach to anomaly detection that reports the subsequence in a TS with the highest pairwise distance to its nearest neighbour as an outlier [20]. It considers subsequences anomalous or unusual in relation to the TS as a reference. Discord detection can be numerically solved as a minimization problem with the matrix profile (MP) [20]. Runtime optimizations exist based on admissible pruning. Frequentist methods further measure the novelty of subsequences by the count of their occurrence, and related information-based algorithms utilize their rate of compressibility as a means of uniqueness.

2.3   Segmentation

The time series segmentation (TSS) task assumes that a TS consists of segments that capture the inherent statistical properties and temporal patterns of the process states at hand. The a priori unknown change points (CPs) between segments are assumed to be abrupt shifts of these properties and indicate state transitions [6]. The TSS problem is to partition a TS into disjoint segments, separated by CPs, corresponding to states of the data-generating process. A number of domain-specific TSS methods that can detect changes in TS with suitable value distributions (e.g. piecewise-constant or Gaussian) have been published in the last decades. Truong et al. [17] present a review of such techniques. They compare methods regarding their cost function, search method, and whether the number of change points is known a priori. Search methods like window-based segmentation (Window) [17] then use such cost functions to find meaningful segmentations that minimize the associated costs. More recently, two domain-agnostic subsequence-based techniques have been proposed, namely FLOSS [6] and ClaSP [5,14]. Both methods use a k-NN to relate similar subsequences and compute a profile, from which CPs can be extracted as local minima (maxima).

2.4 Motif Discovery

Motif discovery in TS (TSMD) has been researched intensively for approximately 20 years [11]. A majority of research is centred on pair motifs, which are defined as the pair of most similar subsequences in a TS. However, substructures commonly do not only occur in pairs but frequently, such as heartbeats in an ECG recording. Thus, it is more natural to think of a motif as a set of frequently appearing and similar subsequences. We will thus focus on those approaches to motif discovery, that aim for finding sets of the most similar subsequences, aka motif sets. EMMA [11] was the first motif set discovery algorithm. It is based on the discretization of subsequences using Symbolic Aggregate approXimation (SAX) [10]. It hashes the discretized SAX words into buckets, where similar subsequences hash into similar buckets, and the buckets are subsequently post-processed to obtain the final motif sets. The concept of Learning Motif (LM) was introduced by Grabocka et al. [7] to better deal with noisy TS. The paper approaches LM discovery as a process which, starting from a random initialization, iteratively modifies a motif core S' to increase its frequency, i.e., the size of the surrounding motif, while keeping its radius fixed. As the frequency function is not differentiable, they propose a smooth Gaussian-kernel approximation that allows using gradient ascent to find the hopefully best hidden motif cores. The LM solution is a heuristic, as the optimization problem is non-convex and the gradient ascent might get stuck in a local optimum.

Table 1. Properties of WSS algorithms.

Method name	Type	Properties	Complexity
DFT	Whole series	Frequency-Domain	$\mathcal{O}(n \log n)$
AC	Whole series	Time-Domain	$\mathcal{O}(n \log n)$
AutoPeriod [18]	Whole series	Hybrid	$\mathcal{O}(n \log n)$
RobustPeriod [19]	Whole series	Hybrid	$\mathcal{O}(n^2)$
MWF [8]	Subsequence	Summary statistics	$\mathcal{O}(m \cdot n)$
SuSS [5]	Subsequence	Summary statistics	$\mathcal{O}(n \log w)$

3   Window Size Selection

Window size selection (WSS) algorithms can be divided into two major categories: (a) whole-series-based and (b) subsequence-based. Whole-series-based methods analyse global properties of a signal in order to detect dominant period sizes. They can further be divided into frequency-based and time-based approaches. While the former decompose a TS into single frequency components, the latter measure the self-similarity of the entire signal when shifted by an offset (lag). A dominant frequency or a high correlation for a certain shift is then used to derive an appropriate window size [4]. Subsequence-based methods, in turn, extract local features from TS. They compare how well statistics computed over temporal patterns (with increasing size) align with the global properties of the signal. A small subsequence width in line with the global TS properties is then chosen as a window size [5,8]. While whole-series-based methods can easily identify strong and repetitive periods in signals, subsequence-based methods are more able to identify window sizes in more diverse TS like with regime changes (different segments) or varying temporal patterns, as they rely on the data set's descriptive statistics as a proxy instead of exact frequencies or shifts (Table 1).

In the following subsections, we discuss four whole-series-based methods, namely Dominant Fourier Frequency, Autocorrelation, AutoPeriod and Robust-Period, as well as two subsequence-based algorithms, Multi-Window-Finder and Summary Statistics Subsequence.

3.1   Dominant Fourier Frequency

The Fourier transform decomposes a signal into a sum of sinusoid waves, also called Fourier coefficients. Each of these coefficients is characterized by its frequency, equal to a period length in the TS, and its phase shift. The main hypothesis of this whole-series-based method is that the most dominant sinusoid wave, i.e. with the largest magnitude, in a signal captures its period best.

Definition 4. *The Discrete Fourier Transformation (DFT) of a TS T, $|T| = n$ is a series of complex coefficients $\mathcal{C} := (c_0, \ldots, c_{n-1}) \in \mathbb{C}^n$, such that $c_k := \sum_{j=1}^{n} T_j \cdot e^{-2\pi i \cdot \frac{jk}{n}}$, for $k = 0, \ldots, (n-1)$ and $i = \sqrt{-1}$. The corresponding series of frequencies is defined as $\mathcal{F} = (f_0, \ldots, f_{\lceil \frac{n-1}{2} \rceil})$, such that $f_k := \frac{k}{n}$, for $k = 0, \ldots, \lceil \frac{n-1}{2} \rceil$.*

A Fourier coefficient c_k describes the phase and magnitude for its associated frequency f_k, with the first c_0 being the mean of the TS T. In order to obtain the magnitude of c_k, we can calculate its modulus $m_k := \sqrt{Re(c_k)^2 + Im(c_k)^2}$. Note that we can only capture $\lceil \frac{n}{2} \rceil$ frequencies because of the Nyquist-Shannon sampling theorem.

Algorithmically (see Algorithm 1), we first transform a TS using the Discrete Fourier Transform (DFT), and then select the most dominant Fourier coefficient, from which we may infer the frequency. Its corresponding period size can then be used as a window size. The quality of this computation can be negatively

---

Algorithm 1. Most dominant Fourier Frequency

1: **procedure** DOMINANTFOURIERFREQUENCY(T)
2:    $\mathcal{C}, \mathcal{F} \leftarrow \mathrm{DFT}(T)$
3:    $\mathcal{M}, \mathcal{W} \leftarrow \sqrt{Re(\mathcal{C})^2 + Im(\mathcal{C})^2}, \frac{1}{\mathcal{F}}$
4:    **return** $\mathcal{W}[\mathrm{ARGMAX}(\mathcal{M})]$
5: **end procedure**

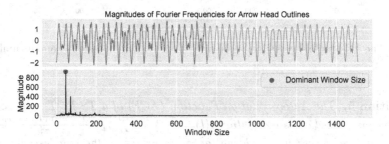

Fig. 2. The magnitudes of the Fourier coefficients show a substantial global maximum for the window size 49 and a smaller local maximum for the window size 72.

affected by spectral leakage in the DFT as well as large (or multiple) dominant periodicities in the signal. However, windowing techniques can be applied to increase the accuracy of the harmonic analysis [18].

The runtime complexity depends on the computation of the DFT, which is in $\mathcal{O}(n \log n)$. The calculation of the magnitudes and window sizes can be performed in $\mathcal{O}(n)$ as well as the linear search for the most dominant frequency. Thus, the overall runtime complexity is in $\mathcal{O}(n \log n)$. Its space complexity is in $\mathcal{O}(n)$ as it uses four additional arrays.

Figure 2 illustrates instances of different arrowhead shapes as blue and orange segments [2]. The corresponding magnitude profile (Fig. 2, bottom) shows a clear global maximum (window size 49, magnitude 921) which captures the period of the signal (between 40–60 data points). The 2nd highest local maximum (window size 72, magnitude 398) also protrudes and captures multiple longer periods containing 70–90 data points.

3.2   Highest Autocorrelation

The autocorrelation (AC) of a TS reports the correlation with a delayed copy of itself. For different time shifts, called lags, it shows how similar the signal is to its shifted version. If the TS has a distinctive period, its AC will be high for the lag that equals the size of the repeated temporal pattern, which in turn can be located and used as a window size.

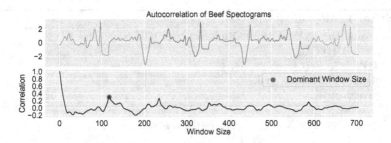

Fig. 3. The AC profile shows substantial deflections for window size 119 and its multiple 236.

Definition 5. *The Autocorrelation Function (ACF) of a TS T, $|T| = n$ defines the zero-normalized cross-correlation $a(l) := \frac{1}{n-l-1} \sum_{j=l+1}^{n} \frac{(T_j - \mu_T) \cdot (T_{j-l} - \mu_T)}{\sigma_T^2}$ for a given lag l and with μ_T, σ_T being the mean or rather the standard deviation of T. The series of cross-correlations $\mathcal{A} := (a(0), \ldots, a(n-1)) \in \mathbb{R}^n$, is the autocorrelation (AC) of T.*

The cross-correlation $a(l)$ captures the similarity of T with its shifted version for a lag of size l. The AC $\mathcal{A}$ of T contains such similarities for all possible lags $0 \leq l \leq n-1$ as a profile. It is highest for no lag and contains local maxima for dominant periods in T as well as their multiples. To determine the period (and hence a window size) for a given TS T, the algorithm calculates the AC $\mathcal{A}$ of T. It then searches for the highest non-trivial local maximum in $\mathcal{A}$ with a peak finding algorithm. Lastly, it reports the lag for the highest peak. While the AC of a signal provides higher quality periodicity estimates, compared to its DFT [18], the selection of the best period size (and not one of its multiples) is more complicated.

The runtime complexity is dominated by the computation of the cross-correlations, which can be reformulated using the Wiener-Khinchin theorem and solved using the FFT in $\mathcal{O}(n \log n)$. The runtime for peak finding using simple baseline approaches utilizing exclusion zones, differencing or shape constraints is in $\mathcal{O}(n)$. Thus, the total runtime is in $\mathcal{O}(n \log n)$. Its space complexity is in $\mathcal{O}(n)$, as it uses one additional array.

As an example of AC based WSS, see Fig. 3. At the top, it shows the concatenation of six beef spectrograms [2] (each consisting of 118 data points) and in the bottom we plotted the corresponding AC profile. It shows the trivial global maximum (for no lag) as well as a distinctive local maximum for a lag of 119 (29.6% correlation) and a more subtle one for a lag of 236 (23.5% correlation), which is an approximate 2× multiple of 119. Its substantial local maximum accurately captures a single instance of a spectrogram, which is the dominant period in this data set.

Algorithm 2. Multi-Window-Finder

1: **procedure** MULTIWINDOWFINDER(T, s, e)
2:     $D_T \leftarrow$ initialize array with INF of size m
3:     **for** $w \leftarrow s$ to e **do**
4:         $\mathcal{M}_w \leftarrow$ MOV_AVG(T, w)
5:         $D_T[w] \leftarrow$ SUM(LOG(ABS($\mathcal{M}_w$ − MEAN($\mathcal{M}_w$))))
6:     **end for**
7:     $M \leftarrow$ FIND_LOCAL_MINIMA(D_T)
8:     $top3 = M_{1,3} \cdot [1, \frac{1}{2}, \frac{1}{3}]$
9:     **return** MEAN($top3$), STD($top3$)
10: **end procedure**

3.3 Hybrids: AutoPeriod and RobustPeriod

It is much easier to extract a signals' top-k frequencies using the DFT rather than its AC. The DFT contains strong peaks, which can be thresholded. It can, however, include false positives due to spectral leakage. In contrast, the AC contains hills and valleys which require a peak finding algorithm (compare Fig. 2 and 3). AC peaks however, when correctly retrieved, capture more accurately the period size estimations [18].

AutoPeriod [18] is a hybrid algorithm that combines both approaches to overcome their own limitations. It computes the DFT, thresholds it to retrieve dominant period size candidates, and then validates them using AC. It filters the Fourier frequencies with a 99% confidence interval and assigns the remaining candidates to their closest AC hills or valleys. It then outputs the top location of the selected hills as the dominant periods. From these, the best autocorrelated frequency can be selected as a window size.

Another hybrid approach is RobustPeriod [19], which first removes the trend in a TS, then decouples its periodicities and lastly detects dominate ones using a bespoke filtered DFT and AC. It uses a Hodrick-Prescott (HP) filter to estimate and remove the TS trend, which can negatively impact the AC computation. The procedure then decomposes a TS into multiple frequency ranges (using maximal overlap discrete wavelet transform) to facilitate the detection of multiple dominant periods. Lastly, RobustPeriod detects periods (in dominant frequency ranges) using bespoke modified variants of DFT and AC that use Fisher's significance test for filtering false positives. From these, the most significant frequency is selected as a window size.

3.4 Multi-Window-Finder

Multi-Window-Finder (MWF) [8] is a subsequence-based approach. Its main hypothesis is that the variance in the moving averages is small given a *suitable* window size. This suitable window size then captures a temporal pattern that repeats throughout a TS. In order to determine the width of this pattern, MWF measures the variance for a range of candidate windows and summarizes the best-fitting ones as the window size for the TS.

Definition 6. *The moving average of a TS T, $|T| = n$ and a window size w, is a series of mean values $\mathcal{M}_w := (m_1, \ldots, m_{n-w+1}) \in \mathbb{R}^{n-w+1}$, such that $m_k := \frac{1}{w} \cdot \sum_{j=0}^{w-1} T[k+j]$, for $k = 1, \ldots, n-w+1$.*

Given a suitable window size w, its variance, measured as the distance of the moving average $\mathcal{M}_w$ to its mean $\mu_{\mathcal{M}_w}$, produces a local minimum compared to smaller (or larger) window sizes.

The Multi-Window-Finder (Algorithm 2) takes a TS T, start offset s and end offset e as input. The procedure then calculates the moving averages $\mathcal{M}_w$ over all window sizes between s and e (line 4). While s is set to a low constant value (e.g. 10), e must either be set using domain knowledge or as a fraction of the TS length (e.g. $\frac{n}{5}$). The absolute distances between the moving averages $\mathcal{M}_w$ and their means are stored in an array D_T at corresponding offsets (line 5). The local minima in these distances represent suitable window sizes. They are located using a differencing technique (line 7), and the first three are selected and weighted by position (line 8). Thereby, the final window size is represented by the three smallest dominant window sizes. These either represent multiples of temporal patterns in the TS or distinct ones. The algorithm reports the final window size as their average, as well as the associated confidence as their standard deviation (line 9–10).

Its runtime complexity is dominated by the calculation of the moving averages and the distances to their means. A single moving average for a given window size can be efficiently computed in $\mathcal{O}(n)$ differencing cumulative sums of the TS. The absolute distance of the moving average to its mean can then simply be computed in $\mathcal{O}(n)$, too. For a total of $m = e - s$ candidate window sizes, this computation takes $\mathcal{O}(m \cdot n)$. The local minima distances are located in $\mathcal{O}(n)$ and the final window size calculation is computed in constant runtime. Hence, the overall runtime complexity is in $\mathcal{O}(m \cdot n)$. The space complexity is in $\mathcal{O}(n)$, as two additional arrays are used.

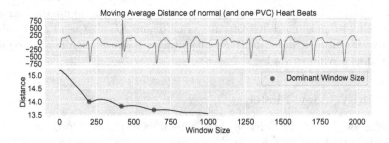

Fig. 4. The moving average distance has distinctive local minima for window size 201 and 416 as well as a more shallow one for 636.

Algorithm 3. Summary Statistics Subsequence

1: **procedure** STATS_DIFF(T, w, $stats_T$)
2:     $stats_w \leftarrow (roll\_mean(T, w), roll\_std(T, w), roll\_range(T, w))$
3:     $stats_{diff} \leftarrow \frac{1}{\sqrt{w}} \cdot$ EUCLIDEAN_DISTANCE($stats_T, stats_w$)
4:     **return** $mean(stats_{diff})$
5: **end procedure**
6: **procedure** SUSS_SCORE(T, w, $stats_T$)
7:     $s_{min}, s_{max} \leftarrow$ STATS_DIFF(T, $\|T\|$, $stats_T$), STATS_DIFF(T, 1, $stats_T$)
8:     $score \leftarrow$ min-max scale STATS_DIFF(T, w, $stats_T$) to $[s_{min}, \ldots, s_{max}]$
9:     **return** $1 - score$
10: **end procedure**
11: **procedure** CALC_SUSS(T, t)
12:     $T \leftarrow$ min-max scale T to range $[0, \ldots, 1]$
13:     $stats_T \leftarrow (mean(T), std(T), 1)$
14:     $lbound, ubound \leftarrow$ EXPONENTIAL_SEARCH(T, $stats_T$, SUSS_SCORE, t)
15:     $w \leftarrow$ BINARY_SEARCH(T, $stats_T$, SUSS_SCORE, $lbound, ubound, t$)
16:     **return** w
17: **end procedure**

Figure 4 shows an example of the moving average distances computed by MWF. The TS (top) shows an ECG recording with normal (and one PVC) heart beats (each one recorded within 250 data points) [9]. The corresponding moving average distances (from 1 to 1k) (Fig. 4 bottom) show a substantial local minimum for window size 200 and 416 as well as a more subtle one for 636. MWF uses these three positions to calculate a final window size of 207 which accurately captures one heart beat.

3.5 Summary Statistics Subsequence

Summary Statistics Subsequence (SuSS) [5] is a recent subsequence-based WSS algorithm that compares summary statistics (mean, standard deviation, range of values) computed over subsequences with those computed over the full TS. Its assumption is that these summary statistics of appropriate subsequences are close to those of the entire TS. Hence, their width is a good choice as a window size.

The pseudocode for SuSS is given in Algorithm 3. It takes a TS T as input and calculates its mean, standard deviation and range as a summary statistics vector $stats_T$ of size 3 (line 13). It uses these global statistics to calculate their distance to the rolling statistics of subsequences with changing length. For a candidate window size $w \in [1, \|T\|]$, the rolling summary statistics $stats_w$ are calculated as a matrix such that the i-th row contains the statistics for $T_{i,i+w}$ (line 2). SuSS calculates the Euclidean distances between $stats_T$ and all rows in $stats_w$ and weighs them with the inverse of the root of the window size (line 3). The normalization of the distances corrects a bias for larger windows that are inherently more similar to the full TS. It creates length-invariant distances comparable across window sizes. The mean distance over all window sizes (line 4) is

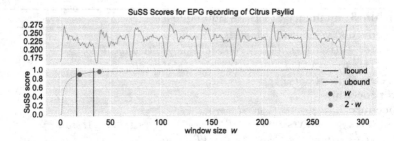

Fig. 5. SuSS locates a narrow range between 16 and 32 (using exponential search) in which the requested window size 20 is found (using binary search), which corresponds to half of the period size.

scaled and represents the final SuSS score for w (line 7–9). These scores monotonically increase with w as the statistics of the windows and the TS eventually align. SuSS first conducts an exponential, followed by a binary search to efficiently find the smallest window size w with a score larger than a pre-defined threshold $t \in [0, \ldots, 1]$, fixed to a domain-agnostic constant value of 89%. The exponential search identifies a small interval $lbound \leq w \leq ubound$, in which the binary search locates the best w (line 14–16).

The runtime complexity is in $\mathcal{O}(n)$ for a given candidate window size. Searching the candidate space is in $\mathcal{O}(n \cdot \log w)$ for the combined search. As the window size is constraint by n, SuSS has a worst-case complexity of $\mathcal{O}(n \cdot \log n)$. In most applications, however, w is a small constant, which leads to a runtime complexity of $\mathcal{O}(n)$. The space complexity is also in $\mathcal{O}(n)$, as the algorithm uses a matrix of shape $n - w + 1 \times 3$ to calculate a SuSS score (which is a single real value) for a given subsequence width.

Figure 5 illustrates an EPG recording of an Asian Citrus Psyllid used for studying its feeding behaviour [9]. In the bottom, we show (for illustration) all the SuSS scores between window size 1 to 300. The scores quickly converge as the appropriate window size is independent of the TS length. For a threshold of 89%, SuSS firstly bounds the search space between 16 and 32 and then finds the window size 20 (score 89,2%) which accurately captures half of a period (see the red dot that captures the entire period).

4   Experimental Evaluation

We experimentally evaluate the six WSS methods for anomaly detection, segmentation and motif discovery. We first describe the data sets, methods and evaluation metrics used for the study (see Subsect. 4.1). We analyse the performance results for anomaly detection (see Subsect. 4.2) and segmentation (see Subsect. 4.3) in a quantitative study, and explore the quality of motifs in Subsect. 4.4. In order to foster the application and development of WSS algorithms in follow-up works, we provide source codes, Jupyter-Notebooks, visualizations and raw measurement sheets on our website [15].

4.1 Setup

Data Sets: We use the two largest benchmark data sets available for the anomaly detection and segmentation task, and two selected TS from the motif discovery literature (Table 2).

Table 2. Benchmark Data sets used. For motif discovery no annotated benchmark exists.

Benchmark name	Type	Number of data sets
HEX UCR Anomaly Benchmark 2021 (HUAB) [9]	Anomaly detection	250
Time Series Segmentation Benchmark (TSSB) [16]	Segmentation	83
ECG heartbeats	Motif discovery	1
Muscle activation	Motif discovery	1

The *HEX UCR Anomaly Benchmark Dataset 2021 (HUAB)* [9] consists of 250 TS from natural, human and animal processes recorded with medical, motion and other sensors. It was released as part of a SIGKDD'21 competition [9] and used to evaluate MWF [8]. Each TS contains an anomaly-free training prefix and a subsequent test suffix, in which exactly one natural or synthetic anomaly is present.

The *Time Series Segmentation Benchmark (TSSB)* [16] contains 83 TS from a wide variety of device, medical, image, motion and other sensors. It was published in [14] and later extended [5]. Each TS is constructed from one UCR data set by grouping TS by label and concatenating them to create segments with controlled distinctive temporal patterns and statistical properties. The offsets, at which the segments are concatenated, are annotated as CPs.

For motif discovery, we present two use cases. *Muscle Activation* was collected from professional in-line speed skating [12] on a large motor driven treadmill with Electromyography (EMG) data of multiple movements. It consists of 29.899 measurements at 100 Hz corresponding to 30 s in total. A muscle activation and recovery takes around 120 ms. *ECG Heartbeats* contains a patient's (ID 71) heartbeat from the LTAF database [13]. It consists of $3k$ measurements at 128 Hz corresponding to 23 s. The heartbeat rate is around 60 to 80 bpm.

Data Mining Methods: We compare three window-based methods from the anomaly detection and segmentation literature, as well as two algorithms for motif discovery. Note, that we are not mainly interested how these methods compare to each other (per task), but rather how window sizes from the different algorithms influence their performance. We use default parameters for all algorithms.

For anomaly detection, we evaluate discord discovery (with the matrix profile) (MP) [20], isolation forest (IF) and a linear one-class support vector machine (SVM). These methods represent a variety of very different approaches to the problem of anomaly detection, and many new techniques extend their principles. For segmentation, we assess window-based segmentation (with mahalanobis cost) (Window) [17], FLOSS [6] and ClaSP [5]. Window is a baseline approach, and FLOSS and ClaSP are the most recent domain-agnostic methods published. From the motif discovery literature, we chose EMMA [11] and Learning Motifs [7], the two reference implementations for K-Motifs and Latent Motifs.

Evaluation Metrics. For the quantitative analysis of TSS and AD, hard and soft metrics exist. The former measures if an algorithm's predictions match the ground truth, while the latter reports the degree to which the predictions precisely match with it. We choose hard metrics suggested in the literature, which provides a fair evaluation in the presence of ties. This is inherently the case for parameter-tuning (in general) and WSS specifically, as all algorithms in Sect. 3 try to estimate a signal's period. In TSDM, it is common practice to consider a prediction (change point or anomaly) to be correct (TP), if it is in proximity to the ground truth.

F1 score for AD: Assume a TS T of length n, with a train segment from $[1, \ldots, l]$ with $l < n$ and a true anomaly subsequence in the interval $[begin, \ldots, end]$ with $l < begin \leq end \leq n$. Assume an algorithm predicts the timestamp p as an anomaly, we label it correct if it is contained in the true anomaly interval $max(1, begin - 100) \leq p \leq min(end + 100, n)$, considering slack, false otherwise. From this matching, we infer the binary F1 score of either 100% or 0%. We choose a slack of 100 as suggested in [9] for HUAB.

F1 score for TSS: Consider again a TS T of size n and sets of ground truth CPs $cpts_T$ and predicted CPs $cpts_{pred}$, with each location in $[1, \ldots, n]$. The F1 score reports the harmonic mean between precision and recall, where precision reflects the fraction of correctly identified CPs over the number of predicted CPs. Recall computes the number of correctly identified CPs over the number of ground truth CPs. We choose a slack of 1%, as suggested in [5], and allow exactly one correctly predicted CP to count as a TP.

For both TSS and AD, we show critical difference diagrams (as introduced in [3]) to compare the average ranks between approaches per benchmark. The best approaches scoring the lowest (average) ranks over all benchmark TS are shown to the right of the diagram. Groups of approaches that are not significantly different in their ranks are connected by a bar, based on a Nemenyi two-tailed significance test with $\alpha = 0.05$.

Motif discovery is an exploratory task applied to unlabelled data. Thus, it is hard to measure the quantitative effect of WSS. Instead, we did a qualitative analysis with weakly labelled TS, and compared the found motifs with the ones reported in the literature.

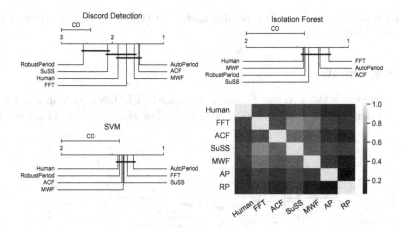

Fig. 6. F1 ranks on 250 benchmark data sets for MP, SVM and IF in combination with human and detected window sizes and window sizes correlation between approaches

4.2 Anomaly Detection

We compare discord detection (with MP), isolation forest (IF) and one-class support vector machine (SVM) in combination with human annotations on the 250 benchmark data sets (HUAB). Figure 6 shows average F1 ranks for the methods.

For discord detection, AutoPeriod ranks first, followed by ACF, MWF, FFT, human, SuSS and RobustPeriod. The first two best-ranking WSS approaches rank significantly better than the last two and the 3rd to 6th approaches rank insignificantly different. The accuracy of the candidates range from 32.8% (RobustPeriod) to 54% (ACF) with high standard deviations between 47–50% (due to the binary scoring). Considering IF (and SVM), the performance differences fade for all WSS algorithms and become statistically indifferent. The mean ranks range minimally, the accuracy is low and between 16.8% and 24.4% (13.2% and 18%) and the standard deviation ranges between 37.5% and 43% (33.9% and 38.5%). Compared to discord detection, MWF and human window sizes perform worse, while FFT and SuSS perform better.

The main finding of these results is that the six WSS methods perform comparably to each other but surprisingly better than human window size annotations. The correlation heatmap in Fig. 6 confirms that FFT, ACF, SuSS and MWF have a moderate to strong correlation, indicating all find similar window sizes. AutoPeriod protrudes with weak correlation, but best-ranking results (rank 1 and 2). Hence, AutoPeriod may be concluded as a favourite for WSS in the TSAD task. AutoPeriod is a hybrid of FFT and ACF and finds anomalies in frequency- and time-domain. This might be the reason for its superior performance. However, the differences are not significant. As such, we expected WSS to perform favourably well for anomaly detection, as a change of the period is indicative of an anomaly. The results underline that it is competitive with or even surpassed human annotations.

4.3   Segmentation

Figure 7 contains the average F1 ranks for ClaSP, FLOSS and Window for the 83 TSSB benchmark data sets as well as a window sizes correlation heatmap.

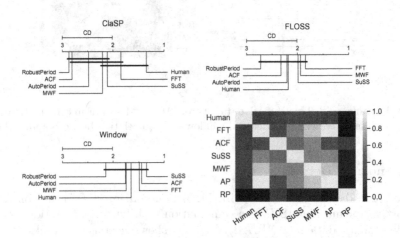

Fig. 7. F1 ranks on 83 benchmark data sets for ClaSP, FLOSS and Window in combination with human and detected window sizes and window sizes correlation between approaches

ClaSP performs best with human windows, followed by FFT, SuSS, MWF, AutoPeriod, ACF and RobustPeriod. While the top-4 approaches do not rank significantly different, only human window sizes perform significantly better than the 3 worst approaches. Performances (standard deviations) range from 69.1% to 88.5% (20.1% to 30.9%). FLOSS (and Window) show only insignificant differences between WSS approaches. The mean ranks are in range of 1.8 to 2.7 (1.4 to 2.1), the mean F1 score is between 56.6% and 62.5% (39.2% and 43.5%) and the standard deviations range in 22.8% to 27.3% (20.7% to 25.3%). In contrast to ClaSP, human annotations rank worse and ACF as well as MWF score better results.

As observed for anomaly detection, the WSS methods perform competitive to human annotations. This is surprising, as the TS have changing periods between segments, such as "running" and "walking" in human activity. All methods except RobustPeriod further show moderate to strong relationships (compare Fig. 7). FFT and SuSS are both within the top-3 ranking approaches and may be concluded as favourites for this task. Interestingly, the WSS by AutoPeriod is more correlated with the ones from other methods, yet it performs worse (rank 5 and 6). This may indicate that the AutoPeriod detection deteriorates in TS with regime changes, as opposed to FFT and SuSS. However, all differences are not significant.

4.4   Motif Discovery

We present the quality of the found motifs of two challenging real-life data sets for EMMA and LM using human and detected window sizes in Fig. 8.

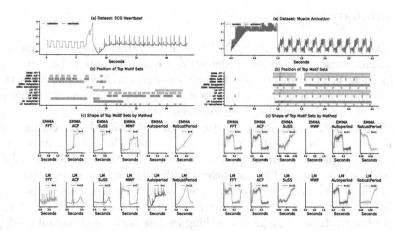

Fig. 8. Found motifs on two popular use cases: ECG heartbeats and inline skating motions

ECG Heartbeats: This data set contains two motifs, a calibration signal with 6 occurrences and the actual heartbeats with 16 occurrences. Two top motif sets as computed by the different methods are shown in Fig. 8 (left). The best results could be achieved using EMMA or LM in combination with ACF and SuSS. Both methods found calibration waves as TOP-1 motif and heartbeats as TOP-2 motif (bottom images). The location of the motifs and its lengths are shown in Fig. 8 (center). The found periods of the other window selection methods result in unrecognizable noisy signals or no motifs found.

Muscle Activation: The two top motif present in this data set are the activation and the recovery phase of the Gluteus Maximus muscle and have 12–13 occurrences as shown in Fig. 8 (right). The best results could be achieved using EMMA and LM using FFT, ACF and AutoPeriod. The TOP-1 motif for EMMA is a whole activation and recovery cycle. The TOP-2 motif found is a shifted variant of the TOP-1 motif and represents - in parts - the recovery phase. MWF failed to find motifs, and SuSS found a too small window size to return meaningful motifs.

Overall, the window lengths of all methods are either too small or too large to distinguish between recovery and activation. ACF, however, seems to find period lengths that produce meaningful motifs on both data sets, the other competitors did not succeed to give good lengths on all data sets. The problem of TSMD is different from that of the other two use cases mentioned before, as the TS are non-periodic. In motif discovery, we search for frequent similar substructures. This substructure may or may not be correlated to a period of the TS. WSS, however, tries to identify a period in the TS. Thus, by design it fails for TSMD. On our supporting website [15], we show the results of two additional (non-periodic) data sets for motif discovery.

5   Summary

We applied window size selection (WSS) to three distinct time series data mining tasks. Segmentation and anomaly detection require the input data to be periodic. As such, WSS even surpasses human annotations. In anomaly detection, a change in the period is even a sign of an anomaly. Segmentation is further characterized by changing window sizes between segments. In motif discovery, the TS itself must not be periodical, but we search for frequently appearing, similar subsequences. As such, we did not see a clear winner for all scenarios covered. From the WSS methods, the window sizes from FFT, ACF, SuSS and MWF are correlated and do not lead to significantly different performances. AutoPeriod, however, ranked highest for anomaly detection and FFT and SuSS are the two best-ranking whole and subsequence-based methods for the segmentation task and have low runtimes. In a global ranking (across both tasks and all methods), FFT ranks first, AutoPeriod and SuSS second, ACF and MWF third, followed by human window sizes, and RobustPeriod. For motif discovery, the presented approaches gave unsatisfactory results, as the size of non-trivial substructures in TS cannot easily be determined by its period size. Hence, more research is needed in data mining domains where the TS is non-periodic or contains changes in its period length. Also, incremental and online detection of changing window sizes is an interesting research area. Future work could further evaluate one of the mentioned TSDM tasks in more detail or explore more of its algorithms, benchmarks and evaluation metrics.

References

1. Blázquez-García, A., Conde, A., Mori, U., Lozano, J.A.: A review on outlier/anomaly detection in time series data. ACM Comput. Surv. (CSUR) **54**, 1–33 (2021)
2. Dau, H.A., et al.: The UCR time series archive. IEEE/CAA J. Automatica Sinica **6**, 1293–1305 (2019)
3. Demšar, J.: Statistical comparisons of classifiers over multiple data sets. J. Mach. Learn. Res. **7**, 1–30 (2006)
4. Elfeky, M.G., Aref, W.G., Elmagarmid, A.K.: Periodicity detection in time series databases. IEEE Trans. Knowl. Data Eng. **17**, 875–887 (2005)
5. Ermshaus, A., Schäfer, P., Leser, U.: ClaSP - Parameter-free Time Series Segmentation. arXiv (2022)

6. Gharghabi, S., et al.: Domain agnostic online semantic segmentation for multi-dimensional time series. DMKD **33**, 96–130 (2018)
7. Grabocka, J., Schilling, N., Schmidt-Thieme, L.: Latent time-series motifs. TKDD **11**(1), 1–20 (2016)
8. Imani, S., Keogh, E.: Multi-window-finder: domain agnostic window size for time series data. MileTS (2021)
9. Keogh, E., Dutta Roy, T., Naik, U., Agrawal, A: Multi-dataset time-series anomaly detection competition (2021). https://compete.hexagon-ml.com/practice/competition/39/
10. Lin, J., Keogh, E., Wei, L., Lonardi, S.: Experiencing sax: a novel symbolic representation of time series. DMKD **15**(2), 107–144 (2007)
11. Lonardi, J., Patel, P.: Finding motifs in time series. In: Workshop on Temporal Data Mining (2002)
12. Mörchen, F., Ultsch, A.: Efficient mining of understandable patterns from multivariate interval time series. DMKD **15**(2), 181–215 (2007)
13. Petrutiu, S., Sahakian, A.V., Swiryn, S.: Abrupt changes in fibrillatory wave characteristics at the termination of paroxysmal atrial fibrillation in humans. Europace **9**(7), 466–470 (2007)
14. Schäfer, P., Ermshaus, A., Leser, U.: ClaSP - Time series segmentation. In: CIKM (2021)
15. Supporting Material (2022). https://github.com/ermshaua/window-size-selection
16. Time Series Segmentation Benchmark (2021). https://github.com/ermshaua/time-series-segmentation-benchmark
17. Truong, C., Oudre, L., Vayatis, N.: Selective review of offline change point detection methods. Sig. Proces. **167**, 107299 (2019)
18. Vlachos, M., Yu, P.S., Castelli, V.: On periodicity detection and structural periodic similarity. In: SDM (2005)
19. Wen, Q., He, K., Sun, L., Zhang, Y., Ke, M., min Xu, H.: Robustperiod: robust time-frequency mining for multiple periodicity detection. In: SIGMOD/PODS (2021)
20. Yeh, C.C.M., et al.: Matrix profile i: all pairs similarity joins for time series: a unifying view that includes motifs, discords and shapelets. In: ICDM (2016)

Poster Presentation

Application of Attention Mechanism Combined with Long Short-Term Memory for Forecasting Dissolved Oxygen in Ganga River

Neha Pant[1]([✉]), Durga Toshniwal[1], and Bhola Ram Gurjar[2]

[1] Department of Computer Science and Engineering, Indian Institute of Technology Roorkee, Roorkee, India
{npant,durga.toshniwal}@cs.iitr.ac.in
[2] Department of Civil Engineering, Indian Institute of Technology Roorkee, Roorkee, India
bhola.gurjar@ce.iitr.ac.in

Abstract. Accurate forecasting of water quality parameters is a significant part of the process of water resource management. In this paper we demonstrate the applicability of Long Short-Term Memory (LSTM) combined with attention mechanism for the long-term forecasting (after 24 h) of Dissolved Oxygen content at various stations of Ganga River flowing through the state of Uttar Pradesh, India. In the given model, the hidden states of the LSTM units are passed to the attention layer. The attention layer then gives different weights to the hidden states based on their relevance. The performance of the models is evaluated using root mean square error, mean absolute error and coefficient of determination. The experimental results indicate that combining attention mechanism with LSTM significantly improves the forecasted values of Dissolved Oxygen when compared with state-of-the-art models like Recurrent Neural Network, LSTM, and bidirectional LSTM. The demonstrated model is particularly useful during the availability of only univariate datasets.

Keywords: Dissolved oxygen · Water quality forecasting · Long short-term memory · Attention

1 Introduction

Water is an essential and irreplaceable resource supporting human, animal, and plant life on earth through its consumption in various forms. Because of rapid urbanization in the recent decades, the number of industrial setups and towns near the rivers has increased substantially in India, causing water quality to deteriorate day by day. This water quality deterioration has called for the efficient management of water resources. Accurate forecasting is an essential step in improving the management of water resources.

Dissolved Oxygen (DO) is one of the many important parameters used to determine the standard of water in rivers and other water bodies. Dissolved Oxygen is the balanced amount of oxygen dissolved in the water bodies left after oxygen-producing processes like absorption from the atmosphere and photosynthesis and oxygen-consuming processes like aerobic respiration and chemical oxidation. Water must contain sufficient DO for the aquatic life to survive. However, continuous anthropogenic activities near the water bodies have led to the depletion of Dissolved Oxygen, thereby resulting in the deterioration of water quality standards.

Currently, many departments managing water resources worldwide have set up sensors to monitor the quality of water at different monitoring stations. However, they cannot be used to forecast the quality of water. However, at the same time, the enormous data collected by these stations can be used to build certain data-based models to predict future values of specific water quality parameters. The forecasts obtained from the models can be used further to control the degree of pollution in the water bodies by encouraging policymakers and government officials to take appropriate actions to manage water resources properly.

In this paper, we have demonstrated the applicability of the attention mechanism combined with LSTM for long-term forecasting of DO content in River Ganga flowing through the state of Uttar Pradesh in India. We also compare the developed model with other state-of-the-art models like Recurrent Neural Network, LSTM, and bidirectional LSTM. The presented method is particularly beneficial when only univariate datasets are available.

2   Related Work

Several studies have used different variations of Artificial Neural Networks for forecasting of different water quality parameters. The employment of artificial neural network (ANN) to determine the amount of biological oxygen demand (BOD) and DO of Gomti river in India has been suggested by Singh et al. in [1]. The study concluded that phosphate, nitrate nitrogen, ammoniacal nitrogen and Chemical Oxygen Demand were the main factors in determining DO. Ruben G. B. et al. [2] recommends the utilization of MLP model with Levenberg-Marquardt algorithm for learning for the forecast the level of COD in Xuxi River, China. I. S. Yeon et al. [3] proposes the use of Levenberg-Marquardt Neural Network (LMNN), Modular Neural Network (MDNN) and Adaptive Neuro-Fuzzy Inference System (ANFIS) models for forecasting DO. Rankovic et al. [4] have conducted a study making use of a feed forward neural network (FFNN) to estimate the strength of DO in the Gruza Reservoir of Serbia. S. Emamgholizadeh et al. [5] suggests the use of various kinds of neural networks like Multi-Layer Perceptron (MLP), Radial basis network (RBF) and ANFIS for water quality forecasting. It is found in the study that pH and temperature have the highest contribution in improving efficiency of the model whereas the nitrates, phosphates and chlorides have been useless in determining the level of DO. Sarkar A. et al. [6] have proposed a study making the use of ANN with feed forward error back propagation to determine the level of DO in Yamuna River in the downstream of Mathura city in India. The authors suggested that better forecasting is possible if higher frequency data is available for training purpose.

A successful demonstration of wavelet neural network (WNN) and artificial neural network models with different combinations of input parameters with different time lags was used to predict DO, temperature, and salinity by Alizadeh et al. [7]. A study comparing linear and non-linear models to forecast the DO levels in the river Danube has been conducted by Csábrági, A. et al. [8]. For this, the authors have employed four different models namely, multi-linear regression, multi-layer perceptron neural network (MLPNN), Radial Basis Function Neural Network, and General Regression Neural Network (GRNN).

Several advanced neural networks have also been used in several studies to find out the complex relationship between the input and output parameters. Zou Q. et al. [9] suggested the use of multi-time scale bidirectional LSTM for prediction of water quality in Beilun River. The authors made use of both water quality and meteorological features in the prediction process. Li et al. 2018 [10] proposed the use of combination of Sparse Auto-encoder and LSTM for predicting DO in a shrimp pond by making use of multivariate dataset containing both water quality and meteorological parameters.

Attention based mechanism was originally used for Natural Language Processing [11]. Nevertheless, the attention mechanism has recently been used for forecasting in several areas like wind power [12], flood [13], electrical loads [14], etc. Liu et al. 2019 [15] makes use of recurrent neural network combined with attention on short and long-term prediction of DO in a pond in Zhejiang Institute of Freshwater Fisheries, Zhejiang province, China. The study makes use of DO, soil parameters and meteorological parameters for short term and long term DO forecasting. The earlier works have made use of historic data consisting of multiple water quality metrics and other external factors like meteorological features. There is a need for methods to be able to handle the non-linear complex relationship between the input and the output features while considering minimal historic data for forecasting DO levels.

3   Data and Methods

3.1   Study Area and Water Quality Data

River Ganga is considered one of the most sacred rivers to the Hindus. The river flows for a length of around 2525 km, flowing through the states of Uttarakhand, Uttar Pradesh, Bihar, and West Bengal in India. The dataset contains values of Dissolved Oxygen for a total of 5 monitoring stations of River Ganga flowing through the Uttar Pradesh region of India. The data is collected from monitoring stations at Ghatiya Ghat bridge (Farrukhabad), Manimau bridge in Kannauj, Bridge at Bithoor, Bridge near Fatehpur (Asni Village) and Bridge in Varanasi. The studied locations are marked on Google maps in Fig. 1. The water quality data is collected from the Uttar Pradesh Pollution Control Board, Lucknow, Uttar Pradesh.

The dataset contains records from 1 April 2017 to 30 April 2021. The dataset available has a sampling rate of one observation per hour for the years 2017 to 2018 and a sampling rate of one observation per 15 min for the years 2019 to 2021. In order to ensure consistency of the sampling rate, we retrieved the records with a sample rate of one observation per hour for all the years. Table 1 illustrates the total number of records in the dataset for each of the monitoring stations. The dataset is divided in such a way that 80 % of the data is used for training and 20 % is used for testing.

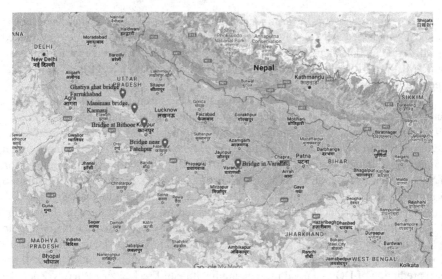

Fig. 1. Study area marked on Google maps

3.2 Data Preprocessing

The dataset contains some random missing values. These missing values are imputed using linear interpolation. The data is further normalized using min-max normalization, thus mapping the values in the range [0, 1]. The following is the equation used for normalizing the dataset:

$$x' = \frac{x - x_{min}}{x_{max} - x_{min}} \tag{1}$$

where, x' is the normalized value, x is the original value, x_{min} is the minimum value and x_{max} is the maximum value of the variable.

Table 1. Number of records in the dataset for the monitoring stations

Station	Number of records
Ghatiya Ghat bridge, Farrukhabad	31970
Manimau bridge, Kannauj	32298
Bridge at Bithoor	33526
Bridge near Fatehpur	35094
Bridge in Varanasi	34938

3.3   Recurrent Neural Network

Recurrent Neural Networks (RNN) are an advancement over simple neural networks making use of sequential data as input. While simple neural network considers input and output to be independent, RNNs takes into account the previous input sequence to determine the current output. The problem with a simple RNN is that it suffers from vanishing and exploding gradients.

3.4   Long Short-Term Memory

To solve the problem of vanishing gradient and gradient explosion, Hochreiter et al. [16] proposed LSTMs. The LSTMs are a special kind of RNNs, with the ability to learn long-term dependencies by storing information related to different time periods using cell states. The cell state at a specific LSTM unit describes the information that has been considered relevant till that particular timestamp. The LSTMs regulate the flow of information to the cell states by making use of forget, input and output gates. The information passed to the gates is a function of hidden states passed from the previous LSTM unit at the previous timestamps and information at the current timestamp.

3.5   Bidirectional Long Short-Term Memory

Bidirectional LSTM is an advancement over the basic LSTM model. The input is passed to the two LSTMs: first through the forward layer and then through the backward layer. In the forward layer, the LSTM is applied on the input in the forward direction and in the backward layer, another LSTM is applied to the input in the backward direction. After learning the sequence in both the directions, merging operation is performed on the two models.

3.6   Long Short-Term Memory with Attention

Originally, attention mechanism was intended for use in Natural Language processing [11] but was quickly adopted in other disciplines as well [12–14]. The basic idea in the attention mechanism is to consider only the most relevant information and to reduce the impact of less important information from further processing.

The LSTM units extract the long-term dependencies. In temporal attention model, the hidden states of the LSTM units are passed to the attention layer. The attention layer assigns different weights to the various hidden states based on their significance for forecasting dissolved oxygen, thus further enhancing the performance of the model. The features thus generated are then further passed to the fully connected layer which finally generates the forecasts. Figure 2 shows the block diagram for our proposed framework.

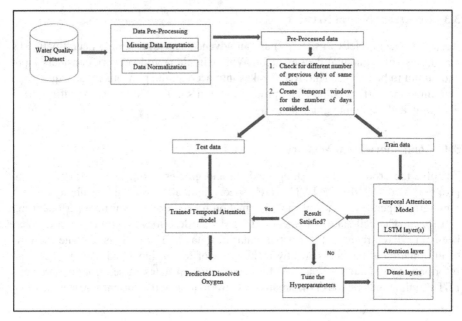

Fig. 2. Block diagram for the proposed framework

4   Results and Discussions

The work has been implemented in Python 3.8 using TensorFlow 2.3.1 and Keras 2.4.3. All the experiments are conducted in Windows 10 operating system with 16 GB RAM and Intel(R) Core (TM) i7-10750H CPU at 2.60 GHz. Adam optimizer is used to accelerate the gradient descent algorithm to minimize the mean squared error. The activation function used is the tanh function for all hidden layers.

The performance of the models is checked on learning rates [0.01, 0.001, 0.0001] and on the batch sizes of [64, 128, 256]. The models perform best with the learning rate of 0.0001 and batch size of 64. The models are also fitted over a variable number of epochs ranging from 10 to 2000. Then a suitable value of epoch is chosen for the model corresponding to each monitoring site. For forecasting DO at a particular time of the day, the DO values measured at the same time for the past n days is taken as input. The performance of the models is also checked by considering a lag of 1 to 5 days as input for each monitoring station. After finding a suitable lag value for each monitoring station, a corresponding window of n previous DO values is given as input for the final building of the model.

The demonstrated model makes use of the LSTM layer as the first hidden layer. The window containing the sequential DO values are first given to the LSTM layer as input. This is followed by the attention layer, which assigns weights to the most relevant hidden states of the previous LSTM layer. The most relevant features generated is then passed to the fully connected dense layer. In the end, an output layer is added, which returns a single forecasted value.

The experiments demonstrate the LSTM combined with attention mechanism performed drastically better than the simple RNN, LSTM and bidirectional LSTM. Moreover, to compare and demonstrate the effectiveness of models, we employed root mean squared error (RMSE), coefficient of determination (R2), and mean absolute error (MAE). Table 2 shows the RMSE values while considering different number of DO values in the input window. The lower values of RMSE and MAE and higher R2 values indicate better models. Table 3 summarizes the results corresponding to RMSE, MAE and R2 for all the models thereby showing that the results obtained by combining LSTM with attention mechanism are significantly better as compared to the other models. The values also indicate that LSTM performs almost similarly or marginally better than the RNN model. Whereas the bidirectional LSTM gives significantly better results as compared to basic RNN and LSTM models. Further, attention combined with LSTM further outperforms all the models.

Table 2. RMSE of LSTM combined with attention model making use of different number of days as lags for River Ganga monitoring stations

Station/Number of days considered as lags	1 Day	2 Days	3 Days	4 Days	5 Days
Ghatiya Ghat bridge, Farrukhabad	0.344	0.343	0.345	0.348	0.347
Manimau bridge, Kannauj	1.771	1.762	1.752	1.758	1.757
Bithoor	0.817	0.823	0.849	0.850	0.853
Fatehpur (Asni Village)	1.276	1.262	1.310	1.257	1.320
Bridge in Varanasi	1.124	1.113	1.088	1.102	1.088

Figure 3 shows the scatter plots for all the stations for the testing phase of the dataset. The x-axis and the y-axis correspond to the measured and predicted values of DO respectively. Figure 4 shows the measured and predicted values of the DO during the testing phase of the model for the month of April 2021.

Table 3. Performance evaluation of models for River Ganga monitoring stations for Train and Test sets

Stations	Models	RMSE		MAE		R^2	
		Train	Test	Train	Test	Train	Test
Ghatiya Ghat Bridge, Farrukhabad	RNN	0.630	0.464	0.337	0.293	0.832	0.904
	LSTM	0.630	0.464	0.338	0.295	0.832	0.904
	Bidirectional LSTM	0.458	0.344	0.226	0.198	0.911	0.947
	LSTM with Attention	0.457	0.343	0.224	0.197	0.911	0.947
Manimau Bridge, Kannauj	RNN	1.854	2.381	1.170	1.570	0.481	0.476
	LSTM	1.852	2.385	1.176	1.573	0.482	0.474
	Bidirectional LSTM	1.305	1.797	0.694	1.066	0.743	0.701
	LSTM with Attention	1.299	1.752	0.680	1.044	0.746	0.716
Bithoor	RNN	1.158	1.191	0.648	0.636	0.785	0.714
	LSTM	1.130	1.179	0.630	0.620	0.796	0.720
	Bidirectional LSTM	0.847	0.821	0.439	0.416	0.885	0.864
	LSTM with Attention	0.843	0.817	0.435	0.414	0.886	0.865
Fatehpur (Asni Village)	RNN	2.018	1.830	1.304	1.172	0.540	0.610
	LSTM	1.994	1.833	1.274	1.148	0.550	0.609
	Bidirectional LSTM	1.315	1.274	0.765	0.755	0.804	0.811
	LSTM with Attention	1.286	1.257	0.732	0.723	0.813	0.816
Bridge in Varanasi	RNN	2.170	1.760	1.452	1.172	0.587	0.794
	LSTM	2.159	1.732	1.438	1.144	0.591	0.801
	Bidirectional LSTM	1.494	1.089	0.920	0.638	0.804	0.921
	LSTM with Attention	1.480	1.088	0.912	0.639	0.808	0.921

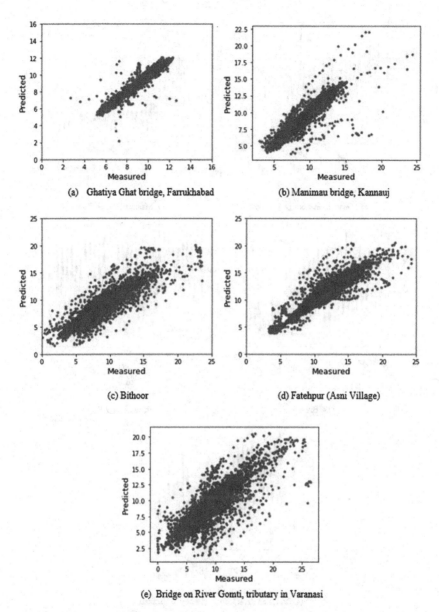

(a)   Ghatiya Ghat bridge, Farrukhabad

(b) Manimau bridge, Kannauj

(c) Bithoor

(d) Fatehpur (Asni Village)

(e) Bridge on River Gomti, tributary in Varanasi

Fig. 3. Scatter plots for the test dataset

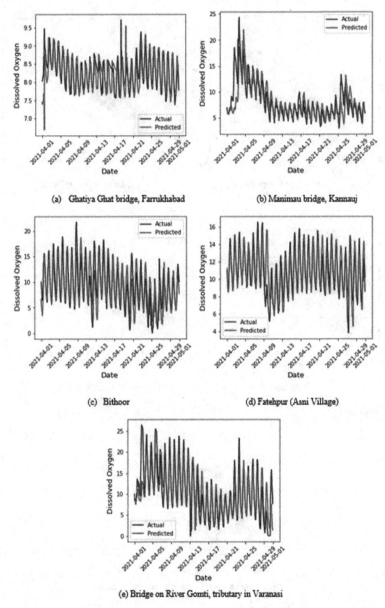

(a) Ghatiya Ghat bridge, Farrukhabad

(b) Manimau bridge, Kannauj

(c) Bithoor

(d) Fatehpur (Asni Village)

(e) Bridge on River Gomti, tributary in Varanasi

Fig. 4. Plots showing measured and predicted Dissolved Oxygen for the test dataset

5 Conclusion

Managing water resources is one of the significant challenges for governments world-wide. Accurate long-term forecasting of water quality parameters like Dissolved Oxygen can help control the degree of pollution by encouraging the officials to make suitable policies and take precautionary actions.

Deep learning models like LSTM have been used successfully in several fields to forecast electricity demand [17, 18], air pollution [19], rainfall [20], etc. Combining LSTM with the attention mechanism can significantly enhance its performance by assigning more weights to certain relevant hidden states for DO forecasting. The results suggest that the suggested temporal attention-based LSTM models perform better than the traditional standalone RNN, LSTM and bidirectional LSTM models. Further, the demonstrated model takes only previous DO values as input features and would therefore be helpful in situations when multivariate datasets are not available. Additionally, because the exhibited model simply relies on historical data, it is simple to extend it to any monitoring station.

References

1. Singh, K.P., Basant, A., Malik, A., Jain, G.: Artificial neural network modeling of the river water quality— a case study. Ecol. Model. **220**, 888–895 (2009). https://doi.org/10.1016/j.ecolmodel.2009.01.004
2. Ruben, G.B., Zhang, K., Bao, H., Ma, X.: Application and sensitivity analysis of artificial neural network for prediction of chemical oxygen demand. Water Resour. Manag. **32**(1), 273–283 (2017). https://doi.org/10.1007/s11269-017-1809-0
3. Yeon, I.S., Kim, J.H., Jun, K.W.: Application of artificial intelligence models in water quality forecasting. Environ. Technol. **29**(6), 625–631 (2008). https://doi.org/10.1080/09593330801984456
4. Rankovic, V., Radulovic, J., Radojevic, I., Ostojic, A., Comic, L.: Neural network modeling of dissolved oxygen in the Gruza reservoir, Serbia. Ecol. Model. **221**(8), 1239–1244 (2010)
5. Emamgholizadeh, S., Kashi, H., Marofpoor, I., Zalaghi, E.: Prediction of water quality parameters of Karoon river (Iran) by artificial intelligence-based models. Int. J. Environ. Sci. Technol. **11**(3), 645–656 (2013). https://doi.org/10.1007/s13762-013-0378-x
6. Sarkar, A., Pandey, P.: River water quality modelling using artificial neural network technique. Aquatic Procedia **4**, 1070–1077 (2015)
7. Alizadeh, M.J., Kavianpour, M.R.: Development of wavelet-ANN models to predict water quality parameters in Hilo Bay, Pacific ocean. Mar. Pollut. Bull. **98**(1), 171–178 (2015)
8. Csábrági, A., Molnár, S., Tanos, P., Kovács, J.: Application of artificial neural networks to the forecasting of dissolved oxygen content in the Hungarian section of the river Danube. Ecol. Eng. **100**, 63–72 (2017). https://doi.org/10.1016/j.ecoleng.2016.12.027
9. Zou, Q., Xiong, Q., Li, Q., Yi, H., Yu, Y., Wu, C.: A water quality prediction method based on the multi-time scale bidirectional long short-term memory network. Environ. Sci. Pollut. Res. **27**(14), 16853–16864 (2020). https://doi.org/10.1007/s11356-020-08087-7
10. Li, Z., Peng, F., Niu, B., Li, G., Wu, J., Miao, Z.: Water quality prediction model combining sparse auto-encoder and LSTM network. IFAC-PapersOnLine **51**(17), 831–836 (2018)
11. Bahdanau, D., Cho, K., Bengio, Y.: Neural machine translation by jointly learning to align and translate. In: ICLR (2015)

12. Niu, Z., Yu, Z., Tang, W., Wu, Q., Reformat, M.: Wind power forecasting using attention-based gated recurrent unit network. Energy **196**, 117081 (2020)
13. Ding, Y.K., Zhu, Y.L., Feng, J., Zhang, P.C., Cheng, Z.R.: Interpretable spatio-temporal attention LSTM model for flood forecasting. Neurocomputing **403**, 348–359 (2020)
14. Zang, H., Xu, R., Cheng, L., Ding, T., Liu, L., Wei, Z., Sun, G.: Residential load forecasting based on LSTM fusing self-attention mechanism with pooling. Energy, 229, 120682, ISSN 0360-5442 (2021). https://doi.org/10.1016/j.energy.2021.120682
15. Liu, Y., Zhang, Q., Song, L., Chen, Y.: Attention-based recurrent neural networks for accurate short-term and long-term dissolved oxygen prediction. Comput. Electron. Agric. **165**, Article 104964 (2019). https://doi.org/10.1016/j.compag.2019.104964
16. Hochreiter, S., Schmidhuber, J.: Long short-term memory. Neural Comput. **9**(8), 1735–1780 (1997)
17. Guo, F.F., Li, L.P., Wei, C.H.: Short term load forecasting based on phase space reconstruction algorithm and bi-square kernel regression model. Appl. Energy **224**, 13–33 (2018)
18. Kim, T.Y., Cho, S.B.: Predicting residential energy consumption using CNN-LSTM neural networks. Energy **182**, 72–81 (2019)
19. Chang, Y.S., Chiao, H.T., Abimannan, S., Huang, Y.P., Tsai, Y.T., Lin, K.M.: An LSTM-based aggregated model for air pollution forecasting. Atmos. Pollut. Res. **11**, 1451–1463 (2020)
20. Xu, Y., Hu, C., Wu, Q., Jian, S., Li, Z., Chen, Y., Wang, S.: Research on particle swarm optimization in LSTM neural networks for rainfall-runoff simulation. J. Hydrol. **608**, Article 127553 (2022). https://doi.org/10.1016/j.jhydrol.2022.127553

Data Augmentation for Time Series Classification with Deep Learning Models

Gautier Pialla[⊠], Maxime Devanne, Jonathan Weber, Lhassane Idoumghar, and Germain Forestier

IRIMAS, Université de Haute-Alsace, Mulhouse, France
{gautier.pialla,maxime.devanne,jonathan.weber,lhassane.idoumghar, germain.forestier}@uha.fr

Abstract. Deep Learning models for time series classification are benchmarked on the UCR Archive. This archive contains 128 datasets. Unfortunately only 5 datasets contain more than 1000 training samples. For most deep learning models, this lead to over-fitting. One way to address this issue and improve the generalization of the models is data augmentation. Although it has been extensively studied and is widely used for images, fewer works have been done on time series. InceptionTime is an ensemble of 5 Inception classifiers and is still regarded as the state-of-the-art deep learning model for time series classification. However, most of the work on data augmentation were not done on the Inception classifier. In this paper we solve this issue by studying 4 different data augmentation methods through 4 experiments on the Inception model. We studied trainings with one or several augmentations at the same time and with or without generating new samples at each epoch. We also conducted experiments with ensembling and benchmarked our results on the UCR Archive. We showed that using a combination of both the scaling and window warping data augmentation methods, we can significantly improve the accuracy of Inception and InceptionTime models.

Keywords: Data augmentation · Time series · Scaling · Window warping · Inception

1 Introduction

As deep learning models get deeper and deeper, training them has become a real challenge. The training part is based on statistics. A distribution of the data is learned on a training set. The aim is to generalize on a test set, unseen by the model. *Generalization* is the main challenge for the training as we expect the model to perform as well on unknown data as on the training set. If a model performs better on the training set than on the test set, we say that it *over-fits*. For this reason, in addition to an important computing power, the training needs quality and quantity of data. This raises the question "For a given task how much data do we need ?". In the literature, this problem is called *sample complexity* as the answer depends on both the complexity of the problem and that of the chosen

© The Author(s), under exclusive license to Springer Nature Switzerland AG 2023
T. Guyet et al. (Eds.): AALTD 2022, LNAI 13812, pp. 117–132, 2023.
https://doi.org/10.1007/978-3-031-24378-3_8

model. In computer vision, state-of-the art models are benchmarked on huge datasets like ImageNet [3], MS-COCO [14] or Open Image [12]. These datasets contain thousands of samples for each different class. Regarding time series, most of the models are benchmarked on the UCR Archive [1]. The latest version of this archive contains 128 datasets regrouped in 7 categories such as Sensor, ECG, or Devices. The downside is their few number of training samples, and the lack of validation sets. As a matter of fact only 5 of them contain more than a 1000 training instances. Thus, it is hard for the models to generalize well because of the over-fitting. In order to improve further generalization and reduce over-fitting, different strategies can be carried out in machine learning. Among them, one can reduce the complexity of a model by simply removing layers or reducing the number of neurons. *Regularization* consists of adding a penalty term to the loss function. Usually, the chosen penalty is the L1 or the L2 norm. Regarding the weigths, the L1 norm minimizes their absolute value while the L2 norm minimizes their squared magnitude. *Early stopping* is also a form of regularization. It entails stopping the training before the appearance of over-fitting. It is widely used for training deep learning models. Differently, *Ensembling* combines several weak independent models in order to obtain a stronger model. Ensembles can have different size, and be composed of different models. It exists several ways to create ensembles. An easy and effective one is to average to predictions of the different models. Another regularization method consists of using more data. One can either collect new data, or increase artificially the amount of training data by creating of modifying existing samples. This is called *data augmentation* (DA). Using synthetic data is particularly useful when it is too difficult to obtain new data. Such data can be created in a realistic way using algorithms, or deep models like Variational Encoders or Generative Adversarial Networks. Most of the time, the augmented data is simply a copy of the training set to which has been applied random transformations. Commonly, for images these transformations are color changes, rotations, zooming, blurring or cropping parts of the images. Increasing the dataset in such a way, helps to provide more context. InceptionTime [8], introduced in 2019, is considered as the state-of-the-art deep learning time series classifier. It is an ensemble of 5 Inception networks. To reduce over-fitting, beside creating an ensemble, Fawaz et al. used early stopping during the training of each separate network. Despite that, InceptionTime still over-fits most of the UCR datasets. To overcome this issue, data augmentation appears like an interesting solution. Unlike in computer vision, where this is widely used, few time series classifiers are using it during training. Iwana et al. [9] benchmarked 12 data augmentation methods over 6 time series classifiers. Some of these methods were adapted from computer vision, but other are specific for time series. As this survey was not conducted on Inception networks and InceptionTime ensembles, we propose to investigate the use of data augmentation on this state-of-the-art architecture. After having selected 4 promising data augmentation methods from [9], our main contributions are:

- We benchmarked them on both Inception and InceptionTime over the entire UCR Archive.

- We went further than existing papers by testing the methods independently but also combined together.
- We created ensembles of Inceptions networks trained with the same data augmentation method but also with different ones.
- Finally, we showed how data augmentation can significantly improve the accuracy of both architectures.

2   Related Work

The aim of using data augmentation is to reduce over-fitting, by improving the generalization of a deep learning model, thus also improving it's accuracy. Many well-known networks have used it to boost their performances and become the state-of-the-art. Among them, AlexNet [11] in 2012 used cropping, mirroring, zooming, blurring and rotation. VGG [16] in 2014 used scaling and cropping. The inception networks [17] introduced in 2014 used cropping and mirroring. ResNet [7] has used cropping and mirroring.

Hence, data augmentation is not a new technique and has been extensively studied for computer vision. Most of the previously cited architectures have been adapted for time series classification. They have given FCN [20], ResNet [20] and InceptionTime [8]. These architectures have all achieved state-of-the-art performances, but unlike their counterparts in computer vision, they have not used data augmentation.

Regarding time series, data augmentation has not been explored in depth until recently. Indeed, two surveys benchmarked most of the existing methods. The first one from Iwana et al. [9] benchmarked 12 data augmentation methods over 6 different classifiers. Similarly, the second study by Weng et al. [21] compared data augmentation methods, but considered not only classification but also anomaly detection and prediction.

Out of the benchmarked methods, most of them are adaptations from the ones used in computer vision. *Jittering* consists of adding to each time step of a time series a random Gaussian noise. *Window slicing* [13] is the process of extracting sub-parts or windows from a time series. Each part is then classified. The majority class obtained within the patches is then assigned to the original series. *Flipping* inverts a time series. Some of these techniques can only be used for specific datasets. Indeed, it does not make sense to apply flipping for every kind of time series, like ECGs. Similarly, for Window slicing, if the discriminative parts are not present in each slice, it can result in false predictions. For this reason, some methods were specifically designed for time series. Guided Warping techniques like *Random Guided Warping* and *Discriminative Guided Warping* [10] use DTW to warp patterns from one time series to another. Forestier et al. [6] introduced weighted DBA which averages a set of time series to create a new one.

Instead of using and modifying existing time series, other methods focus on creating synthetic data. Generative Adversarial Networks (GANs) and Variational Auto-Encoders (VAEs) are popular ways to do so. Regarding GANs,

TimeGAN [22], Recurrent Conditional GAN [5] or Continuous recurrent neural networks [22] are adapted for time series. Regarding auto-encoders we can cite TimeVAE [4], the use of masked autoencoders [23], or the averaging of time series using auto-encoders [18]. Differently, Pialla et al. [15] designed a smooth adversarial attack and showed through adversarial training how adversarial samples can also be used to improve the robustness of deep models.

Although these generative methods can be used as some kind of data augmentation, they require to train new models and often to fine tune them for each dataset. Thus, they do not represent a general and quick approach to implement.

3   Proposed Approach

3.1   Data Augmentation Methods Used

In this paper, we took 4 methods from [9]. We selected the methods that were the most recommended across all deep learning models to asses if they also generalize on the Inception models.

RGW. Random Guided Warping (RGW) has been introduced in [10]. For a given class, two different patterns are selected. Then, these patterns are randomly switched between the samples. The warping between the samples is computed using the DTW algorithm.

DGW. Discriminative Guided Warping (DGW) was also introduced in [10] and is similar to RGW. This time, only the most discriminative pattern is selected inside a batch.

Scaling. The scaling method multiplies a time series with a random scalar α. It can be taken from a random Gaussian distribution $\alpha \sim \mathcal{N}(1, \sigma^2)$. We use the same parameters as in [19]: $\mu = 1$ and $\sigma = 0.1$. This method modifies the magnitude of the time series. An example of a scaled time series is displayed in Fig. 1.

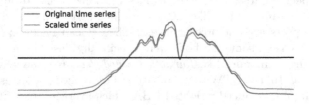

Fig. 1. Example of scaling a time series from the EthanolLevel dataset.

Window Warping. Window warping as been introduced in [13]. It consists of selecting a random window. The window is then sped up by a factor 2 or slowed down by a factor 0.5.

We used a window size equal to 10% of the TS length. An example of Window Warping can be seen below in Fig. 2.

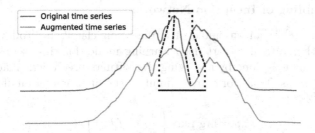

Fig. 2. Example of Window Warping. The part of the original time series in blue has been increased two times. (Color figure online)

3.2 Models Used

The Inception network was first introduced by Fawaz et al. in [8]. It is an adaptation for time series from the famous Inception architecture in computer vision. The model is composed of 6 inception modules, a Global Average Pooling (GAP) and a Dense layer. The architecture is represented in Fig. 3 and the inception modules in Fig. 4.

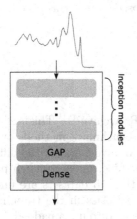

Fig. 3. Inception network.

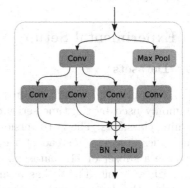

Fig. 4. Inception module.

Each inception module, is composed of several convolutions with different kernel sizes. All the convolutions outputs are concatenated and followed by a Batch Normalization layer and a Relu activation function. The intuition behind the inception module is to make the network wider instead of deeper and prone to over-fitting.

3.3 Ensembling of Inception Networks

InceptionTime [8] is an ensemble of 5 Inception classifiers. Today, it is still regarded as the state-of-the-art deep learning model for time series classification. The ensemble is done by averaging the softmax predictions made by the 5 Inception networks. Thus, for a given input x, the final prediction of the ensemble of n models is:

$$\hat{y} = \arg \max \left(\frac{1}{n} \sum_{i=1}^{n} f_i(x) \right) \tag{1}$$

In this paper, we use InceptionTime to benchmark our ensembling results. We did several kinds of ensemblings: ensemblings of Inception models trained with the same data augmentation method, ensemblings of Inception models trained with different data augmentation methods and finally ensemblings of Inception models trained with several data augmentation methods.

3.4 ROCKET

ROCKET [2], is a non-deep model for time series classification. It is composed of random, unlearnt convolutions. Using theses convolutions, features are extracted using the percentage of positive values (PPV). Finally, the classification is done using a linear classifier. This model is really famous because of its accurate classifications and its exceptionally fast training time, hence the name. As ROCKET is a state-of-the-art time series classifier, we proposed to use it as a benchmark for our best models.

4   Experimental Setup

4.1   Datasets

All our experiments where conducted on the UCR Archive [1]. This archive is commonly used by the time series community to benchmark methods or deep learning classifiers. The 2018 version of the UCR Archive contains 128 different time series datasets. Instead of using the whole archive, many research papers only use a subset of 112 datasets. The reason is that 15 datasets are unequal in length and one, Fungi, has a single instance per class in the training set. Regarding the datasets with unequal length, we decided to use a padded version provided by the same authors. For the Fungi dataset, we could not used it, as the methods RGW and DGW require several training samples of the same class. Thus, in total, we used 127 datasets.

4.2 Implementation

For this work we have reused the code and data from several sources. Regarding the data augmentation, we used the implementation provided by [10]. We used the code and results of Inception and InceptionTime as presented in [8] and the results of ROCKET [2]. As we used several open source codes, we also made freely available all the code and results in our companion GitHub repository[1].

4.3 Protocol and Parameters

If not specified otherwise, we use the same following parameters for each experiment. All trainings where realized using the Adam optimizer during 900 epochs. At each epoch, the training set was randomly shuffled. The objective was to mix the original training samples and the augmented ones. Regarding the training data, we use a mix of original samples and augmented ones. Each original sample has its augmented counterpart generated by each data augmentation method. Thus, if we use 1 data augmentation method, the training set will be twice the size of the original dataset. If we use 2 methods, the amount of training data used is 3 times the size of the training set, and so on. Each training was conducted 5 times. Having several iterations helps to have more consistent results. Indeed the random initialization of the models and the stochasticity of some data augmentation method can have an impact on the trainings. The results presented in Sect. 5, are always an average over the 5 runs. In order to compare the data augmentation with InceptionTime, we created ensembles out of the 5 runs. Theses ensembles average the predictions made by each model composing it. It is the same process used by InceptionTime. These ensembles are unique, and thus, the results presented for those are not an average over several runs.

5 Experiments

5.1 Experiment 1

In the first experiment, we aim to compare the vanilla Inception model, as presented in [8], to Inception models trained with data augmentation.

Results. Figure 5 represents a critical diagram. Such diagrams are useful when comparing multiple methods over several datasets, as it is the case here. The methods are ordered given their average rank over the datasets. A thick horizontal line links a set of classifiers that are not significantly different, according to the Wilcoxon-Holm analysis. With the Fig. 5, we learn that for the Inception classifier, the data augmentations Scaling and Window Warping are both significantly better than DGW and RGW. DGW is the only method significantly worst than the vanilla Inception classifier. Both RGW and Window Warping are not significantly different than the vanilla classifier. Only Scaling is significantly

---

[1] https://github.com/Gpialla/DataAugForTSC.

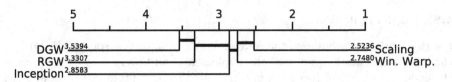

Fig. 5. CD diagram of experiment 1

better than the vanilla classifier. Globally, the Guided Warping methods seems in average to degrade the performances. However these methods are not useless. Indeed, for respectively 43 and 55 datasets, DGW and RGW are still better than the vanilla classifier.

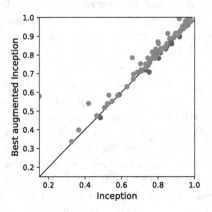

Fig. 6. Pairwise diagram: Inception vs best Inception with augmentation for each dataset. Each dot represent a single dataset. Blue dots represent datasets whose accuracy is improved by at least one data augmentation. Gold dots represent datasets whose accuracies have not changed (same as Inception). (Color figure online)

The Fig. 6 compares for each dataset, the vanilla Inception model to the best augmented Inception model. We can observe that for 92 datasets, using one of the four data augmentation methods improves the accuracy of the Inception model. The vanilla Inception is the best method for only 30 datasets. This shows the relevance of data augmentation for time series. Like for image classification, most of the time series datasets can leverage the use of data augmentation. Using the best data augmentation method improves the average accuracy by +1.40%. The best improvement regards the DodgerLoopDay dataset with an improvement of +43.00% using the RGW data augmentation. For this specific dataset, all data augmentation methods, significantly improve the accuracy, with an average of +41.75%.

Results with Ensembling. Following the previous results, we propose to analyze the impact of data augmentation over ensembling. For each method, we created ensembles in the same way as InceptionTime, by averaging the predictions made by the 5 iterations.

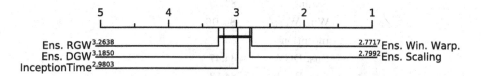

Fig. 7. CD diagram of experiment 1 with ensembling

In Fig. 7 we can see that the methods that were performing the best individually, Scaling and Window Warping, are the ones that provide the best ensembles in term of rank. After ensembling, the rank of the data augmentation methods is conserved. However, all methods are not significantly different and none is significantly better than InceptionTime. Creating an ensemble will smooth and improve the individual performance of the models that compose it. Thus, it is harder to observe any difference between the augmentation methods.

Results with Ensembling of Several Data Augmentation Methods. Previously, we created ensembles using the five trainings of each data augmentation method. Another way to make ensembles is to use different methods. Here we created five ensembles. Within each ensemble, we used four models, each one trained using a different data augmentation method. In the following results, the accuracy of the five ensembles is averaged.

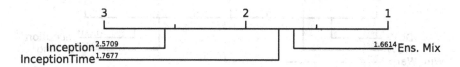

Fig. 8. CD diagram of experiment 1 with ensembling of several data augmentation methods

We called this ensemble Ens. Mix. We can see in Fig. 8 that it significantly outperforms InceptionTime. It seems that using different methods inside the same ensemble leads to better results. Even if the gap between these ensembles and InceptionTime is not huge, this result is important. Before, we should have had to benchmark and select a single data augmentation method, but now we can simply use them all within a single ensemble.

Table 1. Average accuracy

Method	Avg. Accuracy
DGW	83.55
RGW	83.51
Scaling	83.99
Win. Warp	**84.06**
Inception	83.48
Ens. DGW	84.47
Ens. RGW	84.53
Ens. Scaling	84.73
Ens. Win. Warp	**85.13**
Ens. Mix	84.86
InceptionTime	84.24

In Table 1 is recorded the average accuracy for each method presented so far. We observe that all data augmentation method improve the accuracy over their competitor Inception or InceptionTime. Regarding this metric, Window Warping is provide the best results with and without ensembling.

5.2 Experiment 2

This second experiment aims to put in light the importance of the original training set. As all data augmentation methods improve the accuracy of the Inception model, is it efficient to train a model using only augmented data? We reproduced the experiment 1, with the same parameters, but only using augmented data.

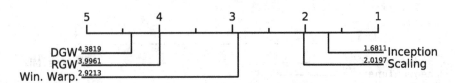

Fig. 9. CD diagram of experiment 2

Results. Figure 9 shows that all methods trained only on augmented data, performs worse than before. The vanilla Inception is significantly better than all of them. The models trained with DGW and RGW are the ones which suffer the most, with a loss in accuracy of respectively -9.63% and -7.89%.

These results underline the importance of the original data. Augmented data can not be used as a substitution of the original data but should be used as a complement.

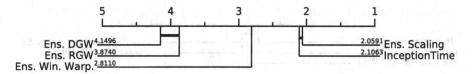

Fig. 10. CD diagram of experiment 2 with ensembling

Results with Ensembling. The previous results are also reflected with ensembling. Only the Scaling ensemble, despite not having been trained on the original data, remains competitive with InceptionTime. The intuition behind this is that Scaling produces augmented samples that are close to the original data. Thus, even without the original data, the model can still generalize over the test set.

5.3 Experiment 3

In image classification, data augmentation is randomly applied at each epoch. As the model never sees several times the same augmented sample, it improves the generalization power of the model. In this experiment we aim to apply this computer vision trick to time series by generating new data augmentation at each epoch. Except for the Discriminative Guided Warping, all presented data augmentation methods use randomness to generate the augmented sample. Thus, we can create almost an infinity of different augmented samples. We only consider the methods Scaling and the Window Warping. As explained before, DGW is not random and both Guided Warping methods are slow at runtime. Indeed, they compute warping paths using the DTW algorithm which is time consuming. Generating augmented samples once, prior to the training does not slow it much, but using them at each epoch would have taken too much time.

Results. Figure11 compares the results from the experiment 1, with their counterpart trained with data augmentation randomly generated at Each Epoch (EE). None of the results are significantly different from Inception. Window Warping seems to be the method that benefits the most from it as *Win. Warp. EE* has a better rank than *Win. Warp..* For the Scaling method, EE data augmentation provides a slightly lower rank.

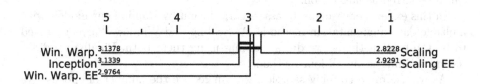

Fig. 11. CD diagram of experiment 3

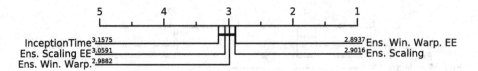

Fig. 12. CD diagram of experiment 3 with ensembling

Results with Ensembling. After ensembling, we notice that once more, Window Warping is the method that benefits the most. Once again the results with EE data augmentation do not outperform the baseline.

Table 2. Detailed results of experiment 3

Method	Avg. Accuracy
Scaling EE	83.84
Win. Warp. EE	**83.89**
Inception	83.48
Ens. Scaling EE	84.66
Ens. Win. Warp. EE	**85.05**
InceptionTime	84.24

When comparing Table 1 and Table 2 we notice that using data augmentation at each epoch results in a slightly lower average accuracy. EE data augmentation should improve the generalization power of the model if used correctly. However, our experiments did not result in significant improvements of the performances, neither in the rank or the accuracy. This shows that this trick, while being efficient in computer vision, does not work well on the UCR archive for time series.

5.4   Experiment 4

Experiment. Until now, we used the different data augmentation methods individually, only one for each training. In experiment 1, we showed that some data augmentation methods are complementary when ensembled together. This can be referred as late fusion.

In this experiment we aim to assess early fusion by training our models with multiple data augmentation methods. As Scaling and Window Warping proved to be the best methods, we did a training using them both. Finally, we did a second training using all four methods.

As we use more training samples, we can reduce the number of epochs. We decided to fix it to 300 epochs.

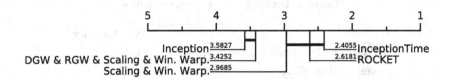

Fig. 13. CD diagram of experiment 4

Results. Figure 13 represents the results of the experiment 4. We can notice that the ensemble *Scaling&Window Warping* is significantly better than the other two methods. *DGW&RGW&Scaling&Win. Warp.* is equivalent to Inception.

This shows that the combined use of several methods can be better than the use of them independently. However the choice of the methods is important. If we use our two best methods this lead to even better results, but using all of them provides the same results as the baseline.

With this early fusion strategy, it is the first time we managed to obtain a single Inception model not significantly worse than the InceptionTime model. As InceptionTime is composed of 5 Inception models, using this training method, we can reduce the training time and the inference time by a factor 5, with similar performances.

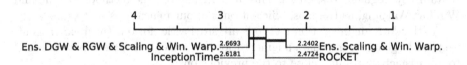

Fig. 14. CD diagram of experiment 4 with ensembling

Results with Ensembling. After ensembling, Fig. 14 shows that *Scaling&Window Warping* is still significantly better than InceptionTime. As this ensemble represent our best result, we also compared it with ROCKET. According to the CD diagram and the Wilcoxon-Holms test, we can not say that it is significantly better than ROCKET but it represents a serious competitor.

In Table 3 we can observe than the combined use of *Scaling* and *Window Warping* provides the best results across all our experiments, for both with and without ensembling.

Table 3. Detailed results of experiment 4

Method	Avg. Accuracy
DGW & RGW & Scaling & Win. Warp	83.16
Scaling & Win. Warp	**84.32**
Inception	83.48
Ens. DGW & RGW & Scaling & Win. Warp	84.18
Ens. Scaling & Win. Warp	**85.34**
InceptionTime	84.24
ROCKET	84.68

6 Conclusion

In this paper, we have shown the relevance of data augmentation for time series classification through four different experiments, each time, with and without ensembling and on the entire UCR Archive.

First, we trained an Inception classifier using the original train sets along with the augmented ones. Then, we repeated the training using only augmented data. These experiments showed the importance of the original training set. Without it, it is much harder for the model to generalize on the test sets which do not contain any augmented samples. This also highlighted the methods Scaling and Window Warping, as the most efficient ones of our benchmark.

As the data augmentation methods are stochastic, for our third experiment, we tried to generate new data augmentation at each epoch. This experience lead to unsatisfactory results, close to the previous ones.

Finally, we did trainings using several data augmentation methods at the same time. Using all four data augmentation methods was not conclusive but using only Scaling and Window Warping lead to our best results. With this method, we manage to train a single Inception model obtaining similar performances to InceptionTime. As InceptionTime is an ensemble of five Inception models, our method requires 5 times less training, and also reduces the inference time by a factor five. When ensembled like InceptionTime, this method becomes significantly better than InceptionTime. Although not significantly better than ROCKET, this method obtain a better average accuracy.

We think that data augmentation will become commonly used for time series classification but still need further improvements. As our future work, we would like to apply data augmentation to Inception and InceptionTime, but for multivariate time series. Moreover, in order to create smarter ensembles, we would like to use weighted ensembles in order to automatically choose the best combination of data augmented models.

Acknowledgment. This work was funded by ArtIC project "Artificial Intelligence for Care" (grant ANR-20-THIA-0006-01) and co-funded by Région Grand Est, Inria Nancy - Grand Est, IHU of Strasbourg, University of Strasbourg and University of

Haute-Alsace. The authors would like to thank the providers of the UCR archive as well as the Mésocentre of Strasbourg for providing access to the GPU cluster.

References

1. Dau, H.A.: The UCR time series archive. IEEE/CAA J. Automatica Sinica 6(6), 1293–1305 (2019)
2. Dempster, A., Petitjean, F., Webb, G.I.: ROCKET: exceptionally fast and accurate time series classification using random convolutional kernels. Data Min. Knowl. Discov. 34(5), 1454–1495 (2020). https://doi.org/10.1007/s10618-020-00701-z
3. Deng, J., Dong, W., Socher, R., Li, L.J., Li, K., Fei-Fei, L.: Imagenet: a large-scale hierarchical image database. In: 2009 IEEE Conference on Computer Vision and Pattern Recognition, pp. 248–255 (2009). https://doi.org/10.1109/CVPR.2009.5206848
4. Desai, A., Freeman, C., Wang, Z., Beaver, I.: Timevae: a variational auto-encoder for multivariate time series generation. arXiv preprint. arXiv:2111.08095 (2021)
5. Esteban, C., Hyland, S.L., Rätsch, G.: Real-valued (medical) time series generation with recurrent conditional gans. arXiv preprint. arXiv:1706.02633 (2017)
6. Forestier, G., Petitjean, F., Dau, H.A., Webb, G.I., Keogh, E.: Generating synthetic time series to augment sparse datasets. In: 2017 IEEE International Conference on Data Mining (ICDM), pp. 865–870. IEEE (2017)
7. He, K., Zhang, X., Ren, S., Sun, J.: Deep residual learning for image recognition. In: Proceedings of the IEEE Conference on Computer Vision and Pattern Recognition, pp. 770–778 (2016)
8. Ismail Fawaz, H.: InceptionTime: finding alexnet for time series classification. Data Min. Knowl. Disc. 34(6), 1936–1962 (2020). https://doi.org/10.1007/s10618-020-00710-y
9. Iwana, B.K., Uchida, S.: An empirical survey of data augmentation for time series classification with neural networks. PLoS ONE 16(7), e0254841 (2021)
10. Iwana, B.K., Uchida, S.: Time series data augmentation for neural networks by time warping with a discriminative teacher. In: 2020 25th International Conference on Pattern Recognition (ICPR), pp. 3558–3565. IEEE (2021)
11. Krizhevsky, A., Sutskever, I., Hinton, G.E.: Imagenet classification with deep convolutional neural networks. In: Advances in Neural Information Processing Systems 25 (2012)
12. Kuznetsova, A.: The open images dataset v4. Int. J. Comput. Vision 128(7), 1956–1981 (2020). https://doi.org/10.1007/s11263-020-01316-z
13. Le Guennec, A., Malinowski, S., Tavenard, R.: Data augmentation for time series classification using convolutional neural networks. In: ECML/PKDD Workshop on Advanced Analytics and Learning on Temporal Data (2016)
14. Lin, T.-Y.: Microsoft COCO: common objects in context. In: Fleet, D., Pajdla, T., Schiele, B., Tuytelaars, T. (eds.) ECCV 2014. LNCS, vol. 8693, pp. 740–755. Springer, Cham (2014). https://doi.org/10.1007/978-3-319-10602-1_48
15. Pialla, G., et al.: Smooth perturbations for time series adversarial attacks. In: Gama, J., Li, T., Yu, Y., Chen, E., Zheng, Y., Teng, F. (eds.) Advances in Knowledge Discovery and Data Mining. LNCS, pp. 485–496. Springer-Verlag, Berlin, Heidelberg (2022). https://doi.org/10.1007/978-3-031-05933-9_38
16. Simonyan, K., Zisserman, A.: Very deep convolutional networks for large-scale image recognition. arXiv preprint. arXiv:1409.1556 (2014)

17. Szegedy, C., et al.: Going deeper with convolutions. In: Proceedings of the IEEE Conference on Computer Vision and Pattern Recognition, pp. 1–9 (2015)
18. Terefe, T., Devanne, M., Weber, J., Hailemariam, D., Forestier, G.: Time series averaging using multi-tasking autoencoder. In: 2020 IEEE 32nd International Conference on Tools with Artificial Intelligence (ICTAI), pp. 1065–1072. IEEE (2020)
19. Um, T.T., et al.: Data augmentation of wearable sensor data for parkinson's disease monitoring using convolutional neural networks. In: Proceedings of the 19th ACM International Conference on Multimodal Interaction, pp. 216–220 (2017)
20. Wang, Z., Yan, W., Oates, T.: Time series classification from scratch with deep neural networks: a strong baseline. In: 2017 International Joint Conference on Neural Networks (IJCNN), pp. 1578–1585. IEEE (2017)
21. Wen, Q., et al.: Time series data augmentation for deep learning: a survey. arXiv preprint. arXiv:2002.12478 (2020)
22. Yoon, J., Jarrett, D., Van der Schaar, M.: Time-series generative adversarial networks. In: Advances in Neural Information Processing Systems **32** (2019)
23. Zha, M.: Time series generation with masked autoencoder. arXiv preprint. arXiv:2201.07006 (2022)

Dimension Selection Strategies for Multivariate Time Series Classification with HIVE-COTEv2.0

Alejandro Pasos Ruiz and Anthony Bagnall[✉]

School of Computing Sciences, University of East Anglia, Norwich, UK
a.pasos-ruiz@uea.ac.uk, ajb@uea.ac.uk

Abstract. Multivariate time series classification (MTSC) is an area of machine learning that deals with predicting a discrete target variable from multidimensional time dependent data. The possible high dimensionality of multivariate time series can affect the training time and possibly accuracy of complex classifiers, which often scale poorly in dimensions. We explore dimension filtering algorithms for high dimensional MTSC used in conjunction with the state of the art MTSC algorithm, HIVE-COTEv2.0. We apply and adapt recently proposed selection algorithms and propose new methods based on the ROCKET classifier built on single dimensions. We find that, for high dimensional MTSC problems, the best approach can on average filter between 50% and 60% of dimensions without significant loss of accuracy, reducing train time by a similar proportion.

1 Introduction

Time series classification (TSC) is an area of machine learning that deals with predicting a discrete target variable from time dependent data. Recently there has been a focus on a specific time series problem called multivariate time series classification (MTSC) i.e. TSC problems where each time series has more than one dimension or channel. MTSC are generally more common than univariate TSC problems, and occur in a wide range of domains such as EEG classification, human activity recognition and classification of medical sensor data. MTSC problems have the added complexity of high dimensionality, which can affect the training time and possibly accuracy of the time series classifier; redundant or highly correlated dimensions may confound the classifier. There have been many recently proposed algorithms for MSTC based on, for example, distance measures, transformation, ensembles and deep learning. A review of MTSC algorithms [18] found that there was no one approach significantly better than the others, when assessed on a benchmark set of data referred to as the UEA MTSC archive [17]. The conclusion of [18] was that an algorithm called the ROCKET [5] was recommended due to its superior speed compared to the rest of the state of the art. Subsequently, a new algorithm, HIVE-COTEv2 (HC2) [16] was shown to be significantly more accurate than all of the algorithms for MTSC evaluated

© The Author(s), under exclusive license to Springer Nature Switzerland AG 2023
T. Guyet et al. (Eds.): AALTD 2022, LNAI 13812, pp. 133–147, 2023.
https://doi.org/10.1007/978-3-031-24378-3_9

in [18], including ROCKET. HC2 represents the current state of the art for both univariate and multivariate TSC, but it does not scale well in terms of number of dimensions. Our aim is to investigate whether we can improve the efficiency (and possibly the accuracy) of HC2 for high dimensional problems using a pipeline approach of filtering dimensions prior to classification.

Standard approaches for classifying high dimensional data are to employ a filter to select a subset of attributes or to transform the data into a lower dimensional feature space using, for example, principal component analysis. Our focus is on dimensionality reduction through filtering. For MTSC, filtering is generally accepted to be selecting the most important dimensions to use before training the classifier. Dimension selection can, on average, either increase, not change or decrease the accuracy of classification. The first case implies that the higher dimensionality is confounding the classifier's discriminatory power. In the second case it is often still desirable to filter due to improved training time. In the third case, filtering may still be desirable, depending on the trade-off between performance (e.g. accuracy) and efficiency (e.g. train time): a small reduction in accuracy may be acceptable if build time reduces by an order of magnitude. We address the task of how best to select a subset of dimensions for high dimensional data so that we can speed up and possibly improve HC2 on high dimensional MTSC problems.

Detecting the best subset of dimensions is not a straightforward problem, since the number of combinations to consider increases exponentially with the number of dimensions. Selection is also made more complex by the fact that the objective function used to assess a set of features may not generalise well to unseen data. Furthermore, since the primary reason for filtering the dimensions is improving the efficiency of the classifier, dimension selection strategies themselves need to be fast. HC2 is not as fast as ROCKET. We investigate whether we can use the speed and competitive accuracy of ROCKET to serve as a dimension filter for HC2. We use a stripped back version of ROCKET to assess and select dimensions through cross validation, then measure the impact this has on HC2 on both the train and the test data. We compare the ROCKET filter to recently proposed algorithms from the literature. Our contribution is to incrementally improve our understanding of how best to classify high dimensional time series: we introduce four new high dimensional MTSC problems to the UEA archive; we propose a hybrid approach for classifying high dimensional MTSC problems using ROCKET as a filter; and we compare our approach to a range of alternative algorithms and analyze the results.

The rest of the document is presented as follows. We review current approaches for dimension selection in Sect. 2, then provide a description of the ROCKET based method in Sect. 3. Section 4 describes the new data we are adding to the archive and our experimental design, and our results are described in Sect. 5. Finally, we draw general conclusions from our experiment and highlight areas of future investigation in Sect. 6.

2 Related Work

Time series classification can be categorized based on the number of dimensions as univariate (1 dimension) or multivariate ($d > 1$ dimensions). In univariate time series classification, an instance is a pair $\{x, y\}$ with m scalar observations $(x_1, \ldots, x_m)$ (the time series) and discrete class variable y with c possible values. A classifier is a function or mapping from the space of possible inputs to a probability distribution over the class variable values. In MTSC, each observation of a time series has d dimensions (or channels), assumed to be aligned in time, so that for a single case $\{x, y\}$, $x = \{x_1, \ldots x_m\}$, where $x_j = (x_{j,1}, x_{j,2}, \ldots, x_{j,d})$. If referring to multiple cases, we denote the jth observation of the ith case of dimension k as the scalar $x_{i,j,k}$.

2.1 MTSC Algorithms

MTSC approaches are often simple extensions of univariate TSC, which is a more extensively researched field. In a review of recently proposed algorithms [18] it was found that the best performing classifiers were Random Convolutional Kernel Transform (ROCKET) [5] and HIVE-COTEv1.0 [1]. Given equality of accuracy, ROCKET was recommended as a starting point for MTSC due to its much faster build time. We use ROCKET in our filtering approach, so a brief overview of the algorithm is appropriate.

ROCKET is based on a large number of random convolution kernels (defaulting to 10,000) used in conjunction with a linear classifier (ridge or logistic regression). It is a pipeline classifier that involves transformation followed by classification. A convolution is a transformation enacted by sliding a weight vector (the convolution) across a series, vector multiplying the weights and the window at each time point to form a new value for each window. Each randomly generated convolution is applied to the time series to create a new series. The maximum value and the proportion of positive values (ppv) are derived from the transformed series and form part of a new feature set. This huge new feature space (by default, 20,000 features for each instance), is used to train the classifier, which internally performs some feature selection/weighting to ignore non-discriminatory features. ROCKET is fast because the convolutions are randomly generated and the classifiers are simple. The original ROCKET was proposed for univariate TSC. However, an approach to enable use on multivariate datasets is available in the sktime toolkit[1]. For multivariate datasets, kernels are randomly assigned dimensions. Weights are then generated for each dimension.

More recently, version 2.0 of the HIVE-COTE classifier (HC2) was shown to be significantly more accurate than ROCKET on the UEA MTSC problems. HC2 is a heterogeneous meta ensemble of four ensemble classifiers built on different data representations: the Shapelet Transform Classifier (STC) [3], the Temporal Dictionary Ensemble (TDE) [14], the Diverse Representation Canonical Interval Forest (DrCIF) [15] and the Arsenal, an ensemble of ROCKET classifiers [16].

---

[1] https://github.com/sktime.

HC2 does not scale very well for high dimensional MTSC. This led us to consider whether we could combine approaches to improve HC2 efficiency. Our aim is to find the simplest approach that speeds up HC2 on high dimensional MTSC problems without significantly decreasing accuracy. Hence, our focus is pipeline approaches that select dimensions prior to classification, rather than wrapper approaches that combine classification and selection.

2.2   MTSC Dimension Selection Algorithms

The Common principal component Loading based Variable subset selection method (CleVer) [20] algorithm is PCA based approach that is adapted for dimension selection for multivariate time series. CleVer uses PCA and clustering techniques to select dimensions. A PCA is performed independently on each instance, and the principal components are extracted. Next, all components that belong to the same class are combined to create common principal components through a process called Common Principal Component Analysis (cPCA). A proportion of the common components are used to create a feature space. These features are clustered, and the closest dimension to each centroid is chosen as selected dimensions. CleVer requires a separate PCA on each series, which is both time and space consuming. It is also complex, and we cannot find an open source implementation. Since we are looking for a lightweight feature selector, we do not evaluate CleVer in this study.

A method based around one nearest neighbour classification with dynamic time warping (1-NN DTW) is described in [10]. A merit score function (MSTS) is used to assess the quality of a subset of dimensions. The DTW distance function between cases and dimensions is precalculated. A prediction for each dimension pair is found through a three fold cross validation of 1-NN DTW. Similarity between each dimension is estimated using the adjusted mutual information (AMI) between the predictions of dimensions (dimension-to-dimension) and for the predictions of each dimension and the class (dimension-to-class). The MSTS for any subset of dimensions is a function of the average of the dimension-to-dimension and dimension-to-class AMI. A subset of features is chosen either through enumerating MSTS for all 2^d feature combinations, or using a wrapper on the top 5% of subsets. The algorithm first calculate the dimension-to-class (DC) correlation for each dimension which is the accuracy of the predictions $\hat{y}$ on train data by cross validation with 3 folds. Second, the dimension-to-dimension (DD) is calculated by the adjusted mutual information (AMI) between the predictions of each pair of dimensions. Finally, for each possible subset, the merit score function is calculated as follows:

$$MS(subset) = \frac{k\overline{DC}}{\sqrt{k + k(k-1)\overline{DD}}} \tag{1}$$

where $\overline{DC}$ is the average of dimension-to-class of each dimension in the subset and $\overline{DD}$ is the average of dimension-to-dimension of each pair of dimensions in the subset. The evaluation of all dimension combinations makes MSTS infeasible

Algorithm 1. MSTS($\boldsymbol{X}, y, |X|$)

Parameters: Training data $\boldsymbol{X}$, labels y, the number of dimensions $|X|$
1: **for** $i \leftarrow 1$ to $|X|$ **do**
2:      $\hat{y}_i \leftarrow$ CrossValidate($\boldsymbol{X}_i$, $classifier : DTW$, $folds : 3$)
3:      $\boldsymbol{DC}_i \leftarrow accuracy(\hat{y}_i, y_i)$
4: **for** (i, j) in $pairs(|X|)$ **do**
5:      $\boldsymbol{DD}_{i,j} \leftarrow AMI(\hat{y}_i, \hat{y}_j)$
6: $bestSubset \leftarrow \varnothing$
7: $bestScore \leftarrow -\infty$
8: **for each** $subset \subseteq |X|$ **do**
9:      $subsetScore \leftarrow MS(subset)$
10:     **if** $subsetScore > bestScore$ **then**
11:         $bestSubset \leftarrow subset$
12:         $bestScore \leftarrow subsetScore$
13: **return** $bestSubset$

for very high dimensional problems. MSTS has recently been applied to sensor data, and used in conjunction with ROCKET [9].

The recent research most closely aligned to our work is described in [7], where dimensions are selected based on distances between series within classes. A synthetic series that characterises each dimension/class combination is found through averaging the relevant dimension of series belonging to that class. A matrix of the pairwise Euclidean distance between all dimension/class centroids is then found. Three algorithms were proposed to use this $d \times c \cdot (c - 1)$ distance matrix for dimension selection.

1. The **KMeans** approach applies k-means clustering (with $k = 2$) on the distance matrix to separate the channels. The cluster centroid represents the mean distance of dimensions across all class pairs and the average of the centroid describes the within cluster variation of dimensions. The kmeans algorithm selects all dimensions in the cluster with the largest average.
2. The **Elbow Class Sum (ECS)** algorithm sums each row of the distance function, then uses the elbow cut method [19] to select dimensions based on the rank order of the sums.
3. The **Elbow Class Pairwise (ECP)** iterates through every class pair, selects the best set of dimensions for that pair using the same elbow cut method as ECS and finally takes the union of dimensions over all pairs.

KMeans, ECS and ECP are compared to full enumeration of dimension subsets and random selection with the accuracy of a range of TSC classifiers, including ROCKET, used to measure performance on evaluate the effectiveness on the multivariate problems in the UEA/UCR time series archive [4].

3 Dimension Selection for HIVE-COTEv2.0

We propose a range of methods for dimension selection, including adaptations of the algorithms described in Sect. 2, with the goal of making HC2 more efficient.

Our classifier pipeline involves dimension selection followed by the HC2 classifier. We want to evaluate the effect of changing the dimension selection mechanism whilst keeping everything else the same. Dimension selection is either through scoring and ranking then selection or dimension subset evaluation.

Our first filtering approach is to employ ROCKET as a mechanism for scoring features from the training data, then using the elbow method to select features. This involves scoring a ROCKET classifier on each dimension independently, then ranking dimensions. We consider three scores all based on ROCKET predictions found through three fold cross validation:

- Accuracy (A): proportion of cases correctly classified.
- Silhouette (S): As alternative to using accuracy the silhouette method used in clustering to determine the optimal numbers of clusters. It is a score that goes from -1 to 1 indicating how good is the clustering based on the distances within a cluster and their differences to the points from other clusters. To use in dimension selection, the train data is cross validated with 3 folds and the predictions are used as clusters. The formula for the silhouette method is:

$$S = \frac{(b-a)}{max(a,b)} \tag{2}$$

  where a is the mean distance between data points in the same cluster and b is the mean distance between all other data points of the next nearest cluster.
- Adjusted Mutual information (M). It is a variation of mutual information that adds an element of chance, usually used in clustering. The formula is:

$$AMI(U,V) = \frac{MI(U,V) - E(MI(U,V))}{avg(H(U), H(V)) - E(MI(U,V))} \tag{3}$$

We also consider using both ECP and ECS as a filtering algorithm for HC2. As another cluster variant, we propose that instead of calculating the centroid distances as with ECP and ECS, we calculate the distance between each instance and the centroid which is calculated as the mean vector of all instances that belong to that class. This method is called CLUSTER. Finally, we also evaluate using MSTS subset selection algorithm, although we make two changes to the version described in Sect. 2.2.

- We use ROCKET instead of DTW as classifier on line 2 of Algorithm 1;
- The exhaustive subset selection done on lines 8–12 of Algorithm 1 is infeasible for some problems, because there are 2^d possible subsets of attributes. Instead, a forward selection procedure is used where the best k subsets starting with size two are selected and one dimension is added per step until the merit score function MSTS stops improving.

Table 1 summarises the attribute selection methods used in our evaluations.

Table 1. Summary of different dimension selection ranking methods with elbow method.

Attribute ranking then selection with elbow method	
Algorithm	Ranking
ECS	Sum of difference between centroid pair distance [7]
ECP	Union of sum of individual centroid pair distances [7]
CLUSTER	Error between centroid and examples
ROCKET$_A$	Accuracy of ROCKET predictions on each dimension
ROCKET$_S$	Sillouette of ROCKET predictions on each dimension
ROCKET$_M$	AMI of ROCKET predictions on each dimension
Attribute subset selection	
MSTS	Subset selection using merit score [10]
KMeans	Cluster distance function [7]

Table 2. Summary of 15 data sets used in experimentation. (*) indicates a padded series, bold indicates a data set new to the UEA archive.

Name	Train size	Test size	Dimensions	Length	Classes
ArticularyWordRecognition	275	300	9	144	25
DuckDuckGeese	50	50	1345	270	5
EMOPain	1093	50	30	180	3
FingerMovements	316	100	28	50	2
MotionSenseHAR	217	144	12	200	6
HandMovementDirection	160	74	10	400	4
Heartbeat	204	205	61	405	2
JapaneseVowels(*)	270	370	12	25	9
MindReading	727	653	204	200	5
MotorImagery	278	100	64	3000	2
NATOPS	180	180	24	51	6
PEMS-SF	267	173	963	144	7
PhonemeSpectra	3315	3353	11	217	39
Siemens	700	395	39	180	10
SpokenArabicDigits (*)	6599	2199	13	65	10

4 Evaluation

We use the time series machine learning toolkit sktime [12] for our experiments.

4.1 Data

The UEA multivariate time series repository contains 30 datasets from a wide range of fields such as EEG classification and human activity recognition [18]. In our experience, filtering does not improve the performance of HC2, so our priority is improving efficiency. Low dimensional data can mask the performance differences of filtering algorithms, so we restrict our attention to higher dimensional problems, which we define as nine or more dimensions. Ideally, we would set the threshold even higher, but there are just nine equal length problems in the archive with nine or more dimensions. There are also two high dimensional data that are unequal length: JapaneseVowels and SpokenArabicDigits. We made these equal length by padding to the longest length. We also include four new high dimensional datasets into the archive to help improve the power of our tests of performance. These four datasets are available on the UEA archive website[2].

EMOPain: The goal of the project that generated this data was the automatic detection of pain behaviours [8] and pain levels, based on data collected from people with chronic pain performing movements that are identical to those that make up daily physical functioning. The data consist of 26 sensor calculating angle positions on distinct parts of the body and 4 electromyography sensor that have the objective of measure the electric signals generated by a muscle when is moved. The sensors are positioned on the upper fibres of trapezium and on the lumbar para spinal muscles approximately at the 4/5 lumbar vertebra.

MindReading: The data consists of MEG recordings [11] of a single subject, made during two separate measurement sessions (consecutive days). In each session the subject was watching five different movie categories without audio. The goal is to predict the category of the movie the subject is watching.

Siemens: This data consist of a group of sensors from four tanks that pumps water from a reservoir tank to three small tanks [2]. The goal is to detect the type of failure the tank is experiencing based on the value of the different sensors.

MotionSenseHAR: This dataset includes time series data generated by accelerometer and gyroscope sensors (attitude, gravity, user acceleration, and rotation rate) [13]. A total of 24 participants in a range of gender, age, weight, and height performed 6 activities in 15 trials in the same environment and conditions: downstairs, upstairs, walking, jogging, sitting, and standing. With this dataset, we aim to look for personal attributes fingerprints in time-series of sensor data, i.e. attribute-specific patterns that can be used to infer gender or personality of the data subjects in addition to their activities.

4.2 Experiments

The experiments were carried out on the High Performance Computing Cluster supported by the Research and Specialist Computing Support service at the University of East Anglia. Each classifier was trained on the same 30 train test resamples of the 15 high dimensional datasets. Build time was limited to 7 days. Our performance metric is test set accuracy. To compare multiple classifiers

---

[2] www.timeseriesclassification.com.

on multiple data sets with use ranks rather than accuracy, and we use critical difference diagrams [6] to display average ranks and cliques: a clique is a group of classifiers that are labelled as not significantly different to each other. We find cliques through pairwise comparison at the 5% alpha level with an adjustment for multiple testing commonly called the Holm correction. This adjustment is less severe than a Bonferroni adjustment: we order classifiers by rank then start with the best performing classifier as our control. We pairwise test using Wilcoxon sign-rank test in order, making the adjustment as to the maximum size of the clique. Thus, if testing 11 classifiers, the maximum number of tests to find the top clique is 10, so we require a p-value of alpha/10 to be considered significantly different. Once we find a classifier that fails the pairwise test, we form a clique of those prior to it. We then repeat the process with the second best classifier, with the caveat that if a clique is found that is contained with one found already, we ignore it.

This is the most robust way we have found to form cliques, but it can still lead to anomalies. Given three classifiers, A, B and C, where A is the highest rank and C the lowest, it is possible that A is significantly better than B but not significantly better than C. However, our approach would put A and C in different cliques. We intend to move towards a more graphical display of pairwise tests and recommend that CD diagrams should only form part of the methodology of presenting results that compare classifiers.

5   Results

Our first experiment defines the scope of further experiments by bounding our expectations as to the accuracy of filtering prior to training HC2. Figure 1 shows the ranks of full HC2, full ROCKET, HC2 with 20% of dimensions selected randomly and HC2 with 60% of dimensions selected randomly.

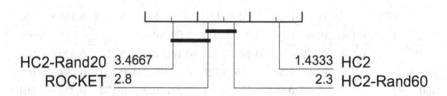

Fig. 1. Critical difference diagram for comparing ROCKET, full HC2 and HC2 with random dimension selection.

Figure 1 illustrates that HC2 is significantly more accurate than ROCKET. We reran the experiments with the sktime implementation of HC2, so this serves to recreate the results reported in [16]. HC2 is, on average, 2.5% more accurate than ROCKET, winning on 11 problems and losing on 4. By default, HC2 is not configured for speed: it takes several hours to complete one resample of experiments, whereas ROCKET takes minutes. Figure 1 also shows that our basic straw man for comparison, randomly selecting 20% or 60% of attributes, results in a significant loss of accuracy in HC2. Our second experiment addresses the question as to whether applying any of the dimension selection algorithms listed in Table 1 can speed up HC2 without loss of accuracy. Figure 2 shows the relative ranked performance of eight different filtering algorithms in addition to the four classifiers shown in Fig. 1. Cliques were formed with the p-values shown in Table 3. The average accuracy data for four classifiers is provided in Table 4, and full results are available in the associated repository.

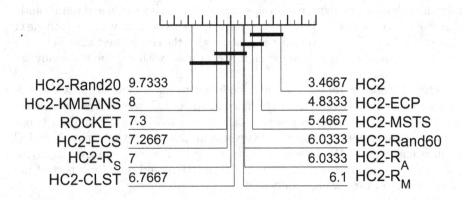

Fig. 2. Critical difference diagram for comparing all dimension selection methods proposed.

Table 3. P-values for pairwise Wilcoxon rank-sum test on 15 high dimensional MTSC problems.

	ECP	MSTS	R60	R_A	R_M	CLST	R_S	ECS	RCKT	KMNS	R20
HC2	0.753	0.198	0.004	0.011	0.016	0.019	0.004	0.096	0.041	0.048	0.001
ECP		0.256	0.272	0.173	0.246	0.124	0.140	0.011	0.100	0.020	0.015
MSTS			0.394	0.570	0.056	0.125	0.173	0.334	0.334	0.281	0.006
R60				0.551	0.551	0.041	0.272	0.246	0.173	0.233	0.001
R_A					0.975	0.096	0.158	0.433	0.307	0.233	0.004
R_M						0.246	0.397	0.551	0.496	0.496	0.015
CLST							0.331	0.510	1.000	0.691	0.140
R_S								0.925	0.910	0.158	0.002
ECS									0.532	0.683	0.061
RCKT										0.826	0.307
KMNS											0.364

Our first conclusion is that our hypothesis that ROCKET could be a good way of filtering dimensions for HC2 is not supported by these results. The three ROCKET variants are significantly worse than HC2, and no better than randomly selecting 60% of dimensions. Table 4 shows that using HC2-R$_A$ results on average in an approximate 1% decrease in accuracy. However, the two filters ECP and MSTS both achieve an accuracy rank that is not significantly worse than HC2. Table 4 shows that HC2-ECP performs very similarly to full HC2, but that HC2-MSTS may slightly reduce accuracy on average.

Table 4. Accuracy of four classifers averaged over 30 resamples of 15 high dimensional datasets.

Name	HC2	HC2-ECP	HC2-MSTS	HC2-R$_A$
ArticularyWordRecognition	**99.51**	**99.51**	99.37	99.27
DuckDuckGeese	55.07	**57.93**	55.2	54
EMO	88.78	**89.87**	89.05	88.77
FingerMovements	**55.57**	52.53	54.5	55
MotionSenseHAR	**99.71**	99.67	99.66	99.67
HandMovementDirection	41.26	**42.48**	41.53	41.89
Heartbeat	73.59	**74.29**	73.06	73.24
JapaneseVowelsEq	93.15	**94.51**	93.06	91
MotorImagery	53.63	52.77	**53.73**	53.53
MindReading	**68.36**	68.17	60.81	60.44
NATOPS	**89.04**	87.54	85.98	87.17
PEMS-SF	**99.96**	97.23	99.92	**99.96**
PhonemeSpectra	**32.01**	31.72	**32.01**	31.67
Siemens	**100**	**100**	99.92	**100**
SpokenArabicDigitsEq	**99.67**	99.62	99.64	99.63
Average	76.62	76.52	75.83	75.68
Wins	9	7	2	2

Of course, filtering will perfectly recreate HC2 results if it selects all dimensions. Table 5 shows the proportion of dimensions selected for three classifiers. On average, HC2-MSTS selects fewer dimensions, and in some cases, massively fewer. For example, with PEMS-SF[3] it selects just 13 out of 963 attributes and achieves an accuracy very close to that of full HC2. Each dimension in PEMS-SF is a single traffic sensor, and the data is measured over time. There will be high correlation between adjacent sensors, and HC2-MSTS is effective at removing a high degree of the redundancy in this data.

Similarly, with DuckDuckGeese[4], HC2-MSTS chooses just 33 of the 1345 attributes, and gets comparable accuracy to HC2, although HC2-ECP actually

---

[3] http://www.timeseriesclassification.com/description.php?Dataset=PEMS-SF.
[4] http://www.timeseriesclassification.com/description.php?
Dataset=DuckDuckGeese.

Table 5. Percentage of dimensions used.

Name	d	HC2-ECP	HC2-MSTS	HC2-R$_A$
ArticularyWordRecognition	9	100	**55.17**	57.09
DuckDuckGeese	1345	29.93	**2.48**	21.08
EMOPain	30	55.29	**31.72**	35.52
FingerMovements	28	38.18	**17.49**	50.49
MotionSenseHAR	12	86.78	**30.75**	65.8
HandMovementDirection	10	83.1	**44.14**	56.21
Heartbeat	61	15.38	**13.85**	45.56
JapaneseVowelsEq	12	75.57	97.41	**62.07**
MotorImagery	64	25.11	**6.25**	54.8
MindReading	204	61.56	**12.81**	16.23
NATOPS	24	79.31	**45.98**	63.07
PEMS-SF	963	35.03	**1.38**	13.8
PhonemeSpectra	11	**18.18**	100	59.25
Siemens	39	30.77	**10.88**	55.61
SpokenArabicDigitsEq	13	53.85	**53.85**	54.91
Average		52.54	**34.94**	47.43

Table 6. Train time in hours, including the time to filter.

Name	HC2	HC2-ECP	HC2-MSTS	HC2-R$_A$
ArticularyWordRecognition	3.80	4.13	**3.42**	3.47
DuckDuckGeese	8.16	5.34	4.09	**3.87**
EMO	23.99	17.72	12.57	**11.52**
FingerMovements	4.15	3.29	**2.98**	3.70
HAR	21.36	21.70	**12.82**	19.39
HandMovementDirection	3.63	3.55	**3.20**	3.46
Heartbeat	6.71	**3.94**	3.96	4.42
JapaneseVowelsEq	3.04	3.07	3.06	**3.00**
MotorImagery	33.06	15.35	**9.32**	26.44
MindReading	42.38	29.9	**14.06**	15.56
NATOPS	3.06	3.00	**2.70**	2.90
PEMS-SF	32.64	13.54	**5.74**	9.44
PhonemeSpectra	112.49	**68.18**	113.20	85.18
Siemens	14.96	7.70	**4.96**	10.16
SpokenArabicDigitsEq	118.89	79.21	78.59	**76.84**
Sum	432.31	279.63	**274.65**	279.33

improves on HC2 when selecting about a third of attributes. DuckDuckGeese contains audio spectrograms of different bird species, and each dimension represents a frequency range. Both HC2-MSTS and HC2-R$_A$ over filter on the problem MindReading, whereas HC2-ECP correctly selects a larger number of dimensions and achieves a similar accuracy to full HC2.

Table 6 summarises the average training time for the HC2 and the three main filtering methods, and includes the time taken to filter. There is hardly any difference in time between the three algorithms, and each method takes about 60% of the time of full HC2.

MSTS and R_A both rely on ROCKET to score dimensions, but differ primarily in how attributes are selected. It seems that the subset selection used by MSTS may be marginally better than the elbow method used by R_A, although our tests do not have the power to reject the null hypothesis that there is no difference. ECP is based on distances between predictions and rather than accuracy, and uses 1-NN DTW to make predictions. It tends to select more attributes that MSTS, but the extra time the resultant HC2 classifier takes is offset by the more time consuming components of MSTS.

Overall, these experiments show that, although there is no significant difference between HC2-ECP, HC2-MSTS and HC2-R_A, only ECP and MSTS reduce dimensionality without reducing the accuracy of HC2 significantly. Both can prove useful tools for filtering prior to using HC2 with high dimensional data, with ECP marginally preferred because it more closely recreates HC2 results.

6 Conclusion

There are of course limitations to this study. We have focused purely on the HC2 classifier, with the justification that this is the current state of the art. However, HC2 is a meta ensemble of four ensemble classifiers, each of which handles multivariate data differently. It may be interesting to explore how filtering may affect each component, and indeed other classifiers. It may be more useful to embed the dimension selection within the component classifiers to create different feature subsets for each. We have also only evaluated dimension selection algorithms. Dimension creation algorithms may also be of use in MSTC.

We have donated four new datasets to the archive, but even then we are limited to evaluation with 15 datasets. Furthermore, many of these are not genuinely high dimensional. More realistic cut off points would be 50 or 100 dimensions. MTSC data is very diverse in origin, and finding algorithms significantly better than others over all problem domains may prove unrealistic. In future work we will continue to seek out new high dimensional problems, and our intention is to focus more specifically on EEG/MEG datasets, to make our research question more specific to that problem domain.

References

1. Bagnall, A., Flynn, M., Large, J., Lines, J., Middlehurst, M.: On the usage and performance of the hierarchical vote collective of transformation-based ensembles version 1.0 (HIVE-COTE v1.0). In: Lemaire, V., Malinowski, S., Bagnall, A., Guyet, T., Tavenard, R., Ifrim, G. (eds.) AALTD 2020. LNCS (LNAI), vol. 12588, pp. 3–18. Springer, Cham (2020). https://doi.org/10.1007/978-3-030-65742-0_1
2. Bierweiler, T., Labisch, D.: Four-tank batch process in smart automation. Tech. rep. (2021). https://github.com/thomasbierweiler/FaultsOf4-TankBatchProcess

3. Bostrom, A., Bagnall, A.: Binary shapelet transform for multiclass time series classification. In: Madria, S., Hara, T. (eds.) DaWaK 2015. LNCS, vol. 9263, pp. 257–269. Springer, Cham (2015). https://doi.org/10.1007/978-3-319-22729-0_20

4. Dau, H., et al.: The UCR time series archive. IEEE/CAA J. Autom. Sin. 6(6), 1293–1305 (2019)

5. Dempster, A., Petitjean, F., Webb, G.I.: ROCKET: exceptionally fast and accurate time series classification using random convolutional kernels. Data Min. Knowl. Disc. 34(5), 1454–1495 (2020). https://doi.org/10.1007/s10618-020-00701-z

6. Demšar, J.: Statistical comparisons of classifiers over multiple data sets. J. Mach. Learn. Res. 7, 1–30 (2006)

7. Dhariyal, B., Nguyen, T.L., Ifrim, G.: Fast channel selection for scalable multivariate time series classification. In: Lemaire, V., Malinowski, S., Bagnall, A., Guyet, T., Tavenard, R., Ifrim, G. (eds.) AALTD 2021. LNCS (LNAI), vol. 13114, pp. 36–54. Springer, Cham (2021). https://doi.org/10.1007/978-3-030-91445-5_3

8. Egede, J.O., et al.: Emopain challenge 2020: multimodal pain evaluation from facial and bodily expressions. In: 2020 15th IEEE International Conference on Automatic Face and Gesture Recognition (FG 2020), pp. 849–856 (2020)

9. Kathirgamanathan, B., Buckley, C., Caulfield, B., Cunningham, P.: Feature subset selection for detecting fatigue in runners using time series sensor data. In: El Yacoubi, M., Granger, E., Yuen, P.C., Pal, U., Vincent, N. (eds) Pattern Recognition and Artificial Intelligence. ICPRAI 2022. LNCS, vol. 13363, pp. 541–552. Springer, Cham (2022). https://doi.org/10.1007/978-3-031-09037-0_44

10. Kathirgamanathan, B., Cunningham, P.: A feature selection method for multidimension time-series data. In: Lemaire, V., Malinowski, S., Bagnall, A., Guyet, T., Tavenard, R., Ifrim, G. (eds.) AALTD 2020. LNCS (LNAI), vol. 12588, pp. 220–231. Springer, Cham (2020). https://doi.org/10.1007/978-3-030-65742-0_15

11. Klami, A.: Proceedings of ICANN/PASCAL2 Challenge: MEG Mind Reading. Tech. rep. (2011). http://urn.fi/URN:ISBN:978-952-60-4456-9

12. Löning, M., Bagnall, A., Ganesh, S., Kazakov, V., Lines, J., Király, F.J.: A unified interface for machine learning with time series. arXiv preprint arXiv:1909.07872 (2019)

13. Malekzadeh, M., Clegg, R.G., Cavallaro, A., Haddadi, H.: Mobile sensor data anonymization. In: Proceedings of the International Conference on Internet of Things Design and Implementation, pp. 49–58. IoTDI 2019, ACM, New York (2019). http://doi.acm.org/10.1145/3302505.3310068

14. Middlehurst, M., Large, J., Cawley, G., Bagnall, A.: The temporal dictionary ensemble (TDE) classifier for time series classification. In: Hutter, F., Kersting, K., Lijffijt, J., Valera, I. (eds.) ECML PKDD 2020. LNCS (LNAI), vol. 12457, pp. 660–676. Springer, Cham (2021). https://doi.org/10.1007/978-3-030-67658-2_38

15. Middlehurst, M., Large, J., Bagnall, A.: The canonical interval forest (CIF) classifier for time series classification. In: 2020 IEEE International Conference on Big Data (Big Data), pp. 188–195. IEEE (2020)

16. Middlehurst, M., Large, J., Flynn, M., Lines, J., Bostrom, A., Bagnall, A.: HIVE-COTE 2.0: a new meta ensemble for time series classification. Mach. Learn. 110(11), 3211–3243 (2021). https://doi.org/10.1007/s10994-021-06057-9

17. Pasos-Ruiz, A., Flynn, M., Bagnall, A.: Benchmarking multivariate time series classification algorithms. arXiv preprint arXiv:2007.13156 (2020)

18. Ruiz, A.P., Flynn, M., Large, J., Middlehurst, M., Bagnall, A.: The great multivariate time series classification bake off: a review and experimental evaluation of recent algorithmic advances. Data Min. Knowl. Disc. 35(2), 401–449 (2020). https://doi.org/10.1007/s10618-020-00727-3

19. Satopaa, V., Albrecht, J., Irwin, D., Raghavan, B.: Finding a "kneedle" in a haystack: detecting knee points in system behavior. In: Proceedings of 31st International Conference on Distributed Computing Systems Workshops, pp. 166–171 (2011)
20. Yang, K., Yoon, H., Shahabi, C.: *CLe Ver*: a feature subset selection technique for multivariate time series. In: Ho, T.B., Cheung, D., Liu, H. (eds.) PAKDD 2005. LNCS (LNAI), vol. 3518, pp. 516–522. Springer, Heidelberg (2005). https://doi.org/10.1007/11430919_60

EDGAR: Embedded Detection of Gunshots by AI in Real-time

Nathan Morsa[1,2]([📧]) [ID]

[1] Department of Electrical Engineering and Computer Science, University of Liège,
Liège, Belgium
nathan.morsa@uliege.be
[2] Research and Development, FN Herstal, Herstal, Belgium

Abstract. Electronic shot counters allow armourers to perform preventive and predictive maintenance based on quantitative measurements, improving reliability, reducing the frequency of accidents, and reducing maintenance costs. To answer a market pressure for both low lead time to market and increased customisation, we aim to solve the shot detection and shot counting problem in a generic way through machine learning.

In this study, we describe a method allowing one to construct a dataset with minimal labelling effort by only requiring the total number of shots fired in a time series. To our knowledge, this is the first study to propose a technique, based on learning from label proportions, that is able to exploit these weak labels to derive an instance-level classifier able to solve the counting problem and the more general discrimination problem. We also show that this technique can be deployed in heavily constrained microcontrollers while still providing hard real-time ($<100\,\text{ms}$) inference. We evaluate our technique against a state-of-the-art unsupervised algorithm and show a sizeable improvement, suggesting that the information from the weak labels is successfully leveraged. Finally, we evaluate our technique against human-generated state-of-the-art algorithms and show that it provides comparable performance and significantly outperforms them in some offline and real-world benchmarks.

Keywords: Event detection · Time series classification · Preventive maintenance · Deep learning · Weak labels · Label proportions · Resource-constrained devices

1 Introduction

1.1 Motivation for Electronic Shot Counters

In recent years, the defence industry has seen an increasing interest in preventive and predictive maintenance. In the context of infantry firearms, the number of rounds fired is the prime contributor to their deterioration. Thus, keeping track of the number of rounds fired is an important part of weapon maintenance as it allows a quantitative measure of wear and tear. While this operation has

T. Guyet et al. (Eds.): AALTD 2022, LNAI 13812, pp. 148–166, 2023.
https://doi.org/10.1007/978-3-031-24378-3_10

historically been done through logbooks updated manually by operators, these are prone to human error and can prove unreliable. Entries might be omitted or subject to inaccurate estimations. The introduction of electronic shot counters to individual weapons allows for much more accurate tracking of weapon usage. These devices are either clipped on or embedded in the firearm and usually rely on MEMS accelerometers, measuring in particular, the acceleration in the firing axis to provide shot detection and counting, burst rate evaluation, and ammunition type discrimination. This allows armourers to perform more accurate maintenance of their inventory by both prioritizing weapons in most need of maintenance and potentially skipping those which have not been operated since their previous maintenance. In addition, the maintenance can more reliably be performed in a data-driven, predictive manner. Modern firearms maintenance guidelines can be broken down into manufacturer-provided estimations for individual parts or components given as an average lifespan in amounts of shots. This allows the armourer to replace those parts preemptively, avoiding potential firearms malfunction during operation. This change in maintenance paradigm is estimated to save up to 50% on armourer labour time, increase weapon availability up to 90%, and reduce operating costs by up to 20%. [3]

While some shot counters employ different types of sensors, our proposed method should be equally applicable to any temporal data from one or a combination of sensors. Although microphones are a popular method of shot counting in controlled environments such as shooting ranges, they require exposing an external sensor that is not compatible with military requirements for weapons which include prolonged exposure to hostile environments such as water, salt, dust, grease or acid. They also suffer from echoes in enclosed environments requiring frequent recalibration. Magnet-based methods have shown very effective; however, the requirement for close proximity to the firing mechanism is often a cause for concern due to either encumbrance or safety reasons. They also require more expensive parts. As a result, accelerometer-based solutions have been preferred by the defence market as these can be fully and invisibly embedded in any part of the weapon, in particular grips and handles, which are often hollow and separated from the firing mechanism.

1.2   Counting Problem

The problem of counting the number of shots in a time series lies firstly in detecting relatively-rare individual events from unrelated ones, such as normal weapon manipulations or falls on hard ground interspersed in-between shots. We illustrate some example inputs in Fig. 1. Example #1 shows a shot that is followed in close proximity by a purely mechanical event which should not be counted. Example #2 illustrate other non-shot events. In addition, shots need to be discerned from each other for proper counting and the start of each one properly identified for burst rate evaluation. However, shots can present a wide variety of signatures depending on external factors (see Sect. 3). Example #3 shows shots fired with the same weapon as #1 presenting differing signatures both from #1 and from each other even though they happen in close succession. Example #4 shows how shots can blend into each other rendering individual detection difficult, with the common occurrence of a mechanical event also blending in at the end of a burst. Mechanical events visually very similar to shots also happen in close proximity. Examples #4, 5 and 6 are taken from different weapons and show how the signature can significantly differ between them.

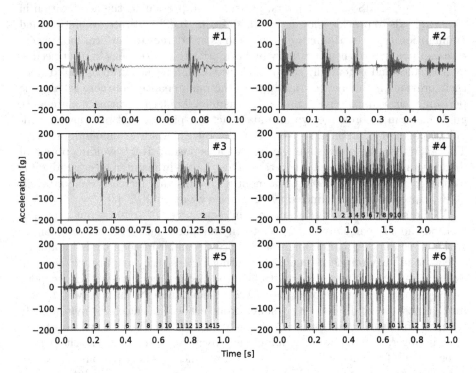

Fig. 1. Example inputs (high resolution available in digital version). Events have been individually labelled by a human expert between shot in green (numbered at the bottom) and non-shot in red. (Color figure online)

1.3   The Case for Machine Learning

As the market for shot counters develops, requests for new types of shot counters have increasingly high requirements and lower accepted lead time. Nowadays, clients of the defence industry expect a higher grade of personalisation, including modifications impacting the core design of the weapon and necessitating new R&D work. On the other hand, fast product delivery is also more and more expected in an increasingly competitive market. This has led to a fundamental restructuring of the manufacturing processes from make-to-stock to assemble-to-order and even engineer-to-order strategies.

In recent public tenders of the firearms market, shot counters have progressively become an important criterion in the attribution process. It is thus growingly important for shot counters to be available with very low delay, ideally at the latest when the weapon prototype is delivered to the client for initial testing so that the shot counter can be evaluated alongside its platform. However, since a shot counter can only be developed when at least one corresponding weapon design prototype is available, the window of time left for development between the end of the weapon R&D work and the first delivery can be slim, sometimes in the order of a few weeks. Combined with the increasing complexity of the many existing weapon variants leading to a correspondingly high required development time as described in Sect. 3, the current techniques of manually written algorithms can result in a failure to meet the market.

The automatisation of the shot counting algorithm generation aims to alleviate this issue by trading labour time from a qualified expert to computation time, which can be scaled through cloud computing according to urgency. In addition, automatically-generated algorithms have been shown to outperform and replace human-generated ones in some situations. However, as further described in Sect. 2, there is currently no publicly available generic technique for automatically deriving shot counting algorithms.

1.4 Contributions

Our paper makes the following contributions:

- We describe a procedure allowing one to use a single-axis accelerometer to construct a dataset representative of a firearm's behaviour with minimal work related to data labelling through weak labels only.
- We propose a new technique that is able to exploit these weak labels to derive an instance-level classifier able to solve the counting problem and the more general discrimination problem.
- To our knowledge, we are the first to propose a neural network structure suitable to solve this problem in real-time on embedded microcontrollers.
- We propose a series of generic and domain-specific improvements to the base technique allowing it to reach much higher performance levels.
- We evaluate our technique against a state-of-the-art unsupervised algorithm and show a very large improvement, suggesting that the information from the weak labels is successfully leveraged.
- We finally evaluate our technique against human-generated state-of-the-art algorithms and show that it provides comparable performance and significantly outperforms them in some offline and real-world benchmarks.

2 Related Work

Owing to the specific nature of the problem and the relatively recent industry interest in embedded shot counters, publicly available academic research on this specific problem is scarce. FN Herstal owns several international patents on the topic since 2006. In particular, one covers the use of successive events in accelerometer data for the purpose of shot counting [4] and has likely hindered further research into exploiting this signal. Loeffler [7] and Reese [11] limit themselves to low scale and sampling frequency, are restricted to a few shots and do not make use of machine learning. Ufer et al. [14] offer a calibration technique on a pre-made expert algorithm. Calhoun et al. [1] propose a method for gunshot detection involving deep learning; however, this technique is aimed solely at acoustic detection (not counting) from a network of city-wide microphones and involves a human in the loop.

Inspiration could be gleaned from the richly studied domain of fall detection. For example, Putra et al. [10] study accelerometer-based fall detection by decomposing the impact into sub-events in the time domain, thereby showing similarities with our problem and applying machine learning techniques. A recent paper by Santos et al. [12] applies deep-learning techniques to this same problem and proposes a CNN with good results when using data augmentation techniques. These approaches however rely on strongly labelled data.

A recent patent application by Weiss et al. [15] for Secubit Ltd. details concurrent work aimed at using deep-learning for shot counting from accelerometer data, facultatively augmented by other sensors. The method proposed in this work differs from the Weiss et al. patent in many aspects:

- A concrete proposition is made for the model structure, data preprocessing, effective input vector selection, dataset construction, training process and an effective method for ammunition type discrimination.
- Our work proposes an innovative technique allowing us to leverage the low-effort data about the number of shots contained in a time series. This allows efficient learning directly from the input dataset in its whole variance without the need for potentially unrepresentative GAN-synthesized data.
- Our technique shows performance best with an input vector significantly smaller than the normal event length.
- Our technique can be entirely performed in an embedded device in real-time, requiring no intermediate representation to be stored and/or transferred.
- The Weiss et al. proposition does not make a concrete description of how their technique can be employed in an embedded device, apart from the flow control system and mentioning possible optimizations through graph pruning and knowledge distillation. Our technique bypasses the need for these optimizations by directly training a network adapted to the target platform.

3   Dataset Acquisition and Construction

For a given model and calibre of firearm, the following external variables are known to have a significant impact on the weapon behaviour: shooting sequence, ammunition type, ammunition load, gas-operated reloading nozzle size, shooter position/mounting mechanism, mounted accessories weight, ammunition loading type, usage of a suppressor, shooting angle, weapon and canon temperature, firearm dirtiness, and firearm wear and tear (by including both new and used weapons).

To acquire a dataset representative of the whole spectrum of possible real-life weapon behaviours, one would ideally have to record and control these external variables independently. However, the number of variables and the large space of possible values for each of them can rapidly lead to an unmanageable number of combinations. As a result, a discrete and possibly reduced number of significantly differing settings for each variable will be chosen according to expert armourer knowledge of the weapon and existing experimental results. A reduced number of combinations will then be chosen according to the development budget, attempting to capture both nominal and extreme behaviours of the weapon.

Raw data can be acquired by recording the sensor output while operating the weapon. However, the labelling of this data presents a significant challenge: Creating strong labels identifying the position of individual shots in the data requires the intervention of a firearms expert to discern shots from unrelated acceleration events. This is a very labour-intensive task and is prone to human error. On the other hand, weak labels in the form of a total number of shots fired in a given recording can be produced cheaply and reliably by manually counting the number of rounds used, especially when these come in pre-numbered containers such as ammunition boxes and magazines.

4   Proposed Method

To exploit our dataset, we need to find a technique allowing us to work from the weak labels. This can be accomplished by finding a way to reformulate the counting problem into a category proportion problem. To do so while keeping a detector with suitable time and space constraints for embedded use, two hypotheses are made:

1. A shot has a finite and known maximum duration.
2. At least one sub-event of a shooting event can always be reliably distinguished from the background noise.

Hypothesis 1 is related to the length of the candidate windows that will be considered. Since it imposes no maximum bound on the duration, a sufficiently large number will always exist to satisfy it. However, larger numbers will negatively impact the performance of the resulting detector. A good number can be easily derived from the minimum theoretical burst rate of the weapon.

Hypothesis 2 allows us to reduce the number of candidate windows that will be considered. It is done by producing candidate windows only when a certain metric is satisfied, preventing useless computations during rest periods where the only input is background noise. The difference between metric and detector is that the metric is not subject to any constraint on the number of false positives it provides. However, a metric with fewer false positives will further reduce the computation time. It is important that the metric avoids false negatives, which would result in a valid candidate not being presented to the detector.

Satisfying hypothesis 2 in practice will depend on the nature of the input signal. For the most common input signal of accelerometer time series, we propose the use of a rolling average on the instantaneous accelerations squared:

$$m[t] = \frac{1}{w} \sum_{i=-w/2}^{w/2} (a[t + i + o])^2 \tag{1}$$

where $a[t]$ is the input acceleration time series, w is a positive integer hyperparameter for the size of the metric window, and o is an optional integer offset that can be applied to shift the position of the metric relative to the input signal.

The input signal and metric are illustrated in Fig. 2. It can then be compared against the high (T_H) and low (T_L) thresholds, whose values are hyperparameters of the model. A candidate would, for example, only be generated when the signal dipped below T_L and increased above T_H.

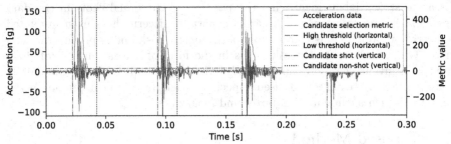

Fig. 2. Example of candidate generation on an ideal input.

Each candidate defines a slice of the input series of a fixed size determined according to Hypothesis 1 at most. In practice, experiments have shown that similar or better classification performance can be obtained with a significantly smaller input vector. A smaller input vector has a major benefit regarding inference-time performance.

Let N be the number of categories of inputs to classify. The classification categories can be arbitrarily decided as long as their number of occurrences can be known for each input series. In the simplest case, a database could be classified as *non-shot* or *shot*, leading to $N = 2$. A more complex example would be classifying between *non-shot, shot with live ammunition*, and *shot with training ammunition* leading to $N = 3$. Shot types could then be further subdivided according to whether or not they include a suppressor with $N = 5$. Given a time series including a shooting sequence with different counts c_i with $i \in \{1, ..., N\}$ being the number of occurrences of each event category. Let its division into candidate slices be $\mathbb{X}$. We can then define event proportions between the known number of events of a certain category and the total number of candidates as $p_i = \frac{c_i}{|\mathbb{X}|}$. A machine-learning-based classifier $f_\theta(\mathbf{x})$ with trainable parameters θ can then be run on each candidate input vector, attempting to classify it into its corresponding category. The resulting predictions over a given time series can then be aggregated into proportions as follows:

$$\hat{\mathbf{p}} = \frac{1}{|\mathbb{X}|} \sum_{\mathbf{x} \in \mathbb{X}} f_\theta(\mathbf{x}) \tag{2}$$

The two proportions can then be compared according to a label proportion technique such as the one described by Tsai et al. [13] to tune the trainable parameters θ to optimal values. In particular, the related part of the loss function will be:

$$\mathcal{L}_{prop} = -\sum_{i=1}^{N} \mathbf{p}_i log(\hat{\mathbf{p}}_i) + \sum_{i=1}^{N} \mathbf{p}_i log(\mathbf{p}_i) \tag{3}$$

The second term is an original addition allowing the loss function to converge to 0 in the case of perfect predictions (i.e., when $\hat{p} = p$). Without it, the minimal achievable loss has different values depending on the ratio of the different proportions. This makes the comparison of loss values across different inputs more meaningful, as well as their aggregation in an average loss over the dataset. Average loss can be viewed as a smooth metric of model quality, whereas the model accuracy can only take discrete values, corresponding to a discrete number of counting errors. This enables us to monitor the model learning evolution more precisely and employ early stopping techniques based on the average loss on the validation dataset. Comparative experiments have shown that its addition provides increased numerical stability and prediction accuracy.

In theory, this formulation does not guarantee the expected assignation of predicted classes in the edge case where the proportion of some of them are systematically equal ($\mathbf{p}_i = \mathbf{p}_j$) in every sample of the training set. However, this is not a practical concern as the natural variability in the number of occurrences of each class will quickly break any potential tie and allow the model to converge appropriately. In addition, it is generally easy to obtain samples containing only non-shot data or a single class of shot data thereby providing some heavily skewed samples preventing this problem from occurring.

This technique allows us to train a model from our weak aggregated labels. Note that our proposed method only relies on a particular definition of the loss function while not imposing any constraints on the type or structure of the model. A proposed model for embedded usage is described in Sect. 4.2, but can be swapped for other types of neural networks or machine learning techniques as long as it is able to train from such a loss function.

4.1 Minimum Cycle Time

An important factor limiting the performance of the technique, as previously described, appears when the metric generates two candidates very close in time. The model will receive two very similar input vectors, different slices of the same shot, which it is likely to both classify as being a shot, leading to false positives in the counting as a typical firearm is only able to shoot one projectile at a time in a cycle. However, we could leverage the known information of the minimum cycle time of the weapon to alleviate these false positives. For example, the modern Minimi 5.56 specifications allow a maximum firing rate of 950 rounds per minute (rpm), corresponding to a 63 ms average cycle time. Since this burst rate can be slightly exceeded in exceptional situations and individual cycle times might vary, it is necessary to incorporate a margin of error over that theoretical number. A value of 40 ms (corresponding to a theoretical cycle rate of 1500 rpm) has been used in our experiments.

While we could consider filtering out candidates at the metric level, at this step, we do not yet know which candidate the model would usually classify as a shot. Doing so thus risks removing the candidate closest to the actual shot ignition in favour of one before or after it. This could lead to non-detections and would diminish the model's ability to precisely identify the position of the shot in the time series. A better approach is to apply this filtering after the network predictions. We first change successive *shot* predictions to *non-shot* if they fall within an exclusion window of the first prediction. Experimental data (see Sect. 5.2) show that this already leads to a significant reduction in error rate. In addition, we can avoid performing model inference on the ignored predictions leading to an overall computational performance increase in deployment. A drawback of implementing this as a post-processing step is that the model has no knowledge of it and remains penalized during training for the duplicate predictions. This might produce a model overall unnecessarily "reluctant" to predict shots. In other words, one can assume that if the model had knowledge of this post-filtering, it would not hesitate to predict a shot for slightly offset candidates, knowing that it would not be penalized for duplicate predictions. We can accomplish this during training by implementing Algorithm 1, which corrects the predictions while ensuring the duplicates do not take part in the loss computation. This process is performed in an iterative fashion since a masked-out shot prediction must not itself create a mask. Redefining Eq. 2 to substitute $f_\theta(\mathbf{x})$ by $f'_\theta(\mathbf{x})$ will then prevent backpropagation for the masked-out predictions. This leads to another significant reduction in error rate in experiments.

Algorithm 1. Remove duplicate predictions in training

Require: t_i: timestamp for each candidate $\mathbf{x}_i$.
Require: T_M: minimum event duration
Require: $f_\theta(\mathbf{x})$: instance-level classifier with trainable parameters θ,
Require: e: vector corresponding to a non-shot prediction with maximum certainty

$\quad \hat{\mathbf{y}}_i \leftarrow \max_{1 \le k \le N} f_\theta(\mathbf{x})_{i,k}$ $\qquad\qquad\qquad$ ▷ Individual category predictions
$\quad \mathbf{m}_i \leftarrow \top$ $\qquad\qquad\qquad\qquad\qquad\qquad\quad$ ▷ Mask to be computed
$\quad$ **for** $i = 1, ..., |\mathbf{x}|$ **do**

$$\hat{\mathbf{y}}'_j \leftarrow \begin{cases} \hat{\mathbf{y}}_j, & \text{if } \mathbf{m}_j \\ 0, & \text{if } \neg\mathbf{m}_j \end{cases}, j \in \{1, ..., |\mathbf{x}|\}$$

$\qquad$ **if** $\hat{\mathbf{y}}'_i$ predicts a shot **then**
$\qquad\qquad$ update$_j \leftarrow (t_j \le t_i) \vee (t_j > t_i + T_M), j \in \{1, ..., |\mathbf{x}|\}$
$\qquad\qquad$ $\mathbf{m} \leftarrow \mathbf{m} \wedge$ **update**
$\qquad$ **end if**
$\quad$ **end for**

$$f'_\theta(\mathbf{x})_j \leftarrow \begin{cases} f_\theta(\mathbf{x})_j, & \text{if } \mathbf{m}_j \\ e, & \text{if } \neg\mathbf{m}_j \end{cases}, j \in \{1, ..., |\mathbf{x}|\}$$

$\quad$ **return** $f'_\theta(\mathbf{x})$

4.2 Model Structure

We have chosen to implement our model as a convolutional neural network (CNN) inspired by the one described by Santos et al. [12], as described in Fig. 3.

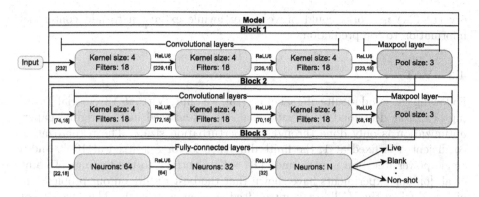

Fig. 3. Neural network structure for an input size of 232. Convolutions do not use strides nor padding. The input size and number of convolution channels depends on the application and the available computational budget.

The illustrated model totals only 33242 parameters, as we look for a small model suitable for real-time embedded inference.

The original ReLU activations have been changed to ReLU6 to make the network more suitable for quantization. ReLU6 activation bounds the values, limiting their possible range. This allows us to use a fixed point representation with more bits allowed to the fractional part, reducing the quantization artefacts and improving overall accuracy. Results outside the scope of this paper have shown the difference in error rate before and after quantization to be reduced both in median and variance when applying ReLU6 activations.

In testing, the maximum value of 6 has shown to produce the best median results, whereas ReLU2 has shown the best best-case performance. Since 6 is not a power of 2, the full [0; 6] range does not quantize efficiently, needing up to 3 bits for the integer part while not making full use of them. However, we speculate that even when the distribution of activation values uses the full range, only a low percentage of values actually falls near the bounds. Better performance can thus be achieved in those cases by only quantizing a 2-bit range around the average, saturating the outliers but leaving one more bit to be used in the fractional part.

As previously mentioned, this paper focuses on the definition of a loss function allowing the leveraging of our weak labels independently of the trained model type. This network serves as a basis proving the viability of the technique on heavily constrained hardware, and the derivation of the optimal model structure will be the subject of future research. While our small model and dataset sizes allow for relatively fast training, we plan on exploring how MINIROCKET [2] could enable us to further reduce it thereby allowing a faster exploration of the hyperparameter space. With proper hardware support, spiking neural networks could also be a good candidate for this type of application. While this work focuses only on instance-level information, long short-term memory (LSTM) networks could prove a worthwhile extension to add contextual information to the prediction.

4.3 VAT

Following the good results of Tsai et al. [13], we apply Virtual Adversarial Training (VAT) as described by Miyato et al. [9]. As advised in the original paper, optimization is only done through the perturbation size ϵ. The regularization coefficient α is fixed at 1, the finite difference factor ξ is fixed at 10^{-6}, and a single power iteration is performed ($K = 1$). Contrary to the findings of Laine et al. [6], our experiments have shown that the best results on our problem are obtained when the VAT loss is introduced as soon as possible. Thus, we do not include any ramping up to the VAT loss component.

5   Experiments

5.1   Methodology

We chose to evaluate the technique on two firearms: the FN Minimi® 5.56 and the FN® M2HB-QCB. The Minimi was selected due both to its availability for in-depth testing and its reputation of being a notoriously difficult weapon to provide counting algorithms for due to its very wide number of possible configurations. In addition, the weapon tends to show low-information signals in some configurations due to its heavy weight regarding the low-power 5.56 ammunition. The M2 was selected as a contrast to the Minimi, being on the higher end of ammunition power and using a completely different action mechanism.

External variables considered for the Minimi were: ammunition type (live/blank), barrel size (short/long), accessory weight (none/3kg accessories), gas-operated reloading nozzle size (minimal/nominal/maximal), shooter position (shoulder/bipod/waist), and firing sequence (semi-automatic, three to six rounds bursts, 4-1-4-1 bursts, full bursts). Data were acquired in groups of ~15 rounds. Non-shot data acquisition includes: dry firing, 1.5m falls onto concrete, opening and closing the top cover, full reloading manipulation, and user randomly bumping the weapon. In addition, similar data were also acquired on the Minimi 7.62.

External variables considered for the M2 were: ammunition type (live/blank), the weight of ammunition belt (minimal belt/100 rounds belt), mount (tripod, fixed mount, elastic mount, deFNder® teleoperated station), and firing sequence (manual rearming, single rounds in automatic mode, 3–6 rounds bursts, 4-1-4-1 bursts, full bursts). Data were acquired in groups of ~10 rounds. Non-shot data acquisition includes: dry firing, rearming and releasing the mobile parts, opening and closing the top cover, and user randomly bumping the weapon.

In all cases, input that contains firing incidents (weapon malfunctions) is rejected. To evaluate the final performance of the algorithm, a validation dataset is split from the input dataset. To ensure that the validation set captures the behaviour of the firearm in a wide range of situations, the input series are first sorted into different bins for each available combination of external variables. The validation set is then constructed by randomly sampling 10% of the data in each bin, rounding in favour of the validation set. The composition of the different datasets is shown in Table 1. Note that the number of non-shot events is not exactly known. This is firstly because there is no easy and reliable way to provide weak labels for these data, meaning we have to rely on operator estimations. In addition, a significant number of non-shot events is also acquired as part normal shooting tests as the operator has to manipulate the weapon before and after firing sequences for both practical and safety purposes. These are unaccounted for in our count. Thus, we only provide a lower bound on the number of non-shot events. A measure of their actual number can be gained from the total number of candidates generated by the preprocessing.

The real-world distribution between shots and non-shots is also unknown, as this will heavily depend on the end user and their doctrine. For example, some users will frequently manipulate the weapon without shooting during training and/or perform dry firings and safety checks before or after shooting, and transport it in vehicles generating significant vibrations. Other users will leave the weapon mostly in storage, and do a minimal number of manipulations around the shooting. We thus evaluate these separately, by including in the firing samples only the minimal number of manipulations and safety checks around the shooting (which also generates unavoidable non-shot candidates due to the inherent behaviour of the weapon). Other non-shot events are ideally sampled separately so that a measure of the number of false positives generated during weapon manipulation can be given. These will be given in the "non-shot only" rows of the following section.

Table 1. Summary of the number of shots per dataset.

	Minimi 5.56		Minimi 7.62		M2	
	Learning	Validation	Learning	Validation	Learning	Validation
Live	4461	1785	4707	1800	5263	729
Blank	2130	719	943	348	4238	529
Non-shot events	>400	>55	>97	>35	>1550	>180
Candidates (total)	14857	5494	12029	2355	60844	8096

Randomly initialized neural networks are then trained in groups of 20. Optimization is done through stochastic gradient descent with fixed 0.9 Nesterov momentum. The learning rate is reduced by a factor of 2 for every 20 epochs without improvement larger than 10^{-5} on the validation loss. A learning phase is stopped if 40 epochs occur without any improvement on the validation loss. Learning occurs in three phases: an optional pre-training phase on a wider dataset, normal training on desired firearm's dataset, and quantization-aware training on the same dataset. After each phase, the best model is selected according to the lowest number of validation errors, then the lowest validation loss in case of a tie and proceeds to the next phase or final evaluation. The resulting network is quantized to eight bits and runs on the target platform through the TFLite for Microcontrollers framework accelerated by the CMSIS-NN [5] library.

To iteratively optimize the different hyperparameters, we start by optimizing individually the preprocessing hyperparameters starting with w from Eq. 1, the associated thresholds T_H and T_L and the network input vector length. We then proceed to optimize the learning rate and VAT perturbation size ϵ. The model can then be reduced according to the desired performance/computational budget tradeoff by reducing the number of convolution channels. A second round of fine-tuning can then be applied. The model shows a single minimal error rate for all hyperparameters, which can thus be optimized by bisection until the minimum is found. The only exception is w which has been shown to produce several local minima requiring a more thorough exploration within the acceptable computational budget. The details of the hyperparameter survey are outside the scope of this article and will be included in a future paper. The values used for our experiments are reports in Table 2.

Table 2. Chosen preprocessing and EDGAR hyperparameters.

Hyperparameter	Minimi 5.56 (#1)	Minimi 5.56 (future)	M2
$|x|$	232	232	360
w	5 ms	5 ms	5 ms
T_H	30	114	114
T_L	10	90	90
Filters	18	18	64
Learning rate	0.002	0.002	0.0032
VAT ϵ	5	5	5

For the Minimi, pre-training is performed on the 5.56 and 7.62 datasets. For the M2, pre-training is performed on all three datasets. Acquisition and testing are done on a custom hardware platform, including a 64 MHz Cortex-M4F microcontroller and a ±200g, 6400 Hz MEMS accelerometer.

Due to technical limitations of our current data collection setup, the extraction of samples currently requires the intervention of a trained technician on the shooting range making it significantly more expensive than autonomous counting operation. As a result, we have chosen to test the final performance of our method in this fashion pending the acquisition of truly independent test datasets.

As detailed in Sect. 2, no ML-based approach or device is currently publicly available for our problem. While the domain of time series classification is well studied, as described in Sect. 3 the lack of labels for individual shots prevents us from using supervised techniques. As a baseline, we include for comparison a method of unsupervised clustering on the candidates based on deep learning:

Deep Temporal Clustering (DTC) as described by Madiraju et al. [8]. Hyperparameters have been fine-tuned following a similar procedure and are reported in Table 3, and pre-training is also applied.

Table 3. Chosen preprocessing and DTC hyperparameters.

Hyperparameter	Minimi 5.56	M2
$|x|$	232	360
w	5 ms	5 ms
T_H	126	114
T_L	119	90
Distance metric	CID	CID
α	17.5	1
γ	90	1
Batch size	64	64
Pool size	4	8
Kernel size	96	10
Filters	50	50

For the human baseline, we compare our technique with FN SmartCore® shot counters, which share the same hardware and sensor, running algorithms generated by human firearm experts. These work by first detecting discrete shocks in the input signal. They then attempt to interpret groups of shocks as sub-events of a firing cycle (such as feeding, locking, firing or rearming) by considering their relative energies, timings, directions and the duration of "calm zones" in-between [4]. These devices have been commercially available since 2012 and are available for a wide range of machine guns and assault rifles.

5.2 Performance

In this section, we examine the performance of our technique on both the validation datasets and real-world testing. Since we are dealing with weak labels, we are unable to verify model predictions at the instance level. Models are evaluated through their error rate, which we define as the sum of the counting differences (category by category) for all time series, divided by the real total count. More formally, we define the error rate E as:

$$E = \frac{\sum_{i,j} |\hat{\mathbf{c}}_{ij} - \mathbf{c}_{ij}|}{\sum_{i,j} \mathbf{c}_{ij}} \tag{4}$$

where c_{ij} is the count of shots (or, if applicable, other countable events) of type i for time series j and $\hat{\mathbf{c}}_{ij}$ is the one estimated by the model.

A model that always predicts non-shots will have an error rate of 100% by this definition. In practical applications, non-shots constitute the majority of candidates (see Table 1). In these conditions, a model that always predicts shots will have an error rate over 100% (**119%** for the Minimi 5.56 and **544%** for the M2 datasets). We can expect applications with a larger class imbalance between non-shots and shots to show a higher base error rate due to the increased number of false positives, denoting a harder problem for shot counters. Note that we could also define the error rate compared to the total number of candidates, resulting in smaller error rates but with identical relative levels for a given dataset.

Another interesting baseline is a classifier that predicts shots randomly according to the relative frequency of shots to non-shots in the learning set, which would be the most trivial exploitation of the weak labels over a random predictor. While such a model would report a fairly accurate total count in identical benchmark situations, it would vary wildly on individual inputs. This is detected in the error rate: the weighed random model obtains $E = \mathbf{31.5\%}$ for the Minimi 5.56 and $E = \mathbf{37.5\%}$ for the M2. Note that since the class imbalance depends on the external conditions and usage, practical applications or different datasets are likely to have a different class distribution which would make such a model increasingly inaccurate. Such a model would also produce a large number of false positives during non-shot usage, which is highly undesirable.

In the experimental results of this section, we also mention (in smaller print) the raw counting result, which is the metric eventually used by the armourer and allows for some desirable error compensation. This also lets the reader know how many real shots an error rate is based on.

Minimi 5.56. Table 4 compares our method with DTC and the human-generated algorithm. Real-world testing (model #1) was performed in similar conditions but with different weapons and sensors. Since then, we have found better values for hyperparameters T_H and T_L, which significantly improved performance, and report the results of this model as "future" as it has not yet undergone real-world testing. The machine-learning model runs in 65ms/inference on our testing platform and the preprocessing runs in 22 μs/sample. It uses 41 kB of program memory and has peak usage of 11 kB of RAM.

We observe that the model significantly outperforms not only the unsupervised baseline but also the human-generated algorithm on the validation set and that the "future" model is even able to obtain a perfect score. The expert model shows better performance in real-world testing on a previously unseen weapon and sensor. We believe this is due to the validation set over-representing extreme cases compared to the nominal-case real-world test. Our machine learning model shows a slightly degraded error rate, falling behind the expert model, but still remains well below the threshold for commercial viability ($E < 5\%$). We assume that this difference is mainly due to an input distribution shift to which the machine learning model is sensitive. In particular, we discovered that our dataset for this weapon did not accurately reproduce the moment at which

Table 4. Error rates and reported count of Minimi 5.56 algorithms on the validation set and during real-world testing, broken down by ammunition type.

	Human		EDGAR			DTC
	Valid.	Real	Valid. (model #1)	Real (model #1)	Valid. (future)	Valid
Live	2.07%	0.41%	0.17%	2%	0%	9.2%
	1752/1785	1205/1210	1788/1785	404/400	1785/1785	1841/1785
Blank	0.69%	0.74%	0.28%	0.75%	0%	11.4%
	714/719	1201/1210	719/719	403/400	719/719	795/719
Total	**1.68%**	**0.58%**	**0.20%**	**1.37%**	**0%**	**9.82%**
Non-shot only (false positives)	30/>55	0/>100	0/>55	6/>100	0/>55	34/>55

our accelerometer starts sampling in practical situations, leading to a slight difference in inputs for the first shot of a burst.

In addition, some false positives were detected. This is not a surprising result as this weapon is notoriously difficult to filter out false positives for, as attested by the result of the expert algorithm on the validation set. We believe that increasing their representation in the learning set would alleviate this issue.

M2. The M2 weapon platform provides a special firing mode allowing the user to manually control the weapon cycle, ensuring only single shots are possible. This functionality fundamentally alters the weapon cycle and, so far, human-generated algorithms have not been able to support it without suffering from a significant number of false-positives. These are currently completely ignored by existing shot counters. With this experiment, we have attempted to solve this problem by training and testing the neural network on the whole dataset, including 20% of samples using this functionality. Results are compared in Table 5. In addition, the M2 platform offered us the unique possibility of mounting two counters in parallel, thus providing directly comparable results.

The machine-learning model runs in 87ms/inference on our testing platform and the preprocessing runs in 22 µs/sample. It uses 52 kB of program memory and has peak usage of 14 kB of RAM.

Following the Minimi results, a greater emphasis was put on including non-shot data in the learning set. This seems to have proven successful as no false-positives have been detected during transport, setup, normal manipulations and over 80 supplementary manipulations and dry firings.

On the validation set, the human-generated algorithm obtains a perfect score on the partial dataset but rises to a 16% error rate when including manually rearmed shots. The EDGAR model shows satisfactory performance ($E < 5\%$) on the partial and full datasets by obtaining a stable 2% error rate on both.

Due to the larger class imbalance of this dataset causing it to report many more false positives, the unsupervised baseline performs very poorly on this dataset and does not manage to beat the previously described weighed random model. This interpretation is supported by the non-shot data on which the DTC

Table 5. Error rates and reported count of M2 algorithms on the validation set and during real-world testing, broken down by ammunition and mount types.

Fixation	Ammun.	Full-auto only					Full-auto + Manual rearm				
		Human		EDGAR		DTC	Human		EDGAR		DTC
		Valid.	Real	Valid.	Real	Valid.	Valid.	Real	Valid.	Real	Valid.
Tripod	live	0%	0%	0%	12%	23%	16%	20%	1%	10%	25%
		160/160	40/40	160/160	35/40	153/160	160/190	40/50	188/190	45/50	193/190
	blank	0%	0%	0%	20%	38%	20%	18%	2%	22%	62%
		160/160	40/40	160/160	32/40	159/160	160/200	40/49	195/200	38/49	262/200
Fixed	live	0%	0%	5%	0%	58%	13%	20%	4%	4%	56%
		209/209	40/40	203/209	40/40	275/209	209/239	40/50	229/239	48/50	318/239
	blank	0%	0%	2%	17%	36%	24%	20%	1%	26%	41%
		130/130	40/40	131/130	33/40	101/130	130/170	40/50	169/170	37/50	159/170
Elastic	live	0%	0%	1%	0%	26%	18%	20%	1%	10%	26%
		140/140	40/40	139/140	40/40	160/140	140/170	40/50	169/170	45/50	185/170
	blank	0%	6%	6%	7%	39%	19%	26%	5%	10%	41%
		129/129	75/80	121/129	37/40	157/129	129/159	75/101	151/159	91/101	182/159
deFNder	live	0%	0%	0%	0%	30%	6%	22%	0%	8%	42%
		110/110	39/39	110/110	40/40	103/110	122/130	39/50	130/130	46/50	144/130
Average		**0%**	**1%**	**2%**	**8%**	**36%**	**16%**	**21%**	**2%**	**13%**	**42%**
Non-shot only (false positives)		$\frac{0}{>110}$	$\frac{0}{>80}$	$\frac{0}{>180}$	$\frac{0}{>80}$	$\frac{314}{>180}$	$\frac{0}{>180}$	$\frac{0}{>80}$	$\frac{0}{>180}$	$\frac{0}{>80}$	$\frac{314}{>180}$

model reports (multiple) shots for every weapon manipulation, which would be unacceptable for practical use. We thus show a large improvement from this baseline.

Real-world testing shows performance falling for both algorithms, especially the machine-learning model rising to 8%. Results on the ammunition discrimination problem outside the scope of this paper suggest that this is at least partly due to a distribution shift in the input, which affects the machine learning model more significantly. Due to equipment availability constraints, only one weapon and three sensors were used to construct the dataset, while testing was done on brand-new, unseen weapons and sensors. Despite this, when including manually rearmed shots, the machine-learning model still shows overall better performance than the human-generated one.

We assume that supplementary testing on a more diverse batch of weapons and sensors could significantly improve the real-world performance of the model.

Breakdown of Performance Improvements. In Fig. 4, we compare the performance of incremental improvements to the base method as discussed in Sect. 4. We start with the base technique. As we move to the right we successively add improvements, conserving all previously enabled ones. Hyperparameters are

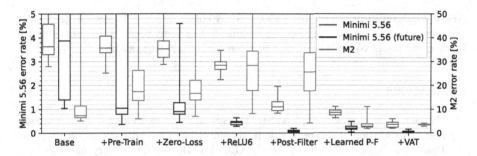

Fig. 4. Effects of incremental improvements. Each box represents the error rate of 20 randomly initialized models on the validation set.

identical to those used to obtain the experimental results in the previous sections. Some models fail to converge at all, especially when zero-loss is disabled; these are treated as 100% error rate and explain the high maximums of some boxes.

We first enable pre-training, add our second term of Eq. 3 in "Zero-Loss", and replace ReLU activations with ReLU6 (see Sect. 4.2). We then enable simple post-filtering (see Sect. 4.1), add our implementation of Algorithm 1 in "Learned P-F", and finally enable VAT (see Sect. 4.3).

6 Conclusion and Future Work

In this study, we have presented an approach that successfully learns an instance-level shot classifier from a weakly-labelled dataset, which we believe opens the way for new machine-learning applications. We showed that it significantly improves predictions from the unsupervised baseline by successfully exploiting the information from weak labels. We also showed that it outperforms human-generated algorithms in most offline testing, reach commercially acceptable levels of performance in real-world testing and are able to solve previously unanswered problems. We expect this to save several weeks of development time per product and enable increased customisation to specific platforms thus further increasing performance. Finally, we showed that our technique could yield models giving this level of performance in real-time on microcontrollers while using less than 14kB of RAM and 87 ms per inference. In the future, we aim to bring real-world performance closer to the one obtained on offline benchmarks by improving the data collection technique and taking systematic measures against input distribution shifts. Outside the scope of this paper, our technique has also shown consistent better-than-human performance on the ammunition discrimination problem. It is already being deployed for that purpose in commercial applications. We hope to bring to light these results and the associate technique improvements in a further study.

Acknowledgements. I would like to thank my colleague Louis Huggenberger for his continuous help in data acquisition. I would like to thank my thesis supervisors Hugues Libotte and Louis Wehenkel for their precious advice and suggestions.

References

1. Calhoun, R.B., Lamkin, S., Rodgers, D.: Systems and methods involving creation and/or utilization of image mosaic in classification of acoustic events (2019)
2. Dempster, A., Schmidt, D.F., Webb, G.I.: MINIROCKET: a very fast (almost) deterministic transform for time series classification. In: Proceedings of the 27th ACM SIGKDD Conference on Knowledge Discovery & Data Mining, pp. 248–257 (2021). https://doi.org/10.1145/3447548.3467231
3. FN Herstal, S.A.: Small arms management: break free of paper chains with a smart, digital armory. White paper (2020)
4. Joannes, R., Delcourt, J.P., Heins, P.: Device for detecting and counting shots fired by an automatic or semi-automatic firearm, and firearm equipped with such a device (2010)
5. Lai, L., Suda, N., Chandra, V.: CMSIS-NN: efficient neural network kernels for arm cortex-m CPUs. arXiv:1801.06601 [cs] (2018). https://doi.org/10.48550/arXiv.1801.06601
6. Laine, S., Aila, T.: Temporal ensembling for semi-supervised learning. arXiv:1610.02242 [cs] (2017). https://doi.org/10.48550/arXiv.1610.02242
7. Loeffler, C.E.: Detecting gunshots using wearable accelerometers. PLoS ONE **9**(9), 1–6 (2014). https://doi.org/10.1371/journal.pone.0106664
8. Madiraju, N.S., Sadat, S.M., Fisher, D., Karimabadi, H.: Deep temporal clustering : fully unsupervised learning of time-domain features. arXiv:1802.01059 [cs.LG] (2018). https://doi.org/10.48550/arXiv.1802.01059
9. Miyato, T., Maeda, S.I., Koyama, M., Ishii, S.: Virtual adversarial training: a regularization method for supervised and semi-supervised learning. arXiv:1704.03976 [cs, stat] (2018). https://doi.org/10.48550/arXiv.1704.03976
10. Putra, I.P.E.S., Brusey, J., Gaura, E., Vesilo, R.: An event-triggered machine learning approach for accelerometer-based fall detection. Sensors **18**, 20 (2017). https://doi.org/10.3390/s18010020
11. Reese, K.A.: A situational-awareness system for networked infantry including an accelerometer-based shot-identification algorithm for direct-fire weapons. Master's thesis, Naval Postgraduate School (2016)
12. Santos, G.L., Endo, P.T., de Carvalho Monteiro, K.H., da Silva Rocha, E., Silva, I., Lynn, T.: Accelerometer-based human fall detection using convolutional neural networks. Sensors **19**, 1644 (2019). https://doi.org/10.3390/s19071644
13. Tsai, K.H., Lin, H.T.: Learning from label proportions with consistency regularization. CoRR abs/1910.13188 (2019). https://doi.org/10.48550/arXiv.1910.13188
14. Ufer, R., Brinkley, K.L.: Self calibrating weapon shot counter (2014)
15. Weiss, I., Hyden, I., Ami, M.: Device system and method for projectile launcher operation monitoring (2021)

Identification of the Best Accelerometer Features and Time-Scale to Detect Disturbances in Calves

Oshana Dissanayake[1,2]([✉]), Sarah McPherson[2,3,4], Emer Kennedy[2,3],
Katie Sugrue[3], Muireann Conneely[3], Laurence Shalloo[2,3],
Pádraig Cunningham[1,2], and Lucile Riaboff[1,2]

[1] School of Computer Science, University College Dublin, Dublin, Ireland
oshana.dissanayake@ucdconnect.ie
[2] VistaMilk SFI Research Centre, Cork, Ireland
[3] Teagasc, Animal and Grassland Research and Innovation Centre, Moorepark,
Fermoy, Co., Cork P61C997, Ireland
[4] Animal Production Systems Group, Wageningen University and Research,
P.O. Box 338, 6700 Wageningen, The Netherlands

Abstract. While human activity has received much attention in time-series analysis research, animal activity has received much less attention. The monitoring of cattle in Precision Livestock Farming is a promising application area as it is reasonable to expect that cattle will be equipped with low-cost sensors for animal welfare reasons. In this paper, we present work on feature selection to detect disturbance in calves such as diseases or stressful events from accelerometer sensors attached to a neck-collar. While the long-term objective is to generate an alert when a disturbance is detected, the work presented here focuses on identifying the most discriminating accelerometer features to detect activity changes associated with a calf stressful event. For that purpose, we used accelerometer data from 47 calves who were dehorned at 16 days $\pm$ 10 days, a routine procedure known to be painful and stressful for calves. We calculated 7 primary features that could change after an occurrence of a disturbance, within a 24 h period before and after dehorning for each calf, falling under the areas of energy expenditure and the structure of the calf activity. These features were explored under 17 time-scales from 1 s to 24 h to find the best time-scale associated with each feature. First filtering with Mutual Information (MI) and Gini index was applied to reduce the candidate set of features for the second features selection with Random Forest Features Importance (RFFI). Performance were evaluated with Random Forest, k-Nearest Neighbor and Gaussian Naive Bayes models on test-sets to assess the relevancy of the selected features. Performance of all classifiers is improved or maintained when features from MI and Gini selection are used but decreased when further feature reduction with RFFI is applied. Therefore, based on MI and Gini selection, the most discriminating features are linked to activity peaks (maximum), amount of dynamic behaviors (standard-deviation) and activity structure (spectral entropy, Hurst exponent) with time-scales ranging from 1 s to 24 h depending on the features, which is consistent with animal welfare literature.

T. Guyet et al. (Eds.): AALTD 2022, LNAI 13812, pp. 167–180, 2023.
https://doi.org/10.1007/978-3-031-24378-3_11

Keywords: Feature selection · Accelerometer time-series data · Animal welfare · Calves · Disturbance detection

1   Introduction

New decision tools are emerging in the context of Precision Livestock Farming (PLF) to improve the efficiency of livestock management [1] and the monitoring of health and welfare [2]. Especially, PLF greatly encourages the development of tools to detect any disease or stressful events in livestock [3]. Early detection would improve animal health and welfare as requested by consumers [4], but would also reduce the costs of treatment for the farmer when it is necessary.

In dairy cattle, several tools are already available to automatically obtain the behaviour over time, such as the time spent grazing, ruminating, resting, and detect heat events (oestrus) [5,6] but no proper tools are available to detect disturbances such as stressful events or diseases in cattle. It is also worth mentioning that no disturbance detection tools exist for calves even though they are prone to a lot of different stressful events during the first few months (separation from the mother, weaning, dehorning, transport, etc.) and vulnerable to certain diseases (neonatal diarrhoea, bovine respiratory disease, etc.) [7]. Thus, improving the welfare and health status of calves through early detection of stressful events or disease would be a major contribution to the field.

Calf activity changes when a disease or distress is experienced [7]. More resting behaviours are usually observed around the time of the diagnosis of diseases [8] while fewer dynamic behaviours such as running or playing are observed after dehorning and after separation from their dams [9,10]. Accelerometer sensors attached to a neck-collar are now used abundantly in livestock management to automatically obtain the behaviour of animals in their daily routines from raw accelerometer time-series data [11–13]. Accelerometers have the advantages of (1) being small enough not to alter the behaviour of the cattle, and (2) collecting accelerometer data over time without interruption over a long period (>1 month) as they have low battery consumption [14]. Accelerometer data collected from a neck collar seems therefore relevant for detecting a disturbance based on a sudden change in calf activity and should be able to support the development of a stress or health event detection model.

Energy expenditure and activity structure are both likely to change after a disturbance in calves [15,16]. Accelerometer features can thus be computed from the raw accelerometer data to account for these two components. Indeed, features like mean, median, standard deviation, motion variation and maximum are related to the energy expenditure levels while features like entropy and fractal patterns are informative about the structure of activity. Such features could thus be used as inputs to a Machine Learning (ML) model to detect disturbances. To develop such a ML model, it is first required to identify the accelerometer features that are altered after a disturbance and that are therefore the most promising for discriminating a normal situation from a disturbed one in calves.

In this context, the objective of this study is to identify the best accelerometer features and the relevant time-scales to detect a disturbance in calves. Especially, we focused on the disturbance related to dehorning, a procedure carried out routinely in farming to comply with Regulations under the Diseases of Animals Act (1966) which prohibits the sale or export of horned animals [17]. Dehorning is known to be stressful and painful in calves [16,18] and is therefore used as a disturbance model to select features in our study.

2   Background Research

2.1   Animal Welfare

2.1.1   Energy Expenditure A decrease of the energy expended by calves can be expected when experiencing a disease. For example, calves with a respiratory disease lay for longer and tended to have longer lying bouts a few days before the diagnosis and during the peak of the disease [8]. Similarly, Hixson *et al.* [15] applied an experimental disease challenge model with *Mannheimia haemolytica (MH)* in group-housed Holstein bull calves and observed less activity following inoculation with MH.

A drop in overall activity level may also be observed after stressful events. An increase in the time spent lying, combined with a decrease of the time spent running, jumping [19] and playing [10] is for example observed in the following days after the separation of the calves from their dams. In the same way, calves may spend more time lying down in hours following dehorning [20,21] and less time playing [9], running or walking [19]. Such a change in the amount of time spent expressing these behaviours may lead to an overall decrease in the energy expended by the calves after these stressful events.

2.1.2   Structure of the Activity An alteration of the activity structure in calves experiencing disease is also expected. Indeed, Hixson *et al.* [15] observed a decrease in grooming, feeding and social interactions in the MH-infected calves. This reduction in the range of expressed behaviours may lead to a loss of complexity in calf activity, as observed in other livestock species experiencing parasitic infection [22].

An alteration of the activity structure in calves after certain stressful events is also expected. Dehorned calves are highly restless in the hours following the procedure and expressed a higher frequency of abnormal behaviors such as tail flicking, head shaking and ear flicking [16,18]. Similarly, the agitation manifested by vocalisation and searching for the dam is observed in calves after separation from the mother [10,23]. These repetitive, unvarying behaviors without apparent biological function may also lead to a loss of activity complexity [22].

2.2   Feature Selection

Model development to classify livestock behavior from raw accelerometer data has been explored elsewhere [11] but only a few studies have focused on disturbance detection in livestock. Calf disturbance detection has been recently investigated from behavioral metrics (e.g., number of daily lying bouts, daily lying time) obtained either from a commercial system [24] or from a behavior classification model applied on raw-time series data [25]. However, relevancy of accelerometer features indicative of the energy expended level and the structure of the activity has never been explored. Furthermore, the focus in these studies is on disease detection and the detection of a stressful event has never been investigated. Features selection would therefore be relevant to gain knowledge about the accelerometer features that would help to address the research question. This requires to identify (i) potential accelerometer features-candidates to feed the model and (ii) a suitable pipeline to select the accelerometer features.

Several accelerometer features have already been investigated to address a similar issue in related communities. For example, the average of acceleration has already been used to classify human motion quality for knee osteoarthritis in humans [26]. Similarly, spectral entropy displayed a good ability to characterize the Parkinson posture at an early stage [27]. Stress detection in humans has also been explored with accelerometer features including statistical features and energy expenditure features with a considerable accuracy [28].

There are several ways to select features in the ML context proposed in the literature, such as filter, wrapper, embedded, hybrid, etc. Filter methods basically use statistic measures to select the best features in the pre-processing step rather than relying on the learning algorithm. This method include techniques such as Information Gain, Gini and the Chi-square metric. Advantages of using filter methods are the low computation time and they usually do not overfit the data. Wrapper methods basically consider the feature selection as a search problem. It creates different combinations of the features and evaluate the outcome in terms of classifier performance to compare it with other combinations. Forward selection, exhaustive feature selection are some of the wrapper methods. Embedded methods combine the advantages of both the filter and wrapper methods. These methods are faster and more accurate than wrappers. Regularization and regression methods such as lasso or ridge regression are some of the techniques of the embedded methods [29–31]. It is worth noting that a common limitation in model development in livestock science is the few animals available to train and validate the model, which usually leads to a drop in performance when the model is applied on new animals [11]. Consequently, features selection with Gini index or Mutual Information (MI) combined with Random Forest Feature Importance (RFFI) sounds promising mainly as we are dealing with a high amount of features and few individuals to train and validate the model [32,33].

3   Materials and Methods

3.1   Time-Series Data Collection Around Dehorning in Calves

The experiment was conducted at Teagasc Moorepark Research Farm (Fermoy, Co. Cork, Ireland; $50°07'N$; $8°16'W$) from January 21 to April 5, 2022. Ethical approval for this study was provided by the Teagasc Animal Ethics Committee (TAEC; TAEC2021-319). All experimental procedures were performed in accordance with European Union (Protection of Animals Used for Scientific Purpose) Regulations 2012 (S.I. No. 543 of 2012).

Forty-seven Holstein Friesian and Jersey calves were used for the trial. All calves were dehorned at the age of 16 ± 10 days using cauterisation and were administrated a local anaesthetic on each side of the head in the corneal nerve (Lidobel; 2 cc/side) 15 min before the procedure. AX3 dataloggers[1] were used for this trial. Activity AX3 are MEMS 3-axis accelerometers and have a flash based on-board memory (512 MB), measuring $23 \times 32.5 \times 7.6$ mm and weighting 11 g. The accelerometers were configured 25 Hz during the experiment. The 47 calves under study were equipped with a AX3 data logger attached to a neck-collar. Accelerometer data were collected from 1–4 weeks before dehorning, during the dehorning procedure, and 4–9 weeks after dehorning.

3.2   Methodology Applied to Calculate and Select Features

The pipeline of the methodology is described in Fig. 1.

3.2.1   Calculate Features from Time-Series Two periods of 24 h of data were selected for the feature selection process:

– The 24 h period immediately preceding the dehorning procedure. No disruption occurred during these 24 h. This period is therefore considered as the baseline period and labeled $D - 1$.
– The 24 h period immediately following dehorning. The disruption has just occurred and the main change in activity due to dehorning is expected at this time [21]. This period is therefore considered as the period after disturbance and labeled $D + 1$.

In each $D - 1$ and $D + 1$ period, the magnitude (see Eq. 1) was first calculated from the 3 axis-accelerometer readings to get a time-series independent of the sensor orientation. A unit value was reduced from the magnitude time-series to remove the gravitational acceleration component.

$$magnitude = |\sqrt{x^2 + y^2 + z^2} - 1| \tag{1}$$

The magnitude scalar of the activities got in pre-dehorning $(D - 1)$ and post-dehorning $(D + 1)$ phases is shown for two calves in Fig. 2.

---

[1] Axivity Ltd.; https://axivity.com/product/ax3.

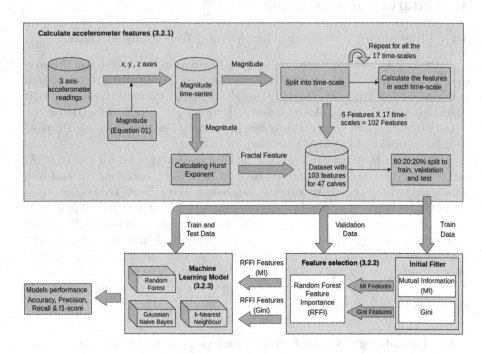

Fig. 1. Pipeline of the methodology followed.

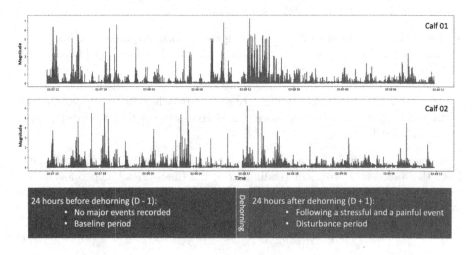

Fig. 2. Behavior of the raw magnitude time-series data in pre-dehorning (D − 1) and post-dehorning (D + 1) phases.

Magnitude time-series were then split into 17 time-scales ranging from 1 s to 24 h. Six features indicative of energy expenditure and activity structure were then calculated in each time-scale in the $D-1$ and $D+1$ periods resulting in 102 different features. The Hurst exponent fractal feature was calculated considering a 24-hour time-scale only, as proposed in Burgunder *et al.* [22]. Thus the final feature dataset consists of 103 features. The details of the features calculated are listed in Table 1.

Table 1. Main feature details

Category	Name	Meaning and Calculation
Energy level/ Activity rate	Mean	Mean of the values present within the time-scale. This feature is indicative of the overall activity level. $$A = \frac{1}{n}\sum_{i=1}^{n} a_i = \frac{a_1 + a_2 + \cdots + a_n}{n}$$
	Median	Median of the values present within the time-scale. This feature is indicative of the overall activity level. $$m(x) = \begin{cases} x_{\frac{n+1}{2}} & n \text{ odd} \\ \frac{1}{2}\left(x_{\frac{n}{2}} + x_{\frac{n}{2}+1}\right) & n \text{ even} \end{cases}$$
	Standard Deviation	Standard Deviation of the values present within the time-scale. This feature is indicative of the amount of dynamic activities of the animal. $$s = \sqrt{\frac{1}{N-1}\sum_{i=1}^{N}(x_i - \bar{x})^2}$$
	Maximum	Maximum value out of the values present within the considered time-scale. This feature is indicative of the scale of the activity peaks for the period.
	Motion Variation	A measure of the variation between the values present within the considered time-scale. This feature is indicative of the amount of dynamic activities of the animal. $MV = \text{mean}(\text{abs}(1^{st} \text{ order discrete difference of the signal window}))$
Structure of the Activity	Spectral Entropy	A measure of disorder or uncertainty. This feature is indicative of the predictability of the time-series (predictable using a few frequencies *versus* hardly predictable with many frequencies, close to a random process [35, 36]. $$SE(F) = \frac{1}{logN_u \sum_u (P_u(F)log_e P_u(F))} \quad [36]$$
	Hurst Exponent	Hurst exponent is used to classify the series as mean-reverting, random walk or as trending [37, 38]. The Hurst exponent features used here is the average of the Hurst exponent obtained with Linear Detrended Fluctuation Analysis and Bridge Detrended Fluctuation Analysis. We refer to [22, 39, 40] for more details about the Hurst exponent calculations. Fathon python package [41] was used to calculate the Hurst exponent.

3.2.2 Two Stages Feature Selection Strategy The data was split into train, test and validation data in a ratio of 60 : 20 : 20%. It was ensured that the labels $D+1$ and $D-1$ for each calf are both in one of the training set, test set or in the validation set.

Features selection was applied with a two stages pipeline (see Fig. 1). A first filter stage was applied with Gini filter and MI filter [32,33] in order to remove the least informative features thereafter. The tree-based structure of the Random Forest model is naturally ranked by how well they improve the purity of the node thus giving an idea itself about the importance of the features considered. In that way, the least informative features can be identified easily based on the features ranking. The training data was first fed into Gini and MI filters separately and the feature importance scores were calculated for each feature.

Next, the bottom 60% of features from the MI and Gini rankings were respectively removed for the rest of the features selection process. Thus, 40 features from MI and Gini filters were fed separately into the RFFI procedure with the validation dataset to obtain the RFFI ranking. This process was carried out in 10 iterations and the features that were outputted in each iteration were recorded. Next, a count of occurrence for each feature was taken and the presence value for each feature was calculated by taking the percentage of occurrences to the number of iterations.

3.2.3 Classification Performance with Selected Features To get a better knowledge of the features selected, five subsets of features were used:

- All the features: As a baseline, the 103 features were used in the training and testing data.
- Initial filtering features from MI (noted *MI* features) and from Gini (noted *Gini* features): Features leading to non-zero MI and Gini scores were used to filter out the training data and the testing data.
- RFFI features from MI (noted *MI+RFFI*) and from Gini (noted *Gini+RFFI* features): Features obtained after the first filtering with a presence value greater than the mean presence value in the RFFI process were used to filter out the training data and the testing data.

For each subset of features, Random forest (RF), K-Nearest Neighbour(k-NN) and Gaussian Naive Bayes (GNB) models were trained with the training data and the model accuracies were assessed.

4 Results

4.1 Model Performance Obtained with Each Subset of Features

Accuracy with the 103 features is above 75% for each model, with the highest achieved with the RF model (87.35%) (Fig. 3).

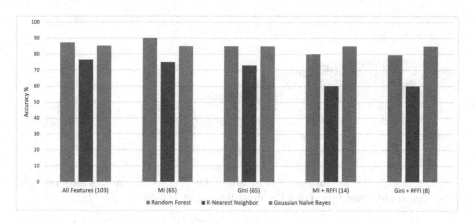

Fig. 3. Model accuracies obtained for all the features, 65 non-zero MI features, 65 best Gini features, best 14 MI + RFFI features and best 8 Gini + RFFI features.

Sixty-five features got a MI score greater than 0 over the 10 iterations (see Fig. 4). The accuracy obtained with the 65 non-zero *MI* features is similar to that obtained with all features for k-NN and GNB and even higher for RF where 90% was achieved (Fig. 3). This suggests that the subset of the 65 non-zero MI features is a relevant one to use in future work. All features got a Gini index greater than 0 over the 10 iterations (see Fig. 5). By analogy with the MI ranking, the *Gini* features used to filter out the training and testing data are the 65 best features from the Gini ranking. The top 65 *Gini* features also lead to similar accuracy to that obtained with all features for the three ML models (Fig. 3).

After removing the 60% of the least informative features based on MI and Gini ranking, RFFI procedure with 10 repetitions led to 14 *MI+RFFI* features and 8 *Gini+RFFI* features with a presence value greater than the mean presence value of the features of the subset. While the performance was maintained or improved after the first filtering with MI and Gini, a drop of performance is observed when models are trained and tested with *MI+RFFI* and *Gini+RFFI* features, especially for RF and k-NN models (Fig. 3), probably due to overfitting.

The accuracy obtained with the different subsets of features suggests that the second stage of feature selection with RFFI does not highlight the most important features and that it is therefore preferable to rely on the first stage of selection with MI and Gini filters to identify the most informative features for the future studies.

4.2 Most Informative Features Based on MI and Gini Selection

Ranking features obtained for MI and Gini selection are displayed in Fig. 4 and Fig. 5, respectively. A visual cut-off to get the most informative features (see highlighted box in Fig. 4 and Fig. 5) leads to the features selection and associated time-scales proposed in Table 2.

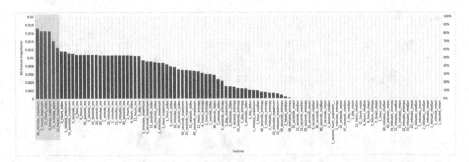

Fig. 4. Mean of MI score for each feature after 10 iterations. 65 features have non-zero MI scores. Highlighted box shows the most important features.

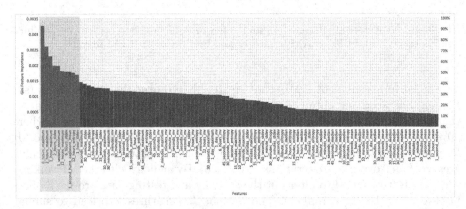

Fig. 5. Mean of Gini score for each feature after 10 iterations. Highlighted box shows the most important features

As per the Table 2, features maximum and standard deviation are both in the top rankings of MI and Gini filtered features. These features are indicative of activity peaks and amount of dynamic behaviors, respectively, which seem to be the most important components of calf activity to discriminate between a 24 h baseline period and a 24 h post-stressful event period. This is also consistent with the Fig. 2 where less peak activity appears to occur from 6 h after dehorning. The lower expression of peak activity and dynamic behaviors suggests less social behaviors such as agonistic behaviors and playing, and less maintenance behaviors such as feeding, over the day following dehorning. This finding is consistent with the calf welfare literature [9]. It is worth noting that 3 time-scales for the feature maximum are common for both the MI and Gini filters (2 h, 6 h and 12 h; Table 2), suggesting that these time-scales should be retained for the future model development. For the standard-deviation feature, there is no time-scale in common between MI and Gini. There is thus no specific time-scale to be preferred, but time-scales from 15 min to 12 h may work properly (see Table 2).

Table 2. Top features and associated time-scales obtained from MI and Gini selection based on their ranking score

Top features	Time-Scale	MI	Gini
Maximum	1 second		■
	30 minutes		■
	1 hour		■
	2 hours	■	
	6 hours	■	
	12 hours	■	
Standard Deviation	15 minutes		■
	1 hour		■
	2 hours		■
	6 hours		■
	12 hours	■	
Hurst Exponent	24 hours		■
Spectral Entropy	12 hours		■

Legend: *Cell background is in orange if the features and time-scales are included in the top ranking for the corresponding feature selection method.*

Hurst exponent with 24-hour time-scale and spectral entropy with 12 h time-scale are also in the top ranking of Gini filter, suggesting that the structure of the activity is also helpful to discriminate between a 24 h baseline period and a 24 h post-stressful event period (see Table 2). It should be noted that the decrease in spectral entropy observed in this study (*data not shown*) suggests a loss of complexity in the calf activity. Similarly, the Hurst exponent increases towards 1 in the post-dehorning period, reflecting a strengthening of the persistent trend after dehorning, and thus less stochasticity, namely less complexity. This can also be seen in the Fig. 2, as we observe a peak of activity in the 6 h after dehorning, probably due to agitation (ear flicking, tail shaking, frequent transitions between standing and lying down), followed by a period without clear activity peaks, reflecting a long and constant state of rest [9]. It is worth noting that loss of complexity of animal activity associated with pathology or stress is also consistent with the animal welfare literature [22].

Finally, mean and median features are not included in the top ranking of neither MI nor Gini. Overall activity level is thus not helpful to discriminate between a 24 h baseline period and a 24 h post-stressful event period.

5   Conclusions

In terms of insights on the problem domain, both features for energy expenditure and structure are included in the most important features with a time scale that is different from one feature to another suggesting that (i) both components of the activity must be considered and (ii) the time scale should be adapted to each feature in the final model.

In terms of the subset to be selected for the development of the model in future work, it seems that the 65 non-zero MI features are the best candidates for the moment as the addition of the second filtering stage with the RFFI procedure decreases the performance of the models. This may be due to the high correlation between features. In future work, we will evaluate correlation-based feature selection [30] and wrappers to address this issue.

Finally, the model that will be developed in the future will also have to take into account the variation of the features animal-wise, which has not been considered in the present study. It is also necessary to consider other sources of disturbances, such as diseases or other stressful procedures (e.g., weaning, transport) to develop a robust model of disturbances detection in calves. This work should contribute to the development of an intelligent model to improve calf welfare by detecting stressful events from accelerometer data, which will be a major addition to the field.

Acknowledgements. This publication has emanated from research conducted with the financial support of SFI and the Department of Agriculture, Food and Marine on behalf of the Government of Ireland to the *VistaMilk SFI Research Centre* under Grant Number 16/RC/3835.

References

1. Rutten, C.J., Steeneveld, W., Vernooij, J.C.M., Huijps, K., Nielen, M., Hogeveen, H.: A prognostic model to predict the success of artificial insemination in dairy cows based on readily available data. J. Dairy Sci. **99**(8), 6764–6779 (2016)
2. Herd monitoring-Medria. Online. Accessed 17 June 2022
3. Andonovic, I., Michie, C., Cousin, P., Janati, A., Pham, C., Diop, M.: Precision livestock farming technologies. In: 2018 Global Internet of Things Summit (GIoTS), pp. 1–6. IEEE (2018)
4. Cardoso, C.S., Hötzel, M.J., Weary, D.M., Robbins, J.A., von Keyserlingk, M.A.: Imagining the ideal dairy farm. J. Dairy Sci. **99**(2), 1663–1671 (2016)
5. Shalloo, L., et al.: A review of precision technologies in pasture-based dairying systems (2021)
6. Saint-Dizier, M., Chastant-Maillard, S.: Towards an automated detection of oestrus in dairy cattle. Reprod. Domest. Anim. **47**(6), 1056–1061 (2012)
7. Hulbert, L.E., Moisá, S.J.: Stress, immunity, and the management of calves. J. Dairy Sci. **99**(4), 3199–3216 (2016)
8. Duthie, C.-A., Bowen, J.M., Bell, D.J., Miller, G.A., Mason, C., Haskell, M.J.: Feeding behaviour and activity as early indicators of disease in pre-weaned dairy calves. Animal **15**(3), 100150 (2021)
9. Morisse, J.P., Cotte, J.P., Huonnic, D.: Effect of dehorning on behaviour and plasma cortisol responses in young calves. Appl. Anim. Behav. Sci. **43**(4), 239–247 (1995)

10. Enríquez, D.H., Ungerfeld, R., Quintans, G., Guidoni, A.L., Hötzel, M.J.: The effects of alternative weaning methods on behaviour in beef calves. Livest. Sci. 128(1–3), 20–27 (2010)
11. Riaboff, L., Shalloo, L., Smeaton, A.F., Couvreur, S., Madouasse, A., Keane, M.T.: Predicting livestock behaviour using accelerometers: a systematic review of processing techniques for ruminant behaviour prediction from raw accelerometer data. Comput. Electron. Agric. 192, 106610 (2022)
12. Swartz, T.H., McGilliard, M.L., Petersson-Wolfe, C.S.: The use of an accelerometer for measuring step activity and lying behaviors in dairy calves. J. Dairy Sci. 99(11), 9109–9113 (2016)
13. Hokkanen, A.-H., Hänninen, L., Tiusanen, J., Pastell, M.: Predicting sleep and lying time of calves with a support vector machine classifier using accelerometer data. Appl. Anim. Behav. Sci. 134(1–2), 10–15 (2011)
14. Godfrey, A., et al.: Instrumented assessment of test battery for physical capability using an accelerometer: a feasibility study. Physiol. Meas. 36(5), N71 (2015)
15. Hixson, C.L., Krawczel, P.D., Caldwell, J.M., Miller-Cushon, E.K.: Behavioral changes in group-housed dairy calves infected with Mannheimia haemolytica. J. Dairy Sci. 101(11), 10351–10360 (2018)
16. Sylvester, S.P., Stafford, K.J., Mellor, D.J., Bruce, R.A., Ward, R.N.: Behavioural responses of calves to amputation dehorning with and without local anaesthesia. Aust. Vet. J. 82(11), 697–700 (2004)
17. Earley, B., McGee, M., O'Riordan, E.G., Marquette, G.: Calf disbudding and castration (2019)
18. Faulkner, P.M., Weary, D.M.: Reducing pain after dehorning in dairy calves. J. Dairy Sci. 83(9), 2037–2041 (2000)
19. Jeffrey Rushen and Anne Marie de Passillé: Automated measurement of acceleration can detect effects of age, dehorning and weaning on locomotor play of calves. Appl. Anim. Behav. Sci. 139(3–4), 169–174 (2012)
20. McMeekan, C., Stafford, K.J., Mellor, D.J., Bruce, R.A., Ward, R.N., Gregory, N.: Effects of a local anaesthetic and a non-steroidal anti-inflammatlory analgesic on the behavioural responses of calves to dehorning. N. Z. Vet. J. 47(3), 92–96 (1999)
21. Theurer, M.E., White, B.J., Coetzee, J.F., Edwards, L.N., Mosher, R.A., Cull, C.A.: Assessment of behavioral changes associated with oral meloxicam administration at time of dehorning in calves using a remote triangulation device and accelerometers. BMC Vet. Res. 8(1), 1–8 (2012)
22. Burgunder, J., Petrželková, K.J., Modrỳ, D., Kato, A., MacIntosh, A.J.: Fractal measures in activity patterns: do gastrointestinal parasites affect the complexity of sheep behaviour? Appl. Anim. Behav. Sci. 205, 44–53 (2018)
23. Johnsen, J.F., et al.: Investigating cow- calf contact in cow-driven systems: behaviour of the dairy cow and calf. J. Dairy Sci. 88(1), 52–55 (2021)
24. Belaid, M.A., Rodríguez-Prado, M., Rodríguez-Prado, D.V., Chevaux, E., Calsamiglia, S.: Using behavior as an early predictor of sickness in veal calves. J. Dairy Sci. 103(2), 1874–1883 (2020)
25. Bowen, J.M., Haskell, M.J., Miller, G.A., Mason, C.S., Bell, D.J., Duthie, C.A.: Early prediction of respiratory disease in preweaning dairy calves using feeding and activity behaviors. J. Dairy Sci. 104(11), 12009–12018 (2021)
26. Taylor, P.E., Almeida, G.J., Kanade, T., Hodgins, J.K.: Classifying human motion quality for knee osteoarthritis using accelerometers. In: 2010 Annual International Conference of the IEEE Engineering in Medicine and Biology, pp. 339–343. IEEE (2010)

27. Palmerini, L., Rocchi, L., Mellone, S., Valzania, F., Chiari, L.: Feature selection for accelerometer-based posture analysis in Parkinson's disease. IEEE Trans. Inf Technol. Biomed. **15**(3), 481–490 (2011)

28. Garcia-Ceja, E., Osmani, V., Mayora, O.: Automatic stress detection in working environments from smartphones' accelerometer data: a first step. IEEE J. Biomed. Health Inform. **20**(4), 1053–1060 (2015)

29. Cai, J., Luo, J., Wang, S., Yang, S.: Feature selection in machine learning: a new perspective. Neurocomputing **300**, 70–79 (2018)

30. Cunningham, P., Kathirgamanathan, B., Delany, S.J.: Feature selection tutorial with python examples. arXiv preprint arXiv:2106.06437 (2021)

31. Chandrashekar, G., Sahin, F.: A survey on feature selection methods. Comput. Electr. Eng. **40**(1), 16–28 (2014)

32. Menze, B.H., et al.: A comparison of random forest and its Gini importance with standard chemometric methods for the feature selection and classification of spectral data. BMC Bioinform. **10**, 213 (2009). https://doi.org/10.1186/1471-2105-10-213

33. Vergara, J.R., Estévez, P.A.: A review of feature selection methods based on mutual information. Neural Comput. Appl. **24**(1), 175–186 (2013). https://doi.org/10.1007/s00521-013-1368-0

34. Powell, G.E., Percival, I.C.: A spectral entropy method for distinguishing regular and irregular motion of Hamiltonian systems. J. Phys. A: Math. Gen. **12**(11), 2053 (1979)

35. Devi, D., Sophia, S., Prabhu, S.B.: Deep learning-based cognitive state prediction analysis using brain wave signal. In: Cognitive Computing for Human-Robot Interaction, pp. 69–84. Elsevier (2021)

36. Qian, B., Rasheed, K.: Hurst exponent and financial market predictability. In: IASTED Conference on Financial Engineering and Applications, pp. 203–209. Proceedings of the IASTED International Conference, Cambridge, MA (2004)

37. Bărbulescu, A., Serban, C., Maftei, C.: Evaluation of Hurst exponent for precipitation time series. In: Proceedings of the 14th WSEAS International Conference on Computers, vol. 2, pp. 590–595 (2010)

38. Domino, K.: The use of the Hurst exponent to predict changes in trends on the Warsaw stock exchange. Phys. A: Stat. Mech. Appl. **390**(1), 98–109 (2011)

39. Alvarez-Ramirez, J., Alvarez, J., Rodriguez, E., Fernandez-Anaya, G.: Time-varying Hurst exponent for US stock markets. Phys. A: Stat. Mech. Appl. **387**(24), 6159–6169 (2008)

40. Bianchi, S.: fathon: a Python package for a fast computation of detrendend fluctuation analysis and related algorithms. J. Open Source Softw. **5**(45), 1828 (2020)

ODIN AD: A Framework Supporting the Life-Cycle of Time Series Anomaly Detection Applications

Niccoló Zangrando, Piero Fraternali, Rocio Nahime Torres, Marco Petri, Nicoló Oreste Pinciroli Vago, and Sergio Herrera(✉)

Department of Electronics, Information, and Bioengineering, Politecnico di Milano, 20133 Milan, Italy
{niccolo.zangrando,piero.fraternali,rocionahime.torres, nicolooreste.pinciroli,sergioluis.herrera}@polimi.it, marco.petri@mail.polimi.it

Abstract. Anomaly detection (AD) in numerical temporal data series is a prominent task in many domains, including the analysis of industrial equipment operation, the processing of IoT data streams, and the monitoring of appliance energy consumption. The life-cycle of an AD application with a Machine Learning (ML) approach requires data collection and preparation, algorithm design and selection, training, and evaluation. All these activities contain repetitive tasks which could be supported by tools. This paper describes ODIN AD, a framework assisting the life-cycle of AD applications in the phases of data preparation, prediction performance evaluation, and error diagnosis.

Keywords: Time series · Anomaly detection · Data annotation · Model evaluation · Evaluation metrics

1 Introduction

With the advent of IoT architectures, the analysis of numerical temporal data series is being increasingly applied in such industries as manufacturing and construction, in which machines, appliances, and whole systems are equipped with sensors producing timestamped numerical data streams. Applications include anomaly detection (AD) [5] whose primary focus is to find anomalies in the operation of working equipment at early stages to alert and avoid breakdowns. AD is also at the core of predictive maintenance (PdM) [29], which aims at optimizing the trade-off between run-to-failure and periodic maintenance, improving the Remaining Useful Life (RUL) of machines, and avoiding unplanned downtime. The development of an AD solution follows the typical life-cycle of a data-driven application, illustrated in Fig. 1. Such a workflow differs from that of a traditional software system because it relies on predefined parametric algorithms that must be fit to the specific task and data at hand [7].

The workflow illustrated in Fig. 1 contains many repetitive tasks. In the preparation stage, the collected data must be annotated with ground truth labels

T. Guyet et al. (Eds.): AALTD 2022, LNAI 13812, pp. 181–196, 2023.
https://doi.org/10.1007/978-3-031-24378-3_12

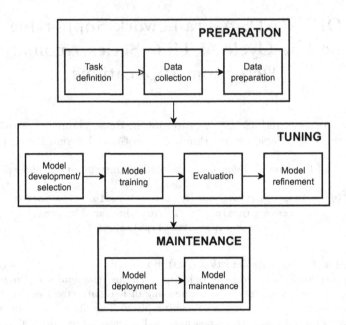

Fig. 1. Life-cycle of a data-driven application

(GT) for training and evaluation purposes. They could also be enriched with additional domain- or task-dependent meta-data, which could be exploited for performance diagnosis purposes [11]. In the tuning stage, the quality of an algorithm is assessed by computing general and task-specific prediction performance metrics. When multiple candidate algorithms are available, their performances must be compared head-to-head on the same data set. Their generalization capability must be checked too, by testing a model trained on the data from a specific source with the data of another distinct source of the same type. Model refinement also entails diagnosing the causes of prediction failures, which may require the categorization of errors into general and task-specific types, the attribution of errors to particular characteristics of the input data, and the quantification of the impact that a certain error type has on the prediction performance metrics.

All these activities are amenable to support by computerized tools. An ideal development environment should enable the data scientist to load multiple data sets and annotate each one with GT labels or with other meta-data, pick the selected algorithms from a library and execute them, and obtain per-algorithm and also comparative performances reports. In the refinement phase, it should be possible to break down the performance metrics based on user-defined criteria, classify errors with user-defined criteria, and assess the impact of the various types of errors on each metrics.

This paper presents ODIN AD, a framework supporting the development of AD applications on numerical uni- and multi-variate data series. ODIN AD offers the following features:

- Data ingestion. Temporal data series can be imported with CSV files. Existing meta-data can be imported too, in CSV format.
- Data annotation. If needed, a data set can be enriched with GT labels and custom meta-data, with a dedicated annotator GUI.
- Algorithm selection and execution. ODIN AD does not support model design and execution but lets the user import the predictions made with any algorithm into the workspace. One or more prediction CSV files can be loaded in the same analysis session.
- Model/algorithm evaluation under multiple configurations. The user can define the configuration of an evaluation session, by choosing the anomaly definition and matching strategy to use and the metrics to compute. ODIN AD implements 5 anomaly definition strategies, 4 anomaly to GT matching strategies, 7 performance metrics and 4 performance curves off-the-shelf. The users can plug in their own strategies and metrics.
- Error diagnosis. Prediction errors can be categorized with user-defined criteria and the impact of a specific type of error on the performance metrics can be quantified.
- Model/algorithm performance visualization and reporting. Prediction performance metrics can be displayed in a visualization GUI and embedded in a performance evaluation report.
- Performance comparison. The visualization and the reporting functions can be applied to a single algorithm or to multiple ones. In the latter case, the head-to-head comparison of the selected algorithms on all the chosen metrics is provided.

ODIN AD is algorithm-agnostic and designed to be extensible. Its architecture allows the integration of other input/output data formats, AD definition strategies, performance metrics, and visualization widgets.

2   Related Work

Statistical and ML algorithms are applied to temporal data series for such applications as forecasting [19], anomaly detection [3,27] and predictive maintenance [33]. The computer-based aid to AD application development mostly focuses on the evaluation phase. Benchmark data sets, such as SKAB [16] and NAB Benchmark [18], annotate data with GT labels and implement common evaluation metrics such as F1 score, NAB score, false alarm rate, and miss alarm rate.

Contributions such as [2,10,34] extend the support beyond the use of the basic performance measures in the evaluation phase. The work [2] generalizes the metrics provided by AD benchmarks by introducing the concept of Preceding Window ROC, which extends the popular ROC diagram to the case of time series. Also, the evaluation process is adapted to better fit the needs of AD algorithm assessment, e.g., by rewarding early anomaly detection. The Darts library [10] assists time series analysis in general. It implements multiple models, from ARIMA to Deep Neural Networks (DNNs). It supports uni- and multi-variate series, meta-learning on multiple series, training on large datasets, model ensembles, and probabilistic forecasting. The library is designed for usability, achieved by wrapping the underlying functions under a simple and uniform Python interface. The RELOAD tool [34] aids the ingestion of data, the selection of the most informative features, the execution of multiple AD algorithms, the evaluation of alternative anomaly identification strategies, the computation of performance metrics, and the visualization of results in a GUI. RELOAD implements multiple metrics and algorithms off-the-shelf and has an extensible architecture. However, it does not support yet the breakdown of performance metrics by user-defined criteria and the characterization of errors.

The PySAD tool [32] supports AD application development on streaming data. It comprises pre-processors for data normalization and enables the execution of AD models and of model ensembles. It also features post-processors to transform model scores for learning purposes. Its evaluator module includes multiple AD metrics (e.g., precision, recall, and window score) and a wrapper to adapt Sklearn metrics so as to allow extensibility. Other tools, such as TagAnomaly [23], Curve [1] or TRAINSET [13], focus mainly on the data preparation step. They let developers annotate anomalies but do not offer the possibility to add meta-data to them. The Wearables Development Toolkit (WDK) [9] is a framework for the analysis of time series produced by wearable and IoT devices. It supports the annotation, the analysis, and the visualization of time series and the performance assessment of activity recognition algorithms.

In the specific field of intrusion detection, the work [22] describes CyberVTI, a client-server tool for AD in network time series. CyberVTI incorporates multiple state-of-the-art unsupervised algorithms and helps the analyst inspect their performances with different parameters. It supports the phases of data ingestion, data preparation, in which the imported data are validated, feature engineering, in which the features are selected, extracted, and normalized, and processing, in which the AD algorithms are executed.

All the mentioned tools that support the evaluation step restrict performance assessment to a few standard metrics. The use of DNNs for AD [3] is evidencing the limits of such a basic approach. DNNs have a complex architecture which makes their behavior hard to understand and debug. This characteristic demands more informative approaches to error diagnosis and model refinement. One possibility is to exploit the semantic richness of time series, which are characterized by many properties (e.g., the sampling frequency, the stationarity, and periodicity of the series, the type and physical characteristics of the signal and of the corresponding acquisition sensor). Such an abundance of significant input properties could be exploited to enable the breakdown of performance indicators and to correlate the errors with specific features of the input and with user-defined categories. The exploitation of data series semantic features, beyond those used for training, and the characterization of errors in user-defined categories are distinctive capabilities of ODIN AD.

3   ODIN AD

In this section we illustrate the main functionalities of ODIN AD. The running example employed to produce the diagrams and the visualizations exploits the time series of the REFIT data set, specifically the fridge consumption data series of house 1 [26]. The GT labels used to compute the performance metrics have been created by three independent annotators. The algorithms used to produce the diagrams are GRU-autoencoder and LSTM-autoencoder [4,20].

3.1   Data Ingestion, Analysis, and Preparation

ODIN AD lets the user import the time series data, the GT labels, and the semantic input annotations. The artifacts follow the formatting guidelines common to most public datasets. Temporal series are imported as CSV files with a timestamp identifier followed by the feature values; GT data are encoded in JSON files listing the timestamps at which anomalies occur; input properties can be imported as CSV files with a timestamp identifier and a column per property.

When the GT labels are not available, ODIN AD lets the user define them with the anomaly annotator GUI shown in Fig. 2. An anomaly is created by selecting a point or an interval on the time axis. Anomalies can be annotated with user-defined meta-data, which can be inserted and/or modified with the annotator GUI. In Fig. 2 the custom annotations refer to a user-defined categorization of the anomalies. The anomaly annotations of the running example include: *Continuous OFF state*, when the appliance is in the low consumption state for a long time, *Continuous ON state*, when the appliance is in the consumption state for an abnormally long time, *Spike*, when the appliance has an abnormal consumption peak, *Spike + Continuous*, when the appliance has a consumption peak followed by a prolonged ON state, *Other*, when the anomaly does not follow a well-defined pattern.

Anomalies and their annotations can be deleted, updated, and exported to a CSV file.

When the same time series is annotated by more than one user, ODIN AD supports the analysis of the inter-annotator agreement over the anomalies and their associated properties, with the help of the diagrams shown in Fig. 3.

In addition to the manually provided properties, ODIN AD supports the automatic extraction of properties from the data series, so as to speed up the annotation process. The current version of ODIN AD implements some basic property extractors: hour of the day, day of the week, month, and duration. The user can add her own extractors to automatically compute custom and domain-dependent properties. As an example, a custom extractor is implemented to automatically derive the anomaly annotations shown in Fig. 2. The user can display and validate or modify the automatically extracted proposals in the annotator GUI. In this way, the GT semantic labeling process is accelerated. Figure 4 shows the distribution of the GT anomalies across the *duration* and *anomaly type* properties of the time series.

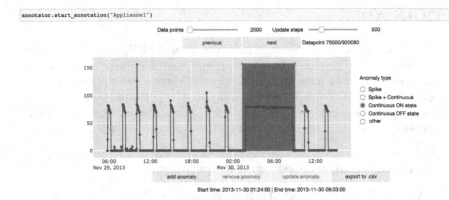

Fig. 2. The interface of the GT anomaly annotator at work on the running example time series. The user can specify the anomalies and add meta-data to them. The user has annotated the currently selected GT anomaly, shown in red, with the *Continuous ON state* label. (Color figure online)

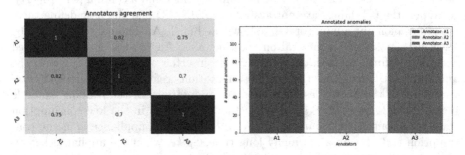

Fig. 3. Diagrams of the inter-annotation agreement: the annotator consensus diagram (left) shows the percentage of data points that are classified in the same way by each pair of annotators. The GT anomalies histogram plots the number of anomalies (points or intervals) created by each annotator.

The temporal data series can be pre-processed before the application of AD algorithms. ODIN AD currently implements the following pre-processors: the stationarity pre-processor, implemented with the Dickey-Fuller test [6], the periodicity pre-processor, implemented with the Fast Fourier Transform method [15], and the seasonality, trend and residual decomposition pre-processor [12]. Residuals decomposition can be done with an additive model (addition of the decomposed values restores the original times series) or with a multiplicative one (the original series is obtained by multiplying the decomposed values). ODIN AD also supports data transformations. The input time series and the output predictions can be manipulated using *scalers*. The current version of ODIN AD implements some predefined scalers (MinMaxScaler, StandardScaler) and can be extended with user-defined ones.

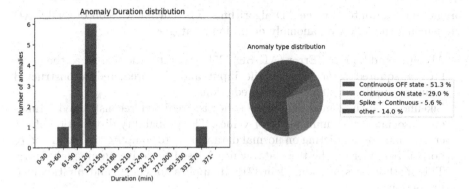

Fig. 4. ODIN AD shows the annotated anomalies in the running example time series distributed by the automatically extracted *duration* property (left) and by the manually refined *anomaly type* property (right).

3.2 Execution

AD algorithms are executed outside ODIN AD and their output is imported into an analysis session. Depending on the AD approach, predictions can be structured as follows:

– If the AD algorithms exploits classification (e.g., OneCLassSVM, LocalOutlierFactor, Isolation Forest), for each timestamp the prediction contains the confidence score.
– If the AD algorithms exploit forecasting (e.g., ARIMA, LSTM) or reconstruction (e.g., LSTMAutoencoder, GRUAutoencoder) the prediction file can contain one value per timestamp (single-valued prediction) or multiple values per timestamp (multi-valued prediction). The latter case is relevant for the methods that exploit a sliding window (e.g., GRU, Autoencoder-based), which assign a different predicted/reconstructed value to the same data point based on the window used to compute the prediction.

3.3 Evaluation and Refinement

ODIN AD supports the assessment of anomaly detectors under multiple anomaly definitions and matching strategies and performance metrics.

Anomaly Definition Strategies. An anomaly definition strategy specifies the way in which the data points of the input time series are compared with the predicted or reconstructed points of the anomaly detector in order to infer whether a point or an interval is anomalous. Each strategy takes in input a pair of entities to compare (points and/or sets of points) and returns a score value s or a score vector s interpretable as the confidence with which the prediction is considered an anomaly. Different strategies can be adopted for the types of predictions computed by the AD algorithms. The current version of ODIN AD implements the following anomaly definition strategies:

- Absolute and Squared Error (AE/SE) [25]: computes the score s as the absolute or squared error between the input and the predicted/reconstructed value. It applies to single-valued predictions.
- Likelihood: each point in the time series is predicted/reconstructed l times and associated with multiple error values. The probability distribution of the errors made by predicting on normal data is used to compute the likelihood of normal behavior on the test data, which is used to derive an anomaly score. This method was introduced in [21]. It applies to single- and multi-valued predictions.
- Mahalanobis: as in the likelihood strategy, each point in the time series is predicted/reconstructed l times. For each point, the anomaly score s is calculated as the square of the Mahalanobis distance between the error vector and the Gaussian distribution fitted from the error vectors computed during validation [20]. It applies to single-valued and to multi-valued predictions.
- Windows strategy: the strategy computes a score vector $\mathbf{s}$ of dimension l associated with each point. Each element s_i of the score vector is the MAE (by default) or the MSE of the i-th predicted/reconstructed window that contains the point [17]. It applies to multi-valued predictions.

The AE, SE, Gaussian, and Mahalanobis strategies compute an anomaly score s. A threshold τ is then applied to such a value for classifying the point as normal or anomalous. The Windows strategy computes an array of anomaly scores and in this case, a point is considered anomalous if each element of the array is above the threshold.

Anomaly Matching Strategies. An anomaly matching strategy specifies the way in which an identified anomaly is compared to the GT, so as to categorize it as a true positive (TP), false positive (FP), true negative (TN), and false negative (FN). ODIN AD implements four strategies:

- Point to point: each anomalous point is compared only to the corresponding data series point using the GT label.
- Interval to interval: the Intersection over Union (IoU) metrics is calculated between the GT anomaly interval and the predicted anomaly interval and a threshold τ is applied to categorize the prediction (IoU $> \tau$ qualifies a TP). By default, the threshold is set to 0.5, but it can be modified.
- Interval to point(s): each predicted anomalous interval is considered a TP if it contains at least X GT anomaly points. By default, X is set to 50% of the interval points.
- Point to interval: each predicted anomaly point is considered TP if it lies within the boundaries of a GT anomaly interval.

Metrics. ODIN AD implements the basic time series metrics and diagrams (accuracy, precision, recall, F1 score, F_{0-1} score, miss alarm rate, false alarm rate, NAB score, Matthews Coefficient, PR and ROC curves). The predefined portfolio can be extended with additional metrics.

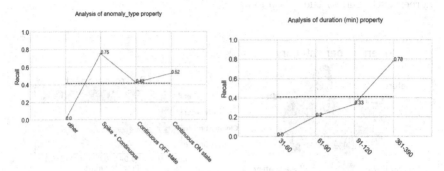

Fig. 5. Break down of the recall metrics based on the values of the *anomaly type* and of the *duration* property. The diagram shows that the algorithm identifies well anomalies of type *spike + continuous* and has more difficulty in detecting the continuous state types. Recall is maximal for long duration anomalies, which are rare and easier to detect.

Analysis, Reporting, and Visualization. The analysis and reports include:

- Performance summary. The values of the selected metrics (standard and custom) are organized in a comprehensive report.
- Performance per confidence threshold value. The performance metrics that exploit a threshold on the anomaly confidence score are plotted for each value used in their computation.
- Performance per IoU threshold value. The performance metrics that exploit a threshold on the overlap between the prediction and the GT interval are plotted for each value used in their computation.
- Confusion matrix. The TPs, FPs, FNs, and TNs are displayed in the usual tabular arrangement.
- Per-property metrics break down. One or more performance metrics are disaggregated by the values of a semantic property of the input. An example is presented in Fig. 5: recall metrics break down by anomaly type and anomaly duration.
- FP error categorization. FP errors are grouped into classes and for each class the performance improvement achievable if such errors were removed is computed. Figure 6 shows an example of FP error categorization and impact analysis predefined in ODIN AD. The user can define other categorizations and apply the break down to any metrics.

– Anomaly duration difference and distribution. The difference of duration between the GT and the TP anomalies and the distribution of the duration of the GT and of all the predicted anomalies are plotted.
– Calibration analysis. The confidence histogram and the reliability diagram [8] enable the assessment of how well the distribution of the predicted anomalies agrees with that of the real anomalies.

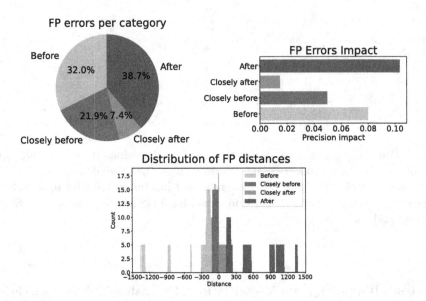

Fig. 6. The FP errors per category diagram (left) shows the distribution of the FPs across four categories. In this breakdown, FPs are grouped by position (before/after) and distance (close/not close) w.r.t. to the closest GT anomaly based on a distance threshold parameter. The FP errors impact diagram (right) shows the contribution of removing each error type on the precision metrics. The distance distribution diagram (bottom) shows the distribution of the distance between FPs and the closest GT anomaly. The analysis shows that most FPs are positioned after more than two hours w.r.t. the closest anomaly and that the post-anomaly false alarms impact the precision metrics the most.

In addition to the performance reports and diagrams, an interface permits the inspection of the data set and of the predictions, as shown in Fig. 7. The user can import a data set and the predictions of one or more AD algorithms, select the feature to display, in the case of multi-variate data series, and scroll the timeline to inspect the anomalies. The visualization can be configured by setting the slice of the time series to show, the number of points per slice and the granularity of the timeline. The default granularity is equal to the sampling frequency of the data set but can be adjusted by aggregating the data points. The user can also set the threshold value used by the anomaly definition strategy.

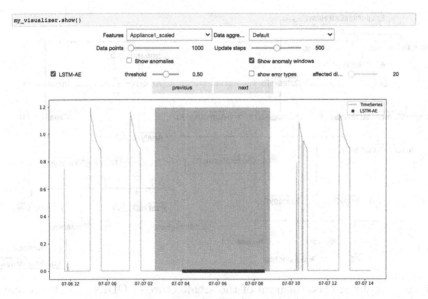

Fig. 7. The user interface of the anomaly visualizer showing the point-wise predictions of one model vs. the GT intervals. A scrollable window lets the user browse the time series. GT interval anomalies are highlighted as colored rectangles and the predicted anomalous points as dots. Adjusting the threshold value used by the anomaly definition strategy updates the diagram.

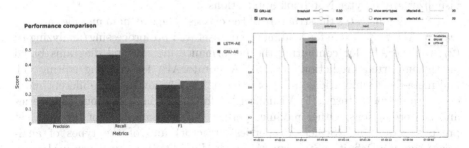

Fig. 8. The user interface of the anomaly visualizer for jointly assessing the results of multiple algorithms: head-to-head display of performance metrics (left) and comparison of identified anomalies (right).

Model Comparison. ODIN AD also supports the comparison of the result of multiple models applied to the same data set. The comparative diagrams can contrast the anomalies detected by the different models and the values of the performance metrics. Figure 8 shows the comparative performance diagram and anomaly visualization.

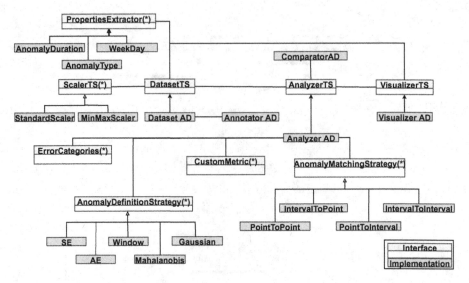

Fig. 9. Simplified class diagram of the architecture of ODIN AD. The components marked with (*) denote the entry points for the extension of ODIN AD.

3.4 ODIN AD Architecture

ODIN AD is open-source[1] and implemented in Python. The annotator and the visualizer are Jupyter Notebook applications.

Figure 9 illustrates the structure of the classes. The five main modules are: (1) DatasetAD, responsible for loading the dataset and pre-processing/analyzing it; (2) AnalyzerAD, for computing the performance metrics and diagrams based on the imported prediction files; (3) AnnotatorAD, for creating/editing GT and meta-data annotations; (4) ComparatorAD, for contrasting different models on the same dataset; (5) VisualizerAD for displaying the input time series and the predictions. Other modules permit the customization of the data set pre/post-processing (Scaler, PropertiesExtractor) and of the types of analysis (AnomalyDefinitionStrategy, AnomalyMatchingStrategy, CustomMetrics, ErrorCategory).

3.5 Extending ODIN AD

ODIN AD is publicly available and the code repository contains a test suite that facilitates extension and bug checking. The "plug&play" architecture enables the customization of the anomaly definition and matching strategies, of the performance metrics, of the pre- and post-data processors, and of the property extractors. Next, we illustrate some examples of how the extension works.

Listing 1 shows how to add a custom anomaly definition strategy. The listing imports the necessary interface (line 1), defines a CustomAnomalyDefinition

---

[1] https://github.com/nahitorres/odin.

class implementing such interface (line 3), and codes the two required functions. The `get_anomaly_score` function computes the anomaly scores (line 5) and the `check_prediction_format` function verifies that the anomaly definition strategy works with the proper prediction formats, single or multi-valued (line 8).

Listing 1. Addition of a custom anomaly definition strategy

```
1 from TOOL.classes.TimeSeries import AnomalyDefinitionStrategy
2
3 class CustomAnomalyDefinition(AnomalyDefinitionStrategy):
4
5   def get_anomaly_scores(self, gt, predictions):
6     # returns the anomaly score for the input time series
7
8   def check_prediction_format(self, predictions):
9     # returns a Boolean indicating if the predictions have the valid
       ↪ type for the strategy
```

Listing 2 shows an example of custom metrics. It declares a new class that implements the `CustomMetricTS` interface (line 3), with the method `evaluate_metric` that actually computes the measure (line 4) given the GT, the predicted anomalies and the matching strategy. An instance of the new metrics is instantiated (line 18) and added to the `Analyzer` module (line 19).

Listing 2. Custom metrics implementation

```
1 from TOOL.classes.TimeSeries import CustomMetricTS
2
3 class MyEvaluationMetric(CustomMetricTS):
4   def evaluate_metric(self, gt, predictions, matchingStrategy):
5     # Parameters:
6     #  gt: contains the GT anomalies
7     #  predictions: contains the predicted anomalies
8     #  matchingStrategy: the selected by the user
9
10    # Returns:
11    #  metric_value: the calculated value in the set
12
13    #TODO: call metrics computation code using the matchingStrategy
14    metric_value = #...
15    std_deviation = # only if apply
16    return metric_value, std_deviation
17
18 my_evaluation_metric = MyEvaluationMetric("my metric name")
19 my_analyzer.add_custom_metric(my_evaluation_metric)
```

4   Conclusions

This paper presents ODIN AD, a framework supporting the life-cycle of AD applications in the phases of data preparation and model evaluation and refinement. Data scientists can load multiple data sets and annotate each one with GT labels or with other meta-data, import the predictions made by the algorithms of their choice, and obtain per-algorithm and also comparative performance reports. In the refinement phase, they can break down the performance metrics based on multiple criteria, classify errors in user-defined types, and assess the impact of the various types of errors on each metrics. ODIN AD is open source and designed with an architecture that eases the customization of such aspects as the anomaly definition and matching strategy, the performance metrics, and the pre- and post-processors.

The future work will focus on extending the support for the analysis of multi-variate time series with algorithms that exploit forecasting and reconstruction. This will require the design and implementation of multi-valued anomaly definition strategies for multi-variate time series in which the user can select the features and the distance function to exploit for the definition of the anomaly. We will also improve the support for the analysis of periodic time series, by implementing more robust approaches to the periodicity detection, such as the one described in [28]. Finally, we aim at integrating interpretability techniques, such as [14,24,30,31], within the performance-oriented analysis functionalities of ODIN AD.

Acknowledgements. This work is supported by the project PRECEPT - A novel decentralized edge-enabled PREsCriptivE and ProacTive framework for increased energy efficiency and well-being in residential buildings funded by the EU H2020 Programme, grant agreement no. 958284.

References

1. Baidu: Curve. https://github.com/baidu/Curve. Accessed 16 June 2022
2. Carrasco, J., et al.: Anomaly detection in predictive maintenance: a new evaluation framework for temporal unsupervised anomaly detection algorithms. Neurocomputing **462**, 440–452 (2021)
3. Chalapathy, R., Chawla, S.: Deep learning for anomaly detection: a survey. arXiv preprint arXiv:1901.03407 (2019)
4. Cho, K., et al.: Learning phrase representations using RNN encoder-decoder for statistical machine translation. arXiv preprint arXiv:1406.1078 (2014)
5. Choi, K., Yi, J., Park, C., Yoon, S.: Deep learning for anomaly detection in time-series data: review, analysis, and guidelines. IEEE Access **9**, 120043–120065 (2021)
6. Dickey, D.A., Fuller, W.A.: Distribution of the estimators for autoregressive time series with a unit root. J. Am. Stat. Assoc. **74**(366a), 427–431 (1979)
7. Gharibi, G., Walunj, V., Nekadi, R., Marri, R., Lee, Y.: Automated end-to-end management of the modeling lifecycle in deep learning. Empir. Softw. Eng. **26**(2), 1–33 (2021). https://doi.org/10.1007/s10664-020-09894-9

8. Guo, C., Pleiss, G., Sun, Y., Weinberger, K.Q.: On calibration of modern neural networks. In: International Conference on Machine Learning, pp. 1321–1330. PMLR (2017)
9. Haladjian, J.: The Wearables Development Toolkit (WDK) (2019). https://github.com/avenix/WDK
10. Herzen, J., et al.: Darts: user-friendly modern machine learning for time series. arXiv preprint arXiv:2110.03224 (2021)
11. Hoiem, D., Chodpathumwan, Y., Dai, Q.: Diagnosing error in object detectors. In: Fitzgibbon, A., Lazebnik, S., Perona, P., Sato, Y., Schmid, C. (eds.) ECCV 2012. LNCS, vol. 7574, pp. 340–353. Springer, Heidelberg (2012). https://doi.org/10.1007/978-3-642-33712-3_25
12. Hyndman, R.J., Athanasopoulos, G.: Forecasting: Principles and Practice. OTexts, Melbourne (2018)
13. Inc, G.: Trainset. https://trainset.geocene.com/. Accessed 17 June 2022
14. Jacob, V., Song, F., Stiegler, A., Rad, B., Diao, Y., Tatbul, N.: Exathlon: a benchmark for explainable anomaly detection over time series. arXiv preprint arXiv:2010.05073 (2020)
15. Kao, J.B., Jiang, J.R.: Anomaly detection for univariate time series with statistics and deep learning. In: 2019 IEEE Eurasia Conference on IOT, Communication and Engineering (ECICE), pp. 404–407. IEEE (2019)
16. Katser, I.D., Kozitsin, V.O.: Skoltech anomaly benchmark (SKAB) (2020). https://www.kaggle.com/dsv/1693952, https://doi.org/10.34740/KAGGLE/DSV/1693952
17. Keras: keras documentation: timeseries anomaly detection using an autoencoder. https://keras.io/examples/timeseries/timeseries_anomaly_detection/
18. Lavin, A., Ahmad, S.: Evaluating real-time anomaly detection algorithms-the Numenta anomaly benchmark. In: 2015 IEEE 14th International Conference on Machine Learning and Applications (ICMLA), pp. 38–44. IEEE (2015)
19. Mahalakshmi, G., Sridevi, S., Rajaram, S.: A survey on forecasting of time series data. In: 2016 International Conference on Computing Technologies and Intelligent Data Engineering (ICCTIDE 2016), pp. 1–8. IEEE (2016)
20. Malhotra, P., Ramakrishnan, A., Anand, G., Vig, L., Agarwal, P., Shroff, G.: LSTM-based encoder-decoder for multi-sensor anomaly detection. arXiv preprint arXiv:1607.00148 (2016)
21. Malhotra, P., Vig, L., Shroff, G., Agarwal, P., et al.: Long short term memory networks for anomaly detection in time series. In: Proceedings, vol. 89, pp. 89–94 (2015)
22. Marques, P., Dias, L., Correia, M.: CyberVTI: cyber visualization tool for intrusion detection. In: 2021 IEEE 20th International Symposium on Network Computing and Applications (NCA), pp. 1–9 (2021). https://doi.org/10.1109/NCA53618.2021.9685543
23. Microsoft: Tag anomaly. https://github.com/microsoft/TagAnomaly. Accessed 16 June 2022
24. Mujkanovic, F., Doskoč, V., Schirneck, M., Schäfer, P., Friedrich, T.: timeXplain-a framework for explaining the predictions of time series classifiers. arXiv preprint arXiv:2007.07606 (2020)
25. Munir, M., Siddiqui, S.A., Dengel, A., Ahmed, S.: DeepAnT: a deep learning approach for unsupervised anomaly detection in time series. IEEE Access 7, 1991–2005 (2018)

26. Murray, D., Stankovic, L., Stankovic, V.: An electrical load measurements dataset of united kingdom households from a two-year longitudinal study. Sci. Data **4**(1), 1–12 (2017)
27. Pang, G., Shen, C., Cao, L., Hengel, A.V.D.: Deep learning for anomaly detection: a review. ACM Comput. Surv. **54**(2), 1–38 (2021). https://doi.org/10.1145/3439950
28. Puech, T., Boussard, M., D'Amato, A., Millerand, G.: A fully automated period- icity detection in time series. In: Lemaire, V., Malinowski, S., Bagnall, A., Bondu, A., Guyet, T., Tavenard, R. (eds.) Advanced Analytics and Learning on Temporal Data, pp. 43–54. Springer International Publishing, Cham (2020). https://doi.org/10.1007/978-3-030-39098-3_4
29. Ran, Y., Zhou, X., Lin, P., Wen, Y., Deng, R.: A survey of predictive maintenance: systems, purposes and approaches. arXiv preprint arXiv:1912.07383 (2019)
30. Rojat, T., Puget, R., Filliat, D., Del Ser, J., Gelin, R., Díaz-Rodríguez, N.: Explainable artificial intelligence (XAI) on timeseries data: a survey. arXiv preprint arXiv:2104.00950 (2021)
31. Schlegel, U., Vo, D.L., Keim, D.A., Seebacher, D.: TS-MULE: local interpretable model-agnostic explanations for time series forecast models. In: Kamp, M., et al. (eds.) Joint European Conference on Machine Learning and Knowledge Discovery in Databases, pp. 5–14. Springer, Cham (2021). https://doi.org/10.1007/978-3-030-93736-2_1
32. Yilmaz, S.F., Kozat, S.S.: PySAD: a streaming anomaly detection framework in python. arXiv preprint arXiv:2009.02572 (2020)
33. Zhang, W., Yang, D., Wang, H.: Data-driven methods for predictive maintenance of industrial equipment: a survey. IEEE Syst. J. **13**(3), 2213–2227 (2019). https://doi.org/10.1109/JSYST.2019.2905565
34. Zoppi, T., Ceccarelli, A., Bondavalli, A.: Evaluation of anomaly detection algo- rithms made easy with reload. In: 2019 IEEE 30th International Symposium on Software Reliability Engineering (ISSRE), pp. 446–455. IEEE (2019)

Author Index

Printed in the United States
by Baker & Taylor Publisher Services